Classic Cold Cuisine

Other cookbooks by Karen Green:

HOW TO COOK HIS GOOSE (And Other Wild Games),
with Betty Black

THE GREAT INTERNATIONAL NOODLE EXPERIENCE

WINNERS!

JAPANESE COOKING FOR THE AMERICAN TABLE

Classic Cold Cuisine

KAREN GREEN

JEREMY P. TARCHER, INC.
Los Angeles
Distributed by Houghton Mifflin Company
Boston

Library of Congress Cataloging in Publication Data

Green, Karen.
  Classic cold cuisine.

  Includes index.
  1. Cookery (Cold dishes)   I. Title.
TX830.G73   1984   641.7'9   84-2752
ISBN 0-87477-322-9
ISBN 0-87477-336-9 (pbk.)

Some of the recipes in this book are based on those by Karen
Green from her cookbooks *How to Cook His Goose (and Other Wild
Games), The Great International Noodle Experience,* and
Japanese Cooking for the American Table.

Jeremy P. Tarcher, Inc.
9110 Sunset Blvd.
Los Angeles, CA 90069

Design by Tanya Maiboroda

Manufactured in the United States of America
D 10 9 8 7 6 5 4 3 2 1
First Edition

To my parents,
who taught me about the finer foods in life.

To my husband,
for whom I perfected my culinary skills.

To my two sons,
who have grown up on my cooking projects.

Acknowledgments

In front of me sit hundreds of manuscript pages, a new cookbook, my fifth, about to be completed. At this time I wish to thank all the marvelous people who helped me. You have all been special people to give of yourselves—your time, advice, ideas, expertise. Thank you for your friendship.

To my husband, Bill, and my sons, Jonathon and Jeffrey, thank you for sipping chilled soups through the winter months and tasting course after course of cold recipes, with very few complaints and with an abundance of smiles and hugs.

To my mother, Betty Schwartz, thank you for listening to my highs and lows, and for your editing advice.

To my editor, Janice Gallagher, thank you for offering your original idea for this book and believing I was the best food writer to do the job. I truly appreciate your constant, loving concern throughout this project. To my agent, Jane Browne, for your professional handling of my contracts and all your advice. To my publisher, Jeremy Tarcher, and to Derek Gallagher and the entire staff of Jeremy P. Tarcher for their encouragement, excitement, and trust in this book.

To my friend Carl Sontheimer and Cuisinarts, Inc., who so generously sent me the newest of equipment to aid in all my chopping, slicing, and pureeing. Your Cuisinart saved me hours of hand work and thus gave me more time for creative exploration.

To my professional food friends, personal friends, and relatives who so generously shared their recipes for this book: my mother, late mother-in-law Anabel Hoy, grandfather Frank Fisher, late grandmother Jean Fisher, Aunt Rose Pitchon, Aunt Sherry Silverman, Aunt Neenie Halpin, Dori Phillips, Evy Darren, Terez Bassenian, Bobbi Felsot, Annie Marino, Rosemary Moses, Pam Mendelsohn, Susan Slack, Christina Hurn, Debbie Pipino, Martha Jean Rutherford, and Jessie Hoy.

I wish you all great happiness, health, and love.

Karen Green
January 1984

Contents

Introduction

After spending several years of intensive study of Japanese cookery and writing *Japanese Cooking for the American Table,* I became interested in continuing my education in the Asian cuisines and then moving on to other foods of the world. My next project—international cold dishes— intrigued me. Not only do I prefer cold or room-temperature foods, but I also feel that a book dedicated to these recipes will be perfect for today's active cook.

Cold foods can and should be made in advance to allow time for a harmonious marriage of the ingredients, seasonings, or dressings. Many of these dishes can be made early in the day and left at room temperature or in the refrigerator, while others need a few further days of refrigeration for proper mellowing. Frozen desserts, for example, can be made a day or two or often longer in advance and frozen until needed.

The joys of cold dishes also involve the use of leftovers with new ingredients or with whatever is on hand in the pantry. Many of today's world-famous recipes, such as Caesar Salad and Veal Tonnato, were actually the tossings or blendings of available ingredients by an ingenious cook. Cooked fish can be transformed into a heavenly mousse or buttery spread. Friday's roasted chicken need not be Saturday's sandwich. Instead, slices of cooked fowl can be tossed with avocados for a California guacamole, torn into shreds to be added to a spicy Szechwan appetizer, or cut into chunks to be combined with homemade mayonnaise and herbs for a delightful French salad. You will look upon your leftovers with an entirely different attitude once you truly appreciate the art of cold cuisine. They will become the artistic beginnings of another delicious recipe.

Thus the busy hostess or host can greatly benefit from a collection of superb cold and room-temperature recipes. For everyday dining, these dishes are ideal for singles and single parents, working couples, and retired people who arrive home after a hectic day at work or play to find their dinner awaiting their pleasure.

Cuisines throughout the world have been greatly influenced by weather conditions. In many tropical countries, cold dishes offer a welcome respite to soaring temperatures. To whet the appetite in sultry climates, recipes have been created incorporating spicy chilies or salty seasonings with meats, fowl, fish, vegetables, and/or fruits. Sugar is often used to balance the spice or salt, and vinegar or fresh lemon or lime juice is sometimes added for tartness. The final dish is not only delicious but also serves to increase thirst as well as appetite. Thus more liquids are consumed, which in turn helps balance the body's fluids.

Yet cold foods should not be thought of merely as hot-weather coolers. In today's contemporary cuisines, they have become year-round fare. With the abundance of produce available to us, we usually eat at

1

least one cold vegetable or fruit, salad, or entree every day, often including the pasta, rice, and potato salads that have now come into their own.
And hostesses have been offering dips with chips or crudités for years.

With *Classic Cold Cuisine,* the innovative cook can prepare a whole
new array of dishes, from appetizers through desserts. The standard sour
cream–onion dip goes into retirement in favor of the Greek cucumber
and yogurt dip tzatsiki, a Mediterranean mélange of ratatouille vegetables, or an Armenian roasted eggplant "caviar" ekra. Instead of meatloaf,
I opt for a country pâté, terrine, or Mexican galatina. A hot minestrone
soup laden with garden vegetables, beans, and pasta takes on a new
identity when served cold, garnished with a dollop of fragrant pesto
sauce. Puddings, custards, mousses, and tarts are all magnificent when
served cold, as are other international classics—Coeur à la Crème, Sicilian Cassata, Almond Torte with Peaches and Cream, Russian Cheese
Pashka.

Instead of preparing a stew when the weather is cold and miserable,
how about offering a tropical curried Senegalese soup followed by an
Indonesian gado gado salad and a Hawaiian coconut custard to transport
your family and friends to warmer exotic lands? And during those dog
days of early autumn when the humidity is in the 90s and it's gray and
sticky, there's nothing more refreshing than a bowl of Greengrocer's
Zucchini Soup or a scoop of Ginger Melon Ice to pick up your energy
level.

Of course, cold foods are ideal hot-weather dishes. In the United
States, where picnicking is a favorite summertime activity, such traditional fare as fried chicken, potato salad, and cole slaw is easy to carry and
can be conveniently prepared ahead.

I cannot emphasize enough how terrific cold and room-temperature
recipes are for entertaining. A bountiful assortment of cold dishes is ideal
for a buffet; if desired, hot dishes can be easily interspersed. This plenti-
ful array of foods is not unique to American cookery. It can be found in
many cuisines, including the rijsttafel rice tables or prasmanan buffets of
Indonesia, the zakuska appetizer tables of Russia, the osechi New Year's
buffets of Japan, the luaus of Hawaii, the smorgasbords of the Scandinavian countries, and the individual thali trays of India.

Classic Cold Cuisine brings together more than 271 well-loved classic
international recipes, covering American, Asian, African, European,
Latin American, Jewish, Russian, Polynesian, Middle Eastern, and
South American cuisines. During my research I became fascinated with
the similarities in so many seemingly dissimilar cuisines. In many cases I
discovered that by altering one or two ingredients a dish could be found
in several countries. Therefore, whenever possible, I have given these
simple variations within the recipe instructions or I have taken one basic
recipe and shown how to internationalize it.

For example, take cucumber salad; a Japanese recipe might include
rice vinegar, ginger, and sugar with the cucumbers; a Mexican recipe,

radishes, lemon juice, mint, and oregano; an American recipe, onions, cider vinegar, and sugar; a Danish recipe, vinegar, water, sugar, and pepper. An Indian tomato salad might mix tomatoes, onions, cilantro, chiles, and ginger; without the ginger it would become Mexican. A favorite egg-based dessert from Brazil calls for fresh coconut cream or milk as the main flavoring, as it does in Indonesia, the Philippines, and other countries where coconuts are abundant. A similar custard can be found in American and many European cuisines with heavy cream or milk, rather than coconut cream or milk, beaten with the eggs. Ice cream, sorbets, sherbets, ices, and gratinées from around the world are quite similar in concept—frozen fruit purees, juices, creams, milks, ices; some are simply fresh fruit pureed with a little sugar and then frozen; others are more complex, with a sugar syrup, meringue, or cooked custard base flavored with spices, candies, fruit pieces, nuts, or liquors.

Ceviche, escabeche, poisson cru, opohi—basically seafood "cooked" in citrus juice—can be found in many cuisines, as can pickled herring or other pickled fish—fish marinated in vinegar. Fresh lemon or lime juice or vinegar is used throughout the world as an ingredient as well as a condiment. A Latin American salsa is very similar to an Indonesian sambal, a Caribbean Island pepper sauce, a Sumatran lado, a Vietnamese nuoc cham, and an Indian tomato chatni (chutney). Soy sauce used in Japanese and Chinese cooking is like nuoc nam in Vietnamese, ketjap-manis or petis in Indonesian, nam plai in Thai, and hot pepper sauce in American. Similarities can be seen between the well-known anchovy paste (American and Italian cuisines) and the lesser-known Thai kapi (shrimp paste), Indonesian trassi, and Filipino bagoong. Cilantro (fresh coriander) is found in many cuisines, including American, Mexican, Chinese, Vietnamese, Indonesian, Russian, and African.

In many cases I have updated the techniques or modified the ingredients of these international recipes to fit today's style of cooking. Thus I have simplified the recipes whenever possible, and made special notations and adaptations throughout the book when an ingredient might be substituted for another that is difficult to find. It is encouraging, however, that with the surge of immigration to the United States of people from other countries, most major supermarkets and specialty stores offer an extensive variety of the international ingredients.

Another liberty I have taken with some traditional recipes is to modernize them, perhaps creating what may become new classics. Because healthful foods and fresh seasonal ingredients are top priorities with most of today's cooks, I have kept these needs in mind with my recipe testing. You will find this in a potato salad or a Waldorf salad in which I have substituted yogurt—low in fat and calories—for mayonnaise; a hearty gazpacho boasting vitamin-rich turnips, peppers, and tomatoes; a California-style piquant curry dip to serve with crudités; and a most pleasant summer squash soup spiked with curry and resembling many classic chilled French vegetable soups that have been enriched with cream. Also, within the instructions of many recipes, I have given the yield of a particular dressing, sauce, or dip so that the creative cook can independently use these with other dishes.

As for the organization of this book, I have divided the chapters in the classic manner in which Americans organize their meals, from appetizers through desserts. I feel menu suggestions are very important to today's busy cook and have therefore given much consideration and space to an extensive listing that precedes the recipes. Then, within each recipe chapter, I have alphabetically grouped each cuisine by country, region, or ethnicity, placing at the end the international recipes, those which are a blend of several cuisines. And, rather than burden this introduction with page after page of background on each cuisine, I felt the readers would prefer more recipes and menus; therefore, I have included this information, along with serving instructions and recipe variations, with the specific recipes, which is where I feel it truly belongs.

Following the recipes there is a section of special ingredients and techniques, where the reader will find descriptions of the less familiar international ingredients, along with substitutions, whenever possible. There are also instructions for several basic international cooking techniques, such as the preparation of coconut milk and cream, making dashi (the basic stock for Japanese recipes), cleaning small squid, and poaching fish in a court bouillon, as well as a cross reference of techniques used throughout the book. Finally, there is an extensive listing of companies from which some hard-to-find ingredients may be ordered by mail.

I think of this book as I have my others—a creative stepping stone for both the novice and the experienced home cook. You can strictly follow my recipes and menus or you can use them for inspiration. I am delighted to share with you hundreds of my favorite classic cold and room-temperature dishes from around the world, and I hope they will become your favorites.

Theme Menus

In this section, I have offered 40 theme menus. In some cases, they are a classic combination of tastes, as in Mother's Day Brunch, where I have suggested a chilled vegetable soup to be followed by a trio of composed salads, and then a grand finale of layers of meringues, whipped cream, chocolate, and fresh fruits. Other menus are an eclectic gathering of international tastes, such as A Meal at the Seashore, with Papaya-Orange Soup, three unusual vegetable salads—mushrooms (Hawaiian mustard dressing), cucumber (Persian dressing), and cherry tomatoes (Italian-French basil vinaigrette)—a main dish of poached fish with avocado sauce (Caribbean), and then crowned by an American pecan pie.

MEXICAN PIÑATA PARTY

Sangria Punch
Scallop Ceviche
León Jícama Salad
Ensalada de Nopales
Cucumber-Radish Salad
Mexicana Guacamole
Galatina
Yucatecan Pickled Onions
Frozen Mango Mousse

CHILDREN'S CHARMER

Chinese Spareribs with
    Sweet-Tart Marinade
Turkey Salad with a Hint of the
    Orient
Toasted Pita Bread Wedges
Cinnamon-Clove Applesauce
Lemon Custard Ice Cream Pie

AN EARLY SPRING PICNIC

Mediterranean Ratatouille
Toast Triangles
Hard-Cooked Eggs Sukiyaki
Parisian Carottes Râpées
Marinated Artichoke Heart and
    Rice Salad
Herb-Baked Chicken
Fresh Strawberry Pie

AFTERNOON TEA

Potted Salmon with Toast
    Triangles
Cold Trout in Aspic
Fresh Mango Chutney Christina
Michael James's Wonderful
    Quiche
Chocolate Mousse–Angel Food
    Cake Dessert
Annie's Very Rich Ginger
    Cheesecake with Strawberry
    Glaze
Strawberry Fool
English Trifle

CHINESE NEW YEAR'S BANQUET

Oriental Asparagus with Sesame
    Seed Sauce
Chinese Tea Eggs
Honey-Soy Marinated Chicken
    Legs
Chinese Spareribs with
    Sweet-Tart Marinade
Flavored Shiitake
Chinese Radish-Cucumber
    Salad
Maifun with Chicken Salad
Ginger Melon Ice

OSECHI BUFFET

Sushi and Sashimi
Onigiri
Spinach with Sesame Dressing
Japanese Eggplants in Miso
    Dressing
Cucumber and Shrimp
    Sunomono
Japanese Pork Loin Roast
Broccoli and Shrimp with
    Transparent Noodles
Candied Sweet Potatoes
Watermelon Ice

MIDDLE EASTERN FESTIVAL

Lassi
Ekra with Toasted Pita Bread
    Wedges
Hummus
Iranian Cucumber, Onion, and
    Yogurt Salad with Raisins
Tabbouleh
Armenian–Russian Salad
Christina's Indonesian Avocado
    Dessert

AN ELEGANT PICNIC

Capitol Hill Pâté
Gravlax with Mustard-Dill Sauce
String Beans and Tomatoes
    Provençale
Marinated Braised Leeks
Vitello Tonnato
Nut Tortes with Zabaglione
    Custard and Berries

TAILGATE PARTY

Ceviche con Alcáparras
Green Almond Sauce
Apple Walnut Salad
Greek Baked and Marinated
    Spring Garden Vegetables
My Mom's Fried Chicken
Double Rich Chocolate Brownie
    Cake

EUROPEAN EPICUREAN AFFAIR

Brandied Game Loaf
Pickled Mushrooms
German Pickled Radish Salad
    Inge
Beet Râpé
String Beans and Tomatoes
    Provençale
Poached Chicken Breasts with
    Tkemali Sauce
Figs with Blueberries

VEGETARIAN FEAST

Tequila-Marinated Avocado
    Appetizers
Sliced Tofu with Condiments
Greengrocer's Zucchini Soup
Cacumbar
Indonesian Gado Gado
Sweet Potato and Almond Halva
Ian Watermelon Ice

CHRISTMAS SWEET TABLE

White Chocolate Cake
Old-Fashioned Fruit Cake
Sicilian Cassata
Cheese Pashka
Double Rich Chocolate Brownie
    Cake

NEW YEAR'S EVE OPEN HOUSE

New Year's Eve Chopped
    Chicken Liver Appetizer
Tuna Pâté with Toast Triangles
Steak Tartare Miniatures
Tapénade
Escabeche of Poached Whitefish
Potato and Roasted Green
    Pepper Salad with Mustard
    Vinaigrette
Mom's Apricot Glazed Baked Ham
English Trifle
Cheesecake Sauce for Fresh Fruits
Coeur à la Crème

BRIDAL WEDDING SHOWER

Salmon Mousse in the Shape of Salmon with Horseradish Sauce and/or Dill Dip
Peas and Onion Salad
Pasta with Garden Vegetables
Mother's Chicken Salad Hawaiian
Almond Torte with Peaches and Cream
Strawberries-in-a-Basket Pavlova

A MEAL AT THE SEASHORE

Papaya-Orange Soup
Marino Marinated Mushroom Salad with Maui Mustard
Persian Cucumber Salad
Cherry Tomatoes in a Basil Vinaigrette Marinade
Caribbean Cold Poached Fish with Avocado Sauce
Pecan Festival Creamy Pecan Pie

A SUNDAY FOOTBALL GATHERING

Acapulco Shrimp Ceviche
Trout Party Dip
Potato Salad with Tangy Blue Cheese Dressing
Red and Green Peppery Cole Slaw
Wonton Chicken Salad
Sherried Onions and Almonds
Pumpkin Chiffon Pie

DELECTABLE DESSERTS

Chocolate Mousse in Mousse Shell
Almond Torte with Peaches and Cream
Pumpkin-Rum Flan
Annie's Very Rich Ginger Cheesecake with Strawberry Glaze
Nut Tortes with Zabaglione Custard and Berries

SOUPS FOR SUPPER

Borscht
Senegalese Soup
Minestra di Verdura with Pesto Sauce
Carrot-Orange Soup
Blueberry Soup

FOR CHOCOLATE LOVERS

Chocolate Mousse–Angel Food Cake Dessert
Boccone Dolce
Banana Cream Pie (with Chocolate)
Chocolate-Dipped Strawberries
Chocolate Bavarian Cream
White Chocolate Cake

PASSOVER TABLE

Chopped Chicken Liver Appetizer
Eggplant and Pepper Salad
Gefilte Fish
Passover Fruit and Nut Charoses
Cambodian Chicken and Tofu Salad
Stewed Rhubarb

PATIO POOLSIDE PARTY

Pacific Coast Curry Dip
Trout Antipasto
Lobio
Caesar Salad
Annie's Very Rich Ginger Cheesecake with Strawberry Glaze

FAMILY DINNER

Farmer Salad
Buba's Fruit Kugel
Cranberry-Orange Delicious Relish
Pork-Stuffed Halibut
French Vanilla-Peach Ice Cream

4TH OF JULY ABUNDANCE

Mexicana Guacamole
Cabbage Slaw with Garden
    Vegetables
Pennsylvania Dutch Beet, Apple,
    and Egg Salad
Cold Poached Salmon in Aspic
    Glaze
Tangy Yogurt Sauce
Lemon Pie

MOTHER'S DAY MENU

Susan's Lemon Squash Soup
Peeled Asparagus with Lemon
    Juice and Olive Oil
Watercress and Walnut Salad
Avocado-Tomato-Bacon Salad
Boccone Dolce

FATHER'S DAY IN THE BACKYARD

Cucumber Refresher
Special Chinese Fried Shrimp
Orange-Avocado Salad
Grandma Fisher's Potato Salad
Szechwan Chicken, Vegetable,
    and Noodle Salad
Pecan Festival Creamy Pecan Pie

SOUTH PACIFIC PLEASURES

Opihi
Lomi Lomi Luau
Senegalese Soup
Pancit Salad
Vietnamese Shrimp and Green
    Papaya Salad
Sea Slaw
Tropical Lime Pie
Haupia

SPICES INTERNATIONAL

Acapulco Shrimp Ceviche
Ecuador Pickled Shrimp
Caribbean Island Hot Pepper
    Sauce
Banana and Raisin Raita
Moroccan String Beans and
    Cilantro
Atjar
Szechwan Chicken Breasts
Pumpkin-Rum Flan

ICE CREAM SOCIAL

French Vanilla-Peach Ice Cream
Ginger Melon Ice
Lemon Custard Ice Cream Pie
Watermelon Ice

MID SUMMER NIGHT'S DELICACIES

Ecuador Pickled Fish
Vichyssoise
Watercress and Mushroom Salad
    with Walnut Oil Dressing
Szechwan Chicken, Vegetable,
    and Noodle Salad
Raspberry Fluff

SCANDINAVIAN SMORGASBORD

Brandied Game Loaf
Pickled Trout
Trout Tempter
Kosher Chopped Herring
Rodkaal
Cucumber in Dilled Cream
Pennsylvania Dutch Pickled Beets
    and Eggs
Asparagus Vinaigrette
Chilled Poached Tuna with
    Cucumber Sauce
Gravlax with Mustard-Dill Sauce
Kaernemaelkskodskaal

SOME LIKE IT "RAW"

Steak Tartare Miniatures
Middle Eastern Lamb Kibbee
Salmon Tartare

Acapulco Ceviche

Fresh Berries with Crème Fraîche

MEDITERRANEAN MÉLANGE

Tzatsiki with Toasted Pita Bread Wedges

Italian Roasted Red and Green Peppers

Mediterranean Marinated Tomato Salad

Green Fettuccine with Tuna, Olives, and Capers

Oasis Fruits

LENTEN SUPPER

Cold Avgolemono

German Beet Salad with Cream

Italian Roasted Red and Green Peppers

New Orleans Shrimp Remoulade in Cream Puff Basket

Cheese Pashka

A SMALL DINNER PARTY

Pheasant Pâté

Spinach-Mushroom Salad with French Dressing

Chirashi-Zushi

African Fish Cone

Frozen Strawberry Souffle

LATE SUPPER ON THE PATIO

Minted Fresh Pea Soup

Salade Niçoise

Strawberry-Rhubarb Compote

Caramel Egg Custard

BUSY-DAY DINNER

Seven Layer Salad

Teriyaki Marinated Steak Slices

French White Bean Salad

Cinnamon-Clove Applesauce

Cheesecake Sauce for Fresh Fruits

CHAMPAGNE BRUNCH

Oriental Asparagus with Sesame Seed Sauce

Chilled Avocado Soup with Tequila

Tomato-Mozzarella-Basil Salad

Orange, Red Onion, Radish Salad

Seafood Pancit Salad

Almond Torte with Peaches and Cream

AUTUMN PICNIC

Spinach and Cheese Pie

Scotch Eggs

Russian Cucumbers with Creamy Dressing

Fettuccine with Marinated Broccoli, Tomato, Olives, and Peppers

Free-Form Apple Tart

VALENTINE'S DAY DINNER

Southwest American Tomato-Cilantro Sorbet

Romaine Salad with Roquefort Dressing

Pasta Primavera

Orange-Avocado Salad

Coeur à la Crème

AN ADULTS ONLY BIRTHDAY DINNER

Mezedaki

Bill's Birthday Party Caponata

Baby Artichokes and Tomatoes in an Herb Vinaigrette

Thai Shrimp Salad

Oven-Poached Pears in a Whiskey Orange Sauce

Appetizers and Hors d'Oeuvres

STEAK TARTARE MINIATURES
NEW YEAR'S EVE CHOPPED CHICKEN LIVER APPETIZER
CAPITOL HILL PÂTÉ
TROUT TEMPTER
PICKLED TROUT
TUNA PÂTÉ WITH TOAST TRIANGLES
OPIHI—SCALLOPS WITH COCONUT CREAM SAUCE
SALMON TARTARE
TROUT PARTY DIP
LOMI LOMI LUAU
SPINACH AND CHEESE PIE
MIDDLE EASTERN LAMB KIBBEE
EKRA—ARMENIAN EGGPLANT APPETIZER
TOASTED PITA BREAD TRIANGLES
ORIENTAL ASPARAGUS WITH SESAME SEED SAUCE
CHINESE TEA EGGS
HONEY-SOY MARINATED CHICKEN LEGS
SPECIAL CHINESE FRIED SHRIMP
CHINESE SPARERIBS WITH SWEET-TART MARINADE
ECUADOR PICKLED FISH
POTTED SALMON
MEDITERRANEAN RATATOUILLE
TAPÉNADE
MEZEDAKI—MARINATED FETA CHEESE
TROUT ANTIPASTO

BILL'S BIRTHDAY PARTY CAPONATA
HARD-COOKED EGGS SUKIYAKI
SLICED TOFU WITH CONDIMENTS
FLAVORED SHIITAKE—ORIENTAL MUSHROOMS
ONIGIRI—COLD RICE BALLS
SUSHI AND SASHIMI
JAPANESE CUCUMBER-TROUT APPETIZER
GEFILTE FISH
AUNT ROSE'S GEFILTE FISH SIMPLIFIED
KOSHER CHOPPED HERRING
CHOPPED CHICKEN LIVER APPETIZER
EGGPLANT AND PEPPER SALAD
CEVICHE/SCALLOP CEVICHE
ACAPULCO SHRIMP CEVICHE
CEVICHE CON ALCÁPARRAS—CEVICHE WITH CAPERS
GALATINA—MEXICAN POACHED "PÂTÉ"
TEQUILA-MARINATED AVOCADO APPETIZERS
LABAN OR MAST—YOGURT
HUMMUS—CHICKPEA-TAHINI SPREAD
PICKLED MUSHROOMS
GRAVLAX WITH MUSTARD-DILL SAUCE
ESCABECHE OF POACHED WHITEFISH
SALMON MOUSSE IN THE SHAPE OF SALMON
GIANT SQUID VINAIGRETTE
PICKLED HALIBUT
BRANDIED GAME LOAF
PHEASANT PÂTÉ

STEAK TARTARE MINIATURES

American   *24 to 26 miniatures*

When dining at some of our country's finest continental restaurants, my husband has always favored steak tartare—a mixture of freshly chopped raw steak with condiments—as his entree. At home I have served it as a main dish in simple patties garnished with a raw egg yolk or, as hors d'oeuvres, in bite-size portions beautifully encased in minced parsley.

1 pound beef sirloin	1 tablespoon capers, drained
1 2-ounce tin anchovies, drained and patted dry, optional	6 to 8 drops hot pepper sauce
1 clove garlic, cut in half	1 teaspoon salt
1 small onion, quartered	Dash freshly ground black pepper
1 egg yolk	1 cup minced fresh parsley
2 tablespoons cognac	
2 teaspoons Dijon-style mustard	

If you are using a food processor, this recipe can be made in a few minutes; by hand it will take longer.

Remove all fat from the steak and cut into small cubes. Using the steel blade with your food processor, add half the steak, half the anchovies, half the garlic, half the onion, half the egg yolk, 1 tablespoon cognac, 1 teaspoon mustard, half the capers, 3 to 4 teaspoons hot pepper sauce, ½ teaspoon salt, and a few grinds of black pepper. Process the mixture, turning the food processor quickly on and off, until everything is well mixed. Do not process so much that the meat becomes a mush. Place the processed mixture in a bowl and process the second half; add to first part.

Shape the steak tartare into small balls, about the size of walnuts. Place minced parsley on a big sheet of wax paper and roll tartare balls in minced parsley until well coated. Refrigerate until serving time.

This appetizer can be made several hours in advance. It is best to remove it from the refrigerator about 15 minutes prior to serving to reduce the chill.

NEW YEAR'S EVE CHOPPED CHICKEN LIVER APPETIZER

American   *Approximately 2 cups*

For the past ten years I have made this chopped chicken liver appetizer for my New Year's Eve buffet tables, and it has become a tradition in our household.

Throughout the hunting season I freeze all the duck livers my husband brings home with his game, and by the holidays I have a nice supply.

1 pound chicken livers
½ pound duck livers,
preferably wild duck livers
(if not available, increase
the quantity of chicken
livers)
4 to 5 tablespoons butter
3 to 4 large onions, finely
grated
6 hard-cooked eggs

6 tablespoons mayonnaise
2 tablespoons dry sherry
1 tablespoon Worcestershire
sauce
½ teaspoon each salt, pepper,
and sugar

Garnish

Minced onion
Chopped hard-cooked egg

Saute the chicken and duck livers over medium heat in a large skillet with 4 tablespoons of butter. When livers are browned on the outside and tender on the inside, remove from skillet and set aside. Add onions and remaining butter, if necessary, to the skillet, cover, and cook over low heat until onions are soft and translucent.

Push cooked livers through a food mill or grinder (or very carefully process in a food processor, taking care not to make a paste) directly into a large bowl. Add cooked onions. Grind eggs and add to livers. Mix everything well with a wooden spoon. Add mayonnaise, sherry, Worcestershire sauce, salt, pepper, and sugar, mixing all ingredients very well.

Spoon liver mixture into a serving bowl or place in a mound shape on a lettuce-lined platter. Refrigerate several hours to allow flavors to mellow.

At serving time, garnish with additional minced onion and grated hard-cooked egg and accompany with sliced pumpernickel or rye bread.

CAPITOL HILL PÂTÉ

American   6 to 8 servings

When I was at college in Washington, D.C., I worked with Mark Talisman, who was both one of the capital's leading congressional assistants and a remarkable cook. He shared many superb recipes with me, including this chicken liver pâté, one of the best I have ever tasted.

1 large Bermuda onion,
quartered
4 to 6 tablespoons butter
4 cloves garlic
4 strips bacon, cut up

1½ pounds chicken livers
4 sprigs parsley, minced
Salt and pepper to taste
4 egg yolks
2 tablespoons cognac

Saute the onion in 3 tablespoons butter. Add garlic and bacon and saute until bacon is transparent. Add livers and saute, adding butter as needed. Add parsley and season lightly with salt and pepper.

When livers are half done (pink on the inside), turn the mixture into a blender or food processor and puree. Add egg yolks to the blender and process again. Add cognac and again process.

Spoon liver mixture into a buttered 9-inch loaf pan and bake 15 to 20 minutes in a preheated 400° oven.

Turn pâté out of pan and cool. Cover and refrigerate several hours until cold.

Serve the pâté on lettuce-lined platter with thin slices of bread.

TROUT TEMPTER

American   *4 to 8 servings*

An unusual trout preparation to serve as an hors d'oeuvre. You can use this same technique with other small fish, and in fact this recipe is very similar to Scandinavian pickled herring.

2 medium trout, cleaned	2 cups vinegar
1 large bay leaf	1 medium onion, sliced into
10 peppercorns	thin rings
8 juniper berries	½ teaspoon dried dillweed
½ teaspoon salt	

Cover trout with cold water and add bay leaf, peppercorns, juniper berries, and salt. Boil gently for about 2 minutes, or until the fish is soft. Drain, bone, and skin the fish and then set aside.

In a second pot, bring the vinegar and sliced onion to a gentle boil. Cook until the onion rings are wilted.

Place the trout in a shallow dish and cover with the hot vinegar and onion. Sprinkle with dillweed and refrigerate at least overnight. Serve chilled in the marinade.

PICKLED TROUT

American   *6 servings*

There are few delicacies in this world to equal fresh-caught trout.

1½ to 2 pounds trout, dressed

Fish Pickling Liquid

    3 cups water
    1 cup cider vinegar
    ⅓ cup sugar
    ½ lemon, thinly sliced
    1 large onion, thinly sliced

2 bay leaves
6 peppercorns
4 whole cloves
4 whole allspice
2 whole garlic cloves

Garnish

    Lemon wedges

Cut off and discard the trout heads. Cut the bodies into thirds and set aside.

To make the pickling liquid: In a medium-size pot or large sauce-pan, combine the ingredients. Bring to a boil, cover with a slight opening, and reduce to a rapid simmer for 15 to 20 minutes. Increase heat to a boil again and add the trout.

Poach trout in the pickling liquid for 3 to 6 minutes, or until barely tender. Remove pot from heat and allow to rest for a few minutes.

Carefully remove trout from pot and place in an attractive refrigerator-to-table bowl or dish with a lip. Pour pickling liquid over top. Cover and refrigerate 12 to 24 hours. At serving time, do not be surprised to find that the pickling liquid has somewhat jelled; this is due to the natural gelatin in the fish bones.

To serve, place dish on dinner table. Or, if desired, drain the trout and place individual pieces on small lettuce-lined salad plates. Garnish with fresh lemon wedges.

TUNA PÂTÉ WITH TOAST TRIANGLES

American

6 to 20 servings, depending on the size of the toast triangles

This tuna pâté is one of my faithful party appetizers. In the unlikely event of leftovers, it is an excellent sandwich spread. You will want to use the recipe for toast triangles with many other dishes, such as steak tartare and other pâtés and mousses.

2 7-ounce cans tuna (preferably white albacore), drained
½ pound butter, cut into pieces
1 onion, peeled and quartered
Juice of 1 lemon
8 drops hot pepper sauce
2 teaspoons fresh dill or 1 teaspoon dried dillweed

Salt and freshly ground pepper to taste
12 pimiento-stuffed green olives
3 tablespoons capers, drained
French or white bread for toast triangles

Garnish

Watercress

Using a blender or a food processor with a steel blade, mix the tuna, butter, onion, lemon juice, pepper sauce, dill, salt, and pepper to a smooth puree. Add the olives and capers and process for a few seconds to combine everything, but do not further puree.

Turn the tuna mixture into a well-oiled mold or round bowl. Cover with plastic wrap and refrigerate for at least 24 hours before unmolding.

To prepare toast triangles: Remove crust from slices of French (not the sourdough variety) or white bread and cut each piece into large triangles. Pour about ¼ inch of olive oil into a large skillet and heat. Add the bread triangles and cook on both sides until they are a light golden color. Drain on paper towels. Triangles will cool within a few minutes and be ready to serve with pâté, or they can be made several hours in advance.

When serving pâté, unmold onto platter and garnish with watercress.

OPIHI—SCALLOPS WITH COCONUT CREAM SAUCE

American   *6 to 12 servings*

In Hawaii this cevichelike scallop dish is made with the native mollusk, opihi, similar to bay scallops, which are small. First the raw shellfish are marinated in lime and lemon juices, and then the acid-cooked fish are tossed with a coconut milk–sour cream sauce. This is a traditional dish at the luau buffet; a very similar appetizer is served in Tahiti. The sauce is also excellent to use as a dip for crudités or tropical fruits.

1½ **pounds scallops (see Note 1)**
¼ **cup each fresh lime and lemon juice**
1 **teaspoon salt**
½ **teaspoon white pepper**
¼ **teaspoon hot pepper sauce**

Coconut Cream Sauce (makes approximately 2 cups)
1 **cup coconut cream (see Index)**
¾ **cup sour cream**
1 **cup chopped green onions**
½ **teaspoon grated fresh ginger (optional—see Note 2)**

Place scallops in a glass or porcelain bowl. In a mixing bowl, combine the juices, salt, pepper, and pepper sauce; pour over scallops and mix well. Cover and refrigerate about 8 hours, or until scallops are opaque, stirring several times.

To prepare the sauce: Combine the coconut milk, sour cream, green onions, and ginger in a large Pyrex measuring cup or bowl. Cover and refrigerate several hours to allow flavors to mellow.

At serving time, remove scallops from marinade and add to the sauce. If you want a thinner sauce, add some of the marinade. Season to taste with salt and pepper, if desired. Spoon individual servings into small glass bowls or "scallop" shells, or serve in a large attractive glass bowl for guests to scoop individual portions.

Note 1: If small bay scallops are not available, cut larger scallops into ½-inch pieces. To somewhat reduce the cost, you can use half scallops and half boneless white fish (firm fish).

Note 2: The ginger is best finely grated, almost to a juice, to offer a mere hint of its pungency to the rich and creamy flavor of the sauce.

SALMON TARTARE

American   *4 servings*

This salmon appetizer is referred to as a tartare because of its resemblance to the classic steak tartare. The ingredients combined with the salmon are quite similar to those used with steak. As with the beef dish, the salmon must be of freshest quality. Also, select a bright red or intense pink salmon, not a light-colored variety, as it makes a more attractive dish.

You can serve this as an appetizer with thin slices of dark bread or use it as a stuffing for hollowed-out cherry tomatoes or green pepper wedges. Individual servings can be placed on a leaf or two of Bibb lettuce for an unusual first course.

8 ounces salmon fillets, boned and skinned	½ teaspoon minced fresh parsley
1 large shallot, finely minced	2 teaspoons lemon juice
1 teaspoon capers	½ teaspoon Dijon mustard
½ teaspoon finely minced fresh dill or 1 teaspoon minced fresh cilantro	Splash each of olive oil and cognac
	Salt and pepper to taste

With a sharp knife, finely chop the salmon. (It is best not to use a food processor, as the salmon easily turns to a mush and the result will be a paste. It's important to retain the salmon's texture.)

Place salmon in a bowl along with the shallot, capers, dill, parsley, lemon juice, and mustard. Carefully mix. Add a splash each of olive oil and of Cognac and season to taste with salt and pepper.

TROUT PARTY DIP

American   *8 to 10 servings*

You can prepare this recipe several days in advance, as it will keep beautifully in the refrigerator for up to ten days.

4 medium-size trout	2 teaspoons salt
Boiling Liquid	½ teaspoon pepper
3 bay leaves	**Cocktail Sauce (makes approximately 1½ cups)**
4 teaspoons minced fresh parsley	¼ cup prepared horseradish
4 tablespoons butter	¼ cup lemon juice
Juice of ½ lemon	1 cup catsup

Clean trout, removing heads and skin. If possible, the flesh should remain intact. To make this easier, you can partially freeze the trout so that it is very cold, and then proceed with the cleaning steps, using pliers. Set trout aside.

Put just enough water in a 2-quart kettle (not larger; the fish should be crowded while they are cooking) to cover the fish—and then remove the fish. Add the boiling-liquid ingredients to the water and bring to a boil, stirring to get a nice mixture and aroma. Drop in the fish.

Cook for 6 to 8 minutes, depending upon the thickness of the trout. Be careful not to overcook. As soon as the trout are tender, take them out of the pot and slit them open; you should be able to remove the bones intact. Reserve the cooking liquid.

In a bowl, break up the flesh with a fork (any remaining bones can easily be picked out) and mix it with ¼ cup of the cooking liquid.

Combine the cocktail sauce ingredients in a separate bowl. The fish and cocktail sauce can be combined together in one bowl or served in separate bowls.

LOMI LOMI LUAU

American
10 to 30 servings, depending on the variety of appetizers served

Lomi lomi, a Hawaiian appetizer made of smoked salmon, resembles a Latin American ceviche. The main difference is that the fish is salt-cured rather than raw. The fillets are then torn by hand into shreds and "massaged" (as described by the Hawaiian word "lomi") with the vegetables and seasonings.

1½ pounds lox (smoked salmon)
4 beefsteak tomatoes, peeled and diced
1 cup minced green onions, including firm green tops

½ cup minced fresh cilantro
Dash hot pepper sauce
Juice of 1 lemon

Several hours before serving time, tear salmon into shreds with your fingers. Place in a mixing bowl along with the tomatoes, green onions, and cilantro. Mix ingredients well with your fingers, as if you were massaging them. Season with hot pepper sauce and lemon juice. Cover and refrigerate until serving time.

Serve lomi lomi in an attractive bowl accompanied by crackers.

SPINACH AND CHEESE PIE

American
4 to 10 servings

This crustless spinach and cheese pie will remind you of a quiche, although it is far lower in calories as it contains neither flour nor cream. Serve wedges as an appetizer, a side dish, or a luncheon or vegetarian entree, or include it with picnic fare, along with a pasta salad studded with garden vegetables and a sinfully rich chocolate dessert.

2 pounds fresh spinach (see
Note)
1 tablespoon butter
1 cup chopped green onions,
including firm green tops

5 eggs
½ pound Monterey Jack
cheese, grated
¼ cup grated cheddar cheese
Salt and pepper to taste

Tear spinach leaves off stems and wash well to remove all dirt and sand. Place spinach leaves in a pot of boiling water and return to a boil for a few seconds, until leaves are barely cooked. Drain and then rinse with cold water and ice cubes to help set the color. Fully drain and chop, squeezing out all excess liquid with the palms of your hands. You should have approximately 8 ounces of cooked spinach leaves. Set aside.

Melt butter in a medium-size skillet over medium heat. Add green onions and cook until soft. Add spinach and cook a few seconds until any remaining moisture has thoroughly evaporated. Set aside to cool.

In a large bowl, beat eggs. Add cheese and the cooled spinach mixture. Season to taste with salt and pepper. (The ingredients for this pie can be assembled several hours in advance and refrigerated until cooking time.)

Pour mixture into a buttered 9-inch pie plate and bake in a preheated 350° oven for about 40 minutes, or until nicely browned. To test, prick with a toothpick; when the toothpick comes out clean, the pie is done. Allow to cool at room temperature. Serve either at room temperature or cold.

Slice pie into wedges or thin slivers, depending upon whether it is an appetizer, side dish, or entree.

Note: If you are pinched for time, you can substitute one 10-ounce box of frozen spinach, defrosted and fully drained, although the taste will not be as fresh.

MIDDLE EASTERN LAMB KIBBEE

Armenian   *6 servings*

Raw lamb and cracked wheat, known as bulgur, are a tasty combination. Since the mixture is mild, serve plenty of chopped radishes and/or onions on the side.

¾ cup fine-grade bulgur
½ pound lean lamb
1 small onion, finely chopped
Seasonings to taste
Salt
Black pepper, freshly
ground
Nutmeg, freshly ground
Allspice

Olive oil

Garnish
Chopped radishes
Chopped onion
Tomato wedges

Place bulgur in a medium-size bowl and cover with cold water to soak for 20 minutes. Meanwhile, finely chop or grind the lamb. Use a food processor, if you have one—or ask your butcher to grind the meat.

To drain the bulgur of excess water, line a sieve with a kitchen tea towel and put the wheat into the sieve. Let excess water drain through into a bowl or kitchen sink. Then squeeze the towel against the sides of the sieve to make certain all liquid is pressed out. (Also refer to the recipe for tabbouleh—see Index.)

Combine the lamb, onion, and bulgur in a mixing bowl and sprinkle with seasonings. With your hands (you will need to dip your hands in ice water from time to time), shape the mixture into 6 small patties or one very large pancakelike patty. Cover with plastic wrap and refrigerate until ready to serve.

At serving time, place the patties on a platter. Make a big indentation in the center of each patty and pour olive oil into each. Garnish the platter with radishes, onion, and tomato wedges, and serve with additional salt.

EKRA—ARMENIAN EGGPLANT APPETIZER

Armenian   *Approximately 4 cups*

There are thousands of variations on eggplant appetizers. In this especially delicious recipe, often prepared in the household of my dear Armenian friend Terez Bassenian, the eggplant is roasted on the barbecue rather than in the oven, a technique used in many Middle Eastern countries.

3 medium eggplants	2 medium tomatoes, chopped
2 large onions, finely chopped	Salt, pepper, and cayenne
2 to 4 tablespoons olive oil	pepper to taste
½ 6-ounce can tomato paste	½ cup minced parsley
(or more to taste)	

Wrap eggplants individually in foil and place on a barbecue rack over hot coals. Cook, turning occasionally, about 20 minutes, or until soft. Eggplant can also be roasted over the open fire of a barbecue or under the broiler or stovetop without the foil. The purple skin will blister and turn brown. This roasting gives eggplant a unique, smoky flavor that cannot be achieved from oven baking. Peel off the skin and scoop out the inside flesh. Chop up eggplant very well and set aside.

Saute onions in olive oil. When soft, add eggplant and continue sauteing, another 5 to 8 minutes. Add tomato paste and tomatoes, stirring well. (More tomato paste can be added, depending upon desired taste and color.) Continue to cook, stirring often, for another 15 minutes. Season to taste with salt, pepper, and cayenne pepper.

Spoon the eggplant mixture into a large serving bowl and stir in half the parsley, mixing well. Garnish with remaining parsley. Allow to cool to room temperature. Ekra can be made in advance and refrigerated. Bring to room temperature before serving.

Serve with pita bread triangles as an appetizer.

Note: In the Greek cuisine, this same recipe is served as a dip, or meze. The eggplant is often pricked and baked rather than broiled. Refer to Eggplant and Pepper Salad (see Index).

TOASTED PITA BREAD TRIANGLES

Armenian   *6 to 8 servings*

Whenever I make these simple homemade pita "crackers," everyone begs for the recipe. My guests are always surprised at how easy they are to make. Served as an accompaniment to ratatouille, eggplant spreads, cucumber dips, hummus, Mexican salsa, and many other dishes, they are healthier and tastier than potato chips.

1 6-pack (8-ounce) package pita bread (preferably plain or sesame)	6 tablespoons butter or margarine at room temperature

Cut pita breads into quarters. (If you are using the larger size, cut into smaller wedges.) Carefully separate the triangles and generously spread the insides with butter. Place them on a foil-lined cookie sheet.

Bake in a preheated 400° oven 7 to 10 minutes, or until crisp.

Serve triangles at room temperature.

These triangles can be prepared several hours ahead and left at room temperature until time to bake.

ORIENTAL ASPARAGUS WITH SESAME SEED SAUCE

Chinese   *4 first-course servings*

An Oriental appetizer or first course featuring asparagus will be the hit of your next dinner party. To make sure the flavors blend, prepare this in the morning and refrigerate it, although it should be brought to room temperature before serving.

1 to 2 pounds asparagus	2 tablespoons soy sauce
	1 tablespoon sugar
Sesame Seed Sauce (makes approximately ¼ cup)	
1 to 1½ teaspoons sesame seeds, toasted	

To roll-cut the asparagus, Chinese-style, use a sharp knife, preferably a Chinese cleaver. Cut off and discard the woody white section of the asparagus. Continue to cut the asparagus into 3 to 4 diagonal lengths, turning the spear as you cut, thus obtaining many angles, which will attract the seasonings and sauce.

Boil asparagus in salted water for a few minutes, or until tender. Immediately drain and rinse with cold water and ice cubes to stop the cooking process. Completely drain again and pat dry with paper towels.

To toast the sesame seeds: Place them in a heavy skillet, without oil, and cook them over high heat, shaking constantly, for 1 to 2 minutes. Wait until you smell the superb aroma of the sesame seeds as they toast! Grind the seeds in a mortar and pestle or Japanese suribachi, or use a baby-food or coffee-bean grinder—although they're a bit messier to clean.

Place soy sauce in a small mixing bowl and add the sugar, stirring completely to dissolve. Stir in the ground sesame seeds and mix well.

Place asparagus in a medium-size bowl, pour the sauce over it, and gently mix. Cover and refrigerate, occasionally spooning sauce over asparagus. Serve at room temperature.

CHINESE TEA EGGS

Chinese   *4 to 8 servings*

These "marbleized" hard-cooked eggs are a classic Chinese appetizer. They are an unusual party dish, especially for a Chinese New Year's gala.

8 medium-size eggs	3 star anise flowers (see
¼ cup Chinese tea leaves	Index)
¼ cup soy sauce	Dash sugar
1 tablespoon salt	

Place eggs in a medium-size saucepan and cover with cold water; slowly bring to a boil, then reduce heat to a simmer. Continue to cook eggs for 30 minutes. Drain and rinse eggs in cold water for 5 to 10 minutes. When eggs have cooled, carefully crack the shells without breaking off any parts. (I use a wooden spoon to crack eggs.) Do *not* peel them.

Return eggs to saucepan, cover with water, and add the tea, soy sauce, salt, star anise, and sugar. Bring liquid to a boil, stir, cover, lower the heat, and simmer for 2 hours. Since the tea rises to the rim of the pot and underneath the lid, it is necessary to scrape it back into the simmering liquid from time to time.

Remove the pan from the heat and allow the eggs to cool in the liquid. This takes several hours. Refrigerate until serving time.

At serving time, peel the eggs, which now have a unique marbled exterior. They can be served whole or cut into halves or quarters.

Tea eggs can be made several days before needed; do not peel until serving time.

HONEY-SOY MARINATED CHICKEN LEGS

Chinese   *4 servings*

These chicken legs should be marinated a minimum of 24 hours. Then, deep-fry them and let them cool at room temperature for excellent party appetizers or picnic fare, garnished with scallion fans.

8 chicken legs

Honey-Soy Marinade (makes approximately ⅔ cup)

¼ cup honey
¼ cup soy sauce
2 tablespoons rice vinegar
1 teaspoon dry mustard
1 teaspoon minced fresh
    ginger

3 tablespoons flour
1 tablespoon cornstarch
Dash salt
1 quart cooking oil, for
    deep-frying

Garnish

Scallions

Place the chicken legs in a medium to large glass dish. Combine the honey, soy sauce, vinegar, mustard, and ginger and spoon it over and around to coat all parts of the chicken. Cover dish and refrigerate for 24 hours, during which time the marinade should be spread over the chicken legs several times.

To cook the chicken, remove it from marinade and pat dry. In a plastic bag or on a sheet of wax paper, combine the flour, cornstarch, and salt. Coat the chicken in the flour mixture.

Heat cooking oil to 350° in a large pot or deep-fryer. Fry four legs at a time, about 12 to 15 minutes or until golden and thoroughly cooked. Drain on paper towels and allow to cool to room temperature.

Scallion fans, a wonderful edible garnish for the chicken legs, can be made early in the day and soaked in ice water until needed. Trim scallions to about 5 or 6 inches in length, discarding both the feathery roots and the excess greens (or reserve for another recipe). Holding a scallion in one hand and a sharp knife in the other, cut vertical slits in both ends, about ½- to 1-inch deep. Place scallions in a large deep bowl with ice water and several ice cubes. In about an hour, both ends of the scallions will begin to curl.

To serve, place chicken legs on a platter, garnished with scallions.

SPECIAL CHINESE FRIED SHRIMP

Chinese   *4 to 6 servings*

Serve these glazed fried shrimp well chilled. They should be eaten in their well-seasoned shells.

1 pound large shrimp
    Cooking oil, for
    deep-frying

1 teaspoon finely minced
    ginger
1 scallion, finely minced

2 tablespoons sake
2 tablespoons soy sauce
1 tablespoon sugar
1 teaspoon rice vinegar

Garnish

Minced green onion stems

Leave shells and tails on shrimp, but remove the legs. Heat oil in a wok for deep-frying, about 375°. Add shrimp and deep-fry very quickly until they turn pink, about 30 to 60 seconds; remove immediately.

Drain oil, reserving for another use. Return wok to heat and add 1 tablespoon of reserved oil. Stir-fry the ginger and scallion for a few seconds to flavor the oil. Return shrimp to wok and stir-fry. Add sake, soy sauce, sugar, and vinegar, and cook, stirring constantly, for a few seconds. Remove shrimp to serving platter. Pour any sauce from the wok on top of them, cover, and refrigerate for several hours.

Serve shrimp well chilled, garnished with green onion stems.

CHINESE SPARERIBS WITH SWEET-TART MARINADE

Chinese   *4 to 6 servings*

These Chinese spareribs are especially terrific party appetizers or picnic fare since they are marinated and baked long in advance of eating. Adults and children alike love their sweet-tart flavor and chewy texture.

2½ to 3 pounds pork spareribs
  (1 sheet of ribs), trimmed
  of any excess fat

**Chinese Sweet-Tart Marinade
(makes approximately 1½ cups)**

  ½ cup soy sauce
  ¼ cup sake
  3 tablespoons beef or
    chicken broth

2 tablespoons hoisin sauce
3 tablespoons honey
1 tablespoon sugar
2 garlic cloves, minced
1 teaspoon minced fresh
  ginger
  Chinese plum sauce
  (optional)

Cut sheet of ribs into 3 or 4 large sections and place in a single layer in a large glass or Pyrex dish. Combine marinade ingredients in a mixing bowl or a large glass measuring cup, stirring to mix everything well. Pour on top of ribs and massage into meat. Cover dish and refrigerate for 24 hours, occasionally turning ribs in marinade.

To cook, bring ribs to room temperature, remove from marinade, and place on a wire rack over a foil-lined cookie sheet. Put the cookie sheet on the center rack in a 325° oven, with a small Pyrex dish or pan of water in the bottom of the oven. Bake spareribs 1½ to 1¾ hours, turning every 30 minutes. Ribs are done when the meat is a rich dark color and crispy.

Cut ribs apart and, using a Chinese cleaver, chop meat end pieces with the small bones into bite-size pieces.

Place ribs on a serving platter. Cover and keep at room temperature until serving. Ribs can also be refrigerated. Serve with Chinese plum sauce, if desired.

Variation: Chinese Sweet-Tart Marinade can be used for other recipes, such as pork chops and chicken pieces.

ECUADOR PICKLED FISH

Ecuadoran   *4 to 8 servings*

A most unusual version of ceviche from South America.

1 pound thin fillets of bass
  or other white fish
¾ cup fresh lime juice
½ cup fresh orange juice
2 tablespoons ketchup
1 medium onion, chopped
1 green pepper, chopped

1 sweet red pepper, chopped
1 serrano chile or other spicy
  green pepper, seeded and
  chopped
¼ cup cooked corn kernels
  Salt to taste

Lay fish fillets side by side in a glass or porcelain dish and pour ½ cup of lime juice on top. Cover and marinate in refrigerator several hours. Drain fillets and place on serving platter.

Combine remaining ingredients and spread over fillets. Refrigerate about an hour before serving.

POTTED SALMON

English   *Approximately 2 cups*

When salmon is at the height of its season, the markets always have an abundance of this fish with its rose-colored flesh at a reasonable price. Although leftover cooked salmon chilled with a fragrant homemade mayonnaise or dill sauce is terrific for lunch or supper, on occasion I have wanted something different. An excellent use of leftover cooked salmon is salmon butter, referred to as potted salmon in England, to be served as an hors d'oeuvre with sliced dark bread or party crackers.

1 pound leftover cooked
  salmon (see Note)
8 tablespoons butter
1 to 2 teaspoons lemon juice

Dash of hot pepper sauce
  or cayenne pepper
Salt and white pepper to
  taste

Salmon butter can easily be made in a food processor with the metal blade, or with a mortar and pestle, in which case the butter should be softened to room temperature. Process all ingredients to the consistency of butter, seasoning to taste with salt and pepper. If desired, add your choice of chopped fresh herbs such as parsley, cilantro, chives, and basil.

Spoon mixture into a decorative crock, cover, and refrigerate. Salmon butter should be served at room temperature so it will easily spread on bread slices or crackers.

Note: If you do not have any leftover salmon, simply poach fish in water to cover, following the Canadian Fisheries Department method of 10 minutes per inch thickness. Water can be seasoned with aromatic vegetables and/or wine. Refer to Fish-Poaching Basics (see Index) for a discussion of court bouillon and fish-poaching techniques.

Variation: This same recipe for making a "butter" can be used with other cooked foods, such as shrimp, fish, or even game birds.

MEDITERRANEAN RATATOUILLE

French   *12 to 18 servings*

This fine Mediterranean dish will remind you of summer's balmy evenings and al fresco European-style dinners. It is very similar to Italian caponata.

When preparing ratatouille, each vegetable should have a distinct taste and texture. Do not overstew them together. Simple seasonal substitutions should be made to ensure the freshest of all ingredients—the main ones being eggplant, tomatoes, zucchini, onions, and peppers. As a lover of mushrooms, I have added them to the classic recipe, resulting in a most successful dish.

Serve this as an hors d'oeuvre, salad, or side dish. You can also use it as a filling for tarts, crepes, and omelets, or toss with pasta.

1 1½-to-2-pound eggplant or several smaller Japanese eggplants, cut into 1-inch cubes
Salt
Approximately ¾ cup olive oil
2 medium to large onions, halved, thinly sliced, and separated into rings
1 large green pepper, seeded and cut into thin strips 2 inches long
1 large sweet red pepper, seeded and cut into thin strips 2 inches long
2 cloves garlic, minced

1 pound small zucchini, cut into ¼-inch slices
1 pound tomatoes, preferably plum, peeled and chopped
1 pound small mushrooms, ends trimmed (if mushrooms are large, cut in half)
2 tablespoons minced fresh basil (or about 2 to 3 teaspoons dried leaves)
2 tablespoons minced fresh parsley
1 teaspoon each dried thyme, rosemary, oregano, and sage leaves

2 bay leaves
1 heaping tablespoon (almost
  2 tablespoons) tomato
  paste
Salt and pepper to taste

Garnish

2 to 4 tablespoons minced
  fresh parsley

Place eggplant in a colander and sprinkle with salt. Allow "bitter" juices to drain for about 30 minutes. Rinse, drain, and pat dry with paper towels.

In a large skillet over low heat, heat 3 tablespoons of oil. Add half the eggplant, in a single layer, and cook over moderate heat, turning until lightly browned on all sides. Remove eggplant with a slotted spoon to a large Dutch oven and repeat process with remaining eggplant, adding another 2 to 3 tablespoons of oil. Remove this eggplant and place in the Dutch oven.

In the same skillet, heat 3 to 4 tablespoons of oil and add the onion, peppers, and garlic. Cook until barely tender, stirring often, for about 10 minutes. Add zucchini and tomatoes, and cook another 5 minutes, stirring often; add oil if necessary. Spoon vegetables into the Dutch oven with the eggplant. Then heat another 3 to 4 tablespoons of oil and cook mushrooms about 5 minutes, until lightly browned on all sides. Spoon into Dutch oven with the other vegetables.

Gently stir all vegetables to mix well. Add fresh basil and parsley. Grind the thyme, rosemary, oregano, sage, and bay leaves in a food processor or blender, or use an electric coffee-bean grinder. Add to vegetable mixture along with tomato paste, and salt and pepper to taste. Mix everything well, but gently.

Place Dutch oven over medium heat, partially cover, and simmer about 15 to 20 minutes, occasionally stirring; the dish should not become soupy or saucy. Uncover and cook another 1 to 2 minutes. Allow vegetables to cool to room temperature.

Serve at room temperature or chill for later use. When serving, garnish with minced parsley.

Ratatouille should be made one or several days in advance, as it tastes even better after flavors have combined.

TAPÉNADE

French

Approximately 1 cup;
6 to 8 servings

Tapénade has been referred to as the poor man's caviar of France. It is a Provençal specialty of minced black olives, anchovies, and capers blended to an aromatic paste with herbs and olive oil. A similar dish, olivada, has roots in Italy's Riviera. Tapénade can be served as a dip or spread for crudités or toast points; as a filling for hollowed-out cherry tomatoes, hard-cooked egg halves, boiled artichoke leaves, or green pepper wedges; or as an unusual dressing with chilled meat slices, chicken, or pasta.

1 cup pitted black olives (preferably a Greek or other Mediterranean variety)

4 anchovy fillets, rinsed, patted dry, and picked over for tiny bones

2 tablespoons capers, drained

¼ cup minced fresh basil (if unavailable, increase parsley)

2 tablespoons minced fresh parsley

1 large clove garlic, minced

1 tablespoon lemon juice

¼ cup olive oil

Tapénade can easily be made in a food processor with the steel chopping blade. Process all ingredients, except the olive oil, until fairly smooth. With the machine running, add the oil in a slow, steady stream until sauce is thick. Spoon tapénade into a bowl, cover, and refrigerate until needed. It will keep about one week.

If serving as a dip, spread, or accompanying sauce, chill well in a serving bowl. To use as a filling, spoon into hollowed-out vegetables or hard-cooked egg halves.

MEZEDAKI—MARINATED FETA CHEESE

Greek   *6 servings*

Most feta cheeses belong to the goat cheese family, as is true of the French chèvre popular in California cuisine. Imported feta comes from Greece, Bulgaria (this variety has received much acclaim), Yugoslavia, Rumania, Sardinia, Hungary, Israel, Denmark, and Holland. Feta is also produced domestically in California, New York, and Wisconsin. It is a white semisoft cheese usually made from goat's milk but also from cow's or ewe's milk.

When you purchase a fine fresh feta from a Middle Eastern market, it is soaking in a brine solution (salt water). Unless you plan to use it immediately, place your feta in a porcelain, plastic, or glass container and cover it with salt water, changing the liquid every few days. By keeping feta in brine, it will remain fresh for several days to weeks. Otherwise, it will quickly dry out.

¾ pound "brick" feta

Greek Marinade (makes approximately ⅔ cup)

½ cup olive oil

1 tablespoon minced fresh mint leaves

1 to 2 tablespoons dried leaf oregano, crumbled through your fingers

1 teaspoon fresh thyme leaves or ½ teaspoon dried

1 teaspoon lemon juice

Salt and pepper to taste

Remove feta from brine and wipe dry. Slice into six ¼-inch-thick pieces and place on a serving dish. Combine the marinade ingredients and pour them over the cheese. Allow to sit at room temperature at least 30 minutes before serving.

Feta cheese is best when marinated only a short time, as it absorbs the marinade during lengthy marination. However, it is possible to marinate several days if olive oil is occasionally poured on top.

Serve with slices of dark, crusty bread. If desired, thinly sliced red onion rings can be sprinkled on top. Or the feta can be cut into small cubes prior to marinating and served at cocktail time with toothpicks.

Variation: Try this same recipe with other goat cheeses, such as a French chèvre.

TROUT ANTIPASTO

Italian

6 to 12 servings, depending on number of other antipasto dishes

Serve as an appetizer with assorted marinated Italian vegetables, sausages, and cheeses.

1 medium onion, chopped	1 tablespoon finely chopped parsley
4 tablespoons olive oil	
2 bay leaves	2 tablespoons capers, drained and rinsed
6 whole cloves	
1 stalk celery, chopped	1 teaspoon salt
1 medium green pepper, chopped	1 teaspoon sugar
3 carrots, scraped and thinly sliced	½ teaspoon freshly ground black pepper
8 pimiento-stuffed green olives, sliced	1 large clove garlic, crushed
2 cups canned peeled tomatoes, with their liquid	1 4-pound trout, cleaned (see Note)

Saute the onion in 2 tablespoons olive oil until soft. Tie the bay leaves and cloves together in a piece of cheesecloth. Add all the ingredients except the trout to the onions and simmer for about 15 minutes.

Meanwhile, place the trout in a large pan. Pour boiling water slowly over the fish and then remove the head, fins, and skin (it should peel off fairly easily). Carefully bone and cut fish into bite-size pieces. Season with salt and pepper and saute lightly in the remaining 2 tablespoons of olive oil until golden brown.

Add fish to the simmering vegetables and continue to cook until the carrots are soft. Discard the bag of herbs. Spoon the mixture into a bowl and refrigerate overnight.

Variation: This appetizer can be made with other fish, such as mackerel.

BILL'S BIRTHDAY PARTY CAPONATA

Italian   *10 to 20 servings*

This Italian eggplant appetizer, similar to the French ratatouille, is one of my favorite party appetizers. It is well worth the cooking steps and time. Fortunately for the busy cook, it is best made several days in advance.

4 medium eggplants (about 1 pound each) or 4 pounds small Japanese eggplants
Salt for draining
2 pounds Italian plum tomatoes (see Note 1)
1 to 1½ cups olive oil
2 medium to large white or yellow onions, coarsely chopped
2 medium to large red onions, coarsely chopped
3 cups diced celery
2 large cloves garlic, finely minced

1 to 1½ cups olive oil
½ cup finely minced parsley
24 pitted small black olives, cut into rings
¼ cup capers
½ cup red wine vinegar
¼ cup water
2 tablespoons sugar
3 tablespoons tomato paste
Salt and pepper to taste

Garnish

¼ cup pine nuts, toasted (see Note 2)

With a sharp paring knife, peel 2 or 3 eggplants; leave the others unpeeled, to add color and texture to the dish. Cut all the eggplant into 1- to 2-inch cubes. Place the eggplant cubes in colanders over paper towels, salt well, and mix the eggplant and salt with your hands. Allow to drain for at least 30 minutes, and preferably for 1 to 2 hours, while preparing the remaining vegetables.

Peel the Italian tomatoes by dipping a few at a time in boiling water for a few seconds and then in cold water. Carefully remove skins with a paring knife and cut tomatoes in half. Remove and discard seeds and dice tomatoes.

In a large heavy skillet, heat about ⅓ cup olive oil and add the onions. Cook over medium heat for about 8 minutes, until onions are soft, not browned, stirring occasionally. Add the celery and garlic and mix thoroughly. Continue to cook over medium heat until everything is soft and tender, about 5 minutes. With a slotted spoon, remove vegetables to a large Dutch oven or roaster.

Pat eggplant dry with paper towels to remove salt and any excess liquid. In the same large skillet, cook a single layer of eggplant, adding olive oil as needed and stirring constantly, for about 8 minutes, until soft, tender, and lightly browned. Remove eggplant to the Dutch oven and brown succeeding batches, adding oil as needed, until all eggplant is done.

Add the diced tomatoes, parsley, olives, and capers to the cooked vegetable mixture. Mix everything well and cook over very low heat for a few minutes.

In a bowl, combine the vinegar, water, sugar, and tomato paste and stir until sugar is fully dissolved. Pour mixture into Dutch oven and stir thoroughly. Cover and cook over low heat for 15 minutes, stirring often. Be careful not to break up mixture to a mush; the vegetables should retain their shape and texture and not become overstewed or soupy. Season to taste with salt and pepper.

Remove from heat and refrigerate, covered, for several days to let all the flavors become mellow.

To serve, spoon mixture into a handsome salad bowl (wood is ideal) and garnish the top with toasted pine nuts. Serve with toasted pita triangles (see Index) or crusty Italian bread.

Note 1: Canned, peeled Italian tomatoes can be substituted, but the fresh are far better.

Note 2: To toast pine nuts, place in a single layer in a dry skillet over very low heat and "toast" until lightly brown, constantly stirring or shaking the skillet.

Variation: Sliced green olives can be used with the black olives (half of each). Pine nuts can be added to the mixture. Additional minced fresh parsley can be used as a garnish. For a spicy touch, add dried red pepper flakes, to taste, during the final 15 minutes of cooking.

HARD-COOKED EGGS SUKIYAKI

Japanese   *8 to 24 servings*

Hard-cooked eggs are a commonly used Japanese ingredient, and are often eaten plain for lunch. For Japanese-style stuffed eggs, you might try mashing the yolks with soy sauce and wasabi (reconstituted green horseradish) and restuffing them. I like to wrap thinly sliced beef around peeled hard-cooked eggs, simmer them in a seasoned liquid, and serve slices as an unusual party appetizer or picnic treat. This recipe also makes excellent use of all the extra hard-cooked eggs found in most American households after Easter.

8 hard-cooked eggs, carefully peeled (see Note 1)	½ cup sake
	⅔ cup soy sauce
½ pound sukiyaki meat (see Note 2)	2 tablespoons sugar
	4 thin slices fresh ginger

Wrap eggs in the meat, encasing them completely. If both eggs and meat are cold, the meat will adhere easily.

In a large skillet, combine the sake, soy sauce, sugar, and ginger. Cook at low heat until sugar has dissolved, stirring constantly. Place the meat-covered eggs in the sauce and cook gently for about 10 minutes, spooning sauce over the eggs; remove.

To cool, place cooked eggs on a rack over wax paper. Excess liquid will drain off. Sliced cooled eggs in halves or thirds, so that each slice has some egg yolk. (If eggs are to be stored for later use, do not slice them until needed. Store in the refrigerator.)

Note 1: For the best way to hard-cook eggs, place eggs in water to cover and bring to a boil. Cover, remove from heat, and steep eggs for 10 minutes. Uncover, rinse in cold water, and peel. This short-steeping technique of cooking prevents a grayish outer rim from forming around the yolks.

Note 2: I use rib eye steak sliced paper thin. At Oriental markets it is available already sliced and called sukiyaki meat; at the supermarket ask the butcher to cut the meat paper thin (sukiyaki style).

SLICED TOFU WITH CONDIMENTS

Japanese   *2 to 4 servings*

One of the simplest and tastiest ways to serve tofu is to drain slices of the fresh bean curd and then garnish it with soy sauce, sesame seeds, and green onions. These slices make an excellent alternative to eggs for breakfast, or they can be served as a snack, side dish, or vegetarian entree. This dish is very popular in Japan during the warm summer months, when the tofu is often chilled with ice cubes.

1 **cake water-packed tofu, quartered**	1 **teaspoon toasted sesame seeds**
1½ **tablespoons soy sauce**	1 **green onion, thinly sliced**

Dry out tofu on paper towels for about 20 minutes. Cut the drained tofu into triangles so that you have 8 equal pieces.

To serve, place on a serving platter and lightly pour soy sauce over all tofu. Sprinkle with sesame seeds and green onion; for a spicy touch, you may also wish to sprinkle with red pepper powder.

FLAVORED SHIITAKE—ORIENTAL MUSHROOMS

Japanese/Chinese   *4 to 8 servings*

Try serving this recipe as an appetizer (zensai) at your next dinner party.

5 **to 10 large dried shiitake**	⅓ **cup soy sauce**
⅓ **cup sake**	1 **tablespoon sugar**

Cover dried mushrooms with warm water and soak for several hours, preferably 24. To cook, bring mushrooms with soaking liquid to a boil, then slightly reduce heat and continue to cook until all water is absorbed. Add sake, soy sauce, and sugar, stirring well to mix ingredients. Continue to cook until all flavors are absorbed.

Let mushrooms cool and remove center core, if desired. If mushrooms are bite-size, serve whole; if they are large, slice into thick strips, about 3 to 4 per mushroom. Serve at room temperature.

ONIGIRI—COLD RICE BALLS

Japanese

20 to 24 rice balls; 5 to 12 servings, depending on number of courses

Onigiri are perfect for a picnic or bento lunch (boxed lunch) or as party hors d'oeuvres. Children like them, too. You can serve them with a simple sprinkling of salted black sesame seeds, or you can put a pinch of filling inside or on top.

3 cups hot steamed white rice

Assorted Fillings and Wrappings

    Salted black sesame seeds
    Nori, cut into thin strips
    Broiled and seasoned fish pieces

    Fermented soy beans
    Umeboshi
    Crushed pineapple or other fruit
    Sweetened and pureed azuki beans

The rice must be very hot to be shaped into balls. It will help you shape the rice to have a bowl of salted or vinegared water handy to dip your hands into as you work.

Place about 1 tablespoon of rice in the palm of your hands and shape. If a filling is desired, press it into the center of the rice ball as you are shaping it. If the filling is to be placed on top, make an indentation in the rice ball. If desired, balls may be wrapped with strips of nori. Salted black sesame seeds are primarily used to sprinkle on the outside.

Serve at room temperature, with soy sauce if desired. Leftovers can be stored at room temperature for several hours.

SUSHI AND SASHIMI

Japanese

The very popular sushi and sashimi are attractively arranged bite-size slices of fish—most often raw. The basic difference between the two is that sushi comes with a cold vinegar-dressed rice (sushi meshi) whereas sashimi stands alone.

If you have never savored these delicacies, don't let the rawness turn you away. Think about oysters or clams on the half shell, perhaps more familiar raw-fish appetizers. Incidentally, for the novice or the timid, there are several shellfish, such as crab, lobster, or shrimp, which are generally cooked for sushi preparation.

As far as fish selection, saltwater fish and shellfish are the best. Raw freshwater fish and salmon are not recommended, as they may carry parasites. At a sushi bar, these are smoked, salt-cured, or cooked.

Both sushi and sashimi are served with several condiments and garnishes. A small dab of green horseradish paste, wasabi, is generally placed between the rice and fish when sushi is made. For sashimi, the wasabi is served on the side. (Wasabi is made by reconstituting horseradish powder; water is added drop by drop until the proper pastelike consistency is achieved. Wasabi is very pungent; be stingy with it!) Shredded daikon that has been crisped in ice water, sweet pickled ginger (gari), and a small container of soy sauce generally accompany both sushi and sashimi. Other common garnishes or condiments include cucumber, parsley, lettuce or greens, red pepper, watercress, seaweed, Japanese pickles, minced green onions, and carrot or lemon slices.

In making sushi or sashimi, it is essential to understand how to cut the fish. Slightly dampen both the knife and the cutting board to aid in the slicing. When you slice, use a cutting rather than a sawing motion. Do not tear the fish; the cuts should be clean. It is best to use the tip and bottom one-third to two-thirds of the knife blade. Occasionally wipe the blade clean with a moist towel.

In most cases, fish fillets should be cut into bite-size pieces, approximately ¼- to ½-inch-thick rectangles. Cut straight down and then pull the knife toward you. Thick loins of fish, such as tuna, can easily be cut in this manner.

Halibut and other firm white fish are typically cut into very thin, nearly transparent slices, about ⅙-inch thick. To cut like this, the blade must be slanted at an almost horizontal angle and the fish sliced across the grain.

Once you are comfortable with slicing fish, you can serve sashimi at any time. Sashimi makes a wonderful party appetizer, the most common combinations being tuna, whitefish, and octopus. Allow at least five slices of fish per person.

In order to prepare sushi, you must make the special vinegar-dressed rice. Short-grained rice should be washed and steamed, allowed to rest uncovered, and then mixed with the dressing. The proper marriage of the dressing, called awaze-zu, with the cooked rice is of utmost necessity.

While the rice is cooking, combine the dressing ingredients. A good formula for this dressing is 4 parts rice vinegar, 2 parts sugar, ½ part salt. To estimate your vinegar needs, calculate approximately 10 percent of the original rice measurement. Thus for 2 generous cups of uncooked rice, use ¼ cup vinegar, 2 tablespoons sugar, and 1 to 1½ teaspoons salt. Mix ingredients together in a small bowl, stirring with chopsticks until the sugar has dissolved. Taste the dressing, adjusting the ingredients to taste. Some people prefer equal parts of vinegar and sugar. A sweet-sour flavor is desired.

After the rice has been properly steamed and allowed to rest, turn it into a wooden tub or a glass, porcelain, or plastic bowl. Do not use metal as it may interact unfavorably with the vinegar. Fan rice with a sturdy piece of cardboard and slowly pour the dressing over the rice. Do not add all the dressing at once; the rice should absorb the dressing without becoming soupy.

Using a wooden rice paddle or spatula, turn the rice over, a small amount at a time, as if you were cutting through the rice from top to bottom (a motion similar to that of folding in egg whites). At the same time, continue to cool the rice with the fan so that the rice absorbs the dressing and becomes shiny. This process takes about 10 minutes.

Sushi rice can be made a couple of hours in advance. Cover the mixture with a damp kitchen tea towel and leave at room temperature. Unfortunately, the seasoned rice does not refrigerate or freeze well, so use it within one day.

There are four basic categories of sushi: (1) fingers or ovals (nigiri-zushi), (2) rolls generally made with nori wrappers (maki-zushi), (3) pressed loaves (oshi-zushi), and (4) scattered (chirashi-zushi).

In my Japanese cookbook, *Japanese Cooking for the American Table* (published by J. P. Tarcher, Inc.), I have devoted an entire chapter to the preparation of sushi and sashimi. Please refer to that book for a more in-depth discussion of the techniques, with illustrations. Also refer to the index of this book for Chirashi-Zushi—Scattered Sushi Salad, which I feel is best suited to parties and entertaining.

JAPANESE CUCUMBER-TROUT APPETIZER

Japanese   *6 to 8 servings*

A novel sunomono (vinegared vegetable dish) combining fresh trout with cucumbers, this is an unusual appetizer to serve at your next dinner party.

¼ cup rice vinegar	1 cup finely chopped trout
¼ cup soy sauce	fillets
2 teaspoons sugar	3 medium cucumbers
1 teaspoon finely chopped fresh ginger	

Combine the soy sauce, vinegar, sugar, and ginger in a ceramic or glass bowl, stirring to make sure sugar is fully dissolved. Stir in chopped fish. Marinate one hour. Peel cucumbers, cut in half lengthwise, and scoop out seeds. Slice very thin and add to fish mixture. Set aside for 15 minutes and serve in individual small bowls.

GEFILTE FISH

Jewish   *Approximately 30 gefilte fish;*
                                       8 to 10 servings

One of the most traditional of all Jewish dishes, chilled gefilte fish (fish balls) is often served for special holidays and celebrations, particularly after sundown on

Yom Kippur, a day of fasting. Gefilte fish is best made several days in advance and refrigerated until serving time.

Gefilte Fish Stock

Fish heads, bones, and skin (see Note)
1 onion, cut in half
2 large stalks of celery (with leaves), chopped
3 carrots, chopped
2 bay leaves
6 peppercorns

Fish Dumplings

2 pounds whitefish fillets

1 large onion, finely chopped
1 hard-cooked egg, finely chopped
Salt and white pepper to taste
2 to 3 teaspoons matzo meal or fine bread crumbs

Garnish

Cooked carrots
Horseradish sauce

Place fish parts in a large stock pot and add water to cover. Add the onion, celery, carrots, bay leaves, and peppercorns. Bring stock to a boil, then reduce to a simmer and allow to simmer for at least 30 minutes. This fish stock can be made in advance and refrigerated or frozen.

Meanwhile, chop the fish fillets by hand or with the aid of a food processor; be careful to chop the fish and not turn it into a mush. Place chopped fish in a large bowl and add the finely chopped onion, egg, salt, and pepper. Bind the mixture with the matzo meal. With your hands, form fish mixture into small balls, using about ¼ cup for each (have a bowl of ice water handy and keep your hands moist).

Place fish balls in the simmering pot of stock. There should be enough liquid to cover the fish balls (add water if necessary). Return liquid to a boil, then reduce to a simmer and cook fish for 2 hours, occasionally basting fish balls with the stock.

Remove fish balls and chill. If you wish to reserve the stock for another use, strain and refrigerate or freeze.

At serving time, place several fish balls on each plate; garnish with cooked carrots and horseradish sauce.

Note: Call your fishmonger or butcher in advance and request that he save you some fish heads, bones, and skin to use for a fresh fish stock. If you have a friendly relationship with your supplier, there's generally no charge for these parts. Plan this in advance, and reserve in your freezer.

AUNT ROSE'S GEFILTE FISH SIMPLIFIED

Jewish   *6 to 8 servings*

There are several excellent brands of jarred gefilte fish. If you wish to save yourself the many hours of preparing homemade fish balls, you can season and further cook the commercially made ones according to the following excellent recipe.

1 large onion, thinly sliced
3 carrots, thinly sliced
  Salt, pepper, and paprika
  to taste
1 24-ounce jar gefilte fish
  with its liquid

Garnish
  Cooked carrots
  Horseradish sauce

Place the onion and carrots in a large, heavy stove-to-oven pot. Season with salt, pepper, and paprika, and add water to cover. Bring to a boil. Add fish and liquid. Cover pan and simmer for an hour. Uncover and place in a 350° oven for 30 minutes. Refrigerate until serving time. Serve chilled, as in the preceding recipe, with vegetables and horseradish.

KOSHER CHOPPED HERRING

Jewish   *6 or more servings*

From my Philadelphia family comes this recipe for Jewish-style chopped herring. These marinated fillets can also be used to make Scandinavian herring dishes.

3 whole herrings in brine
½ cup cider vinegar
2 tart apples, peeled, cored,
  and diced
2 hard-cooked eggs, chopped
2 onions, chopped
2 slices white bread, soaked
  in water and squeezed dry,
  then crumbled

1 teaspoon sugar (or more to
  taste)
  Freshly ground pepper and
  salt to taste

Soak herring overnight in a stainless steel bowl with cold water to cover. Occasionally drain and add fresh cold water to cover. Drain well. Remove skin and bones and cut herring into 1- to 2-inch pieces. Combine all ingredients and marinate for several hours before serving.

    Serve chilled as an hors d'oeuvre or appetizer with thinly sliced dark bread.

    Scandinavian variation: After herring has marinated for several hours, remove it from the marinade, reserving the marinade for other use. Combine herring with 1 red onion sliced into thin rings, 1 cup sour cream, ¼ cup finely chopped fresh dill, and, if desired, ¼ to ½ cup Dijon-style mustard.

CHOPPED CHICKEN LIVER APPETIZER

Jewish   *3 cups*

Every Jewish household has its favorite recipe for chopped chicken liver. This one is from my family's personal collection.

1 pound chicken livers	4 hard-cooked eggs, peeled
¾ cup chicken fat (available from your butcher)	1 teaspoon salt
	Dash pepper
1 cup coarsely chopped onions	

Wash chicken livers and pat dry with paper towels; set aside.

Cut up chicken fat and place in a skillet with the onions. Saute, stirring occasionally, to prevent burning the onions. Cook until the onions are lightly browned and fat is melted. Remove onions and set aside. Pour liquid chicken fat into a cup and set aside.

Place livers in the same skillet with 3 tablespoons of the liquid chicken fat and saute until well done. Add additional chicken fat, if necessary. Cool slightly.

Using a food grinder with a fine blade, a food blender at high speed, a food processor with a metal blade, or a chopping bowl, finely grind or chop the livers, hard-cooked eggs, and onions. Place mixture in a bowl, add salt, pepper, and about ¼ cup liquid fat. If additional fat is necessary, add salad oil, one tablespoon at a time, to the mixture. Mix until all ingredients are well blended.

Fill a well-oiled 3-cup mold or shape into a simple ball and refrigerate. Serve with cocktail-size rye bread slices.

EGGPLANT AND PEPPER SALAD

Jewish   *Approximately 2 cups*

Eggplant appetizer and salad recipes are found throughout the Middle East and north into the Soviet Union as well as in the Far East. The base of all these dishes is primarily roasted eggplant combined with peppers, onions, and oil. Some cultures add tomatoes, as in ekra (see Index), while others serve them on the side. The plump, round-bellied, deep purple eggplants are used in the Middle East and Eastern Europe, whereas the Oriental cuisines prefer the small cylindrical variety.

Every household has its favorite eggplant recipes. This one is from my great aunt Sherry Silverman's collection.

1 large eggplant (about 1¼ pounds)	1 small to medium onion, finely minced
1 large green pepper	1 tablespoon lemon juice or

white vinegar	Garnish (optional)
2 tablespoons salad or olive oil	Quartered tomatoes
Salt and pepper to taste	

Prick eggplant all over with the tines of a fork to prevent it from explod-
ing in the oven. Place eggplant and green pepper on a cookie sheet and
bake at 450° for 40 to 45 minutes, occasionally turning the vegetables.
The eggplant is done when it has deflated, the skin is brownish, and the
center feels very soft. The pepper is done when it is blackened on the
outside. (In several cuisines, the eggplant and pepper are placed on a grill
over hot coals or over a gas burner until charred.) Allow vegetables to
cool.

Peel eggplant and pepper, discarding the skins. Finely chop the
eggplant pulp, including the seeds, and place in a medium to large
serving bowl. Discard pepper seeds and finely chop the flesh, reserving
any pepper juice. Stir both the pepper and juice into eggplant; the mixture will resemble a chunky paste. Add minced onion, mixing thoroughly. Add first the lemon juice and then the oil, stirring thoroughly
each time. Season to taste with salt and pepper. Cover bowl and refrigerate several hours before serving.

To serve, accompany with quartered tomatoes, if desired, and offer
triangles of pita bread or chunks of a hearty, crusty bread on which to
spread the eggplant mixture.

Variation: This salad has Rumanian Jewish roots, and some cooks
of that region add more green pepper. Crushed garlic may also be added.
I have tasted a Greek version in which peeled, seeded, and chopped
tomatoes were added. Cayenne pepper to taste may also be added. For
baba ganoush, a Middle Eastern eggplant relish found in Lebanon, Syria,
and Jordan, ¼ cup tahini (sesame paste) is added instead of green pepper, along with an additional 2 tablespoons of olive oil. A little olive oil is
also dribbled over the top and sides of the dish, and it is garnished with
minced green onions at serving time. To transform this recipe into an
Indian bhurta, you can add a few tablespoons of plain yogurt and season
to taste with fresh and/or dried chiles.

CEVICHE/SCALLOP CEVICHE

Mexican   *3 to 4 servings*

*When investigating the origin of ceviche, I found a strong Oriental heritage.
Many of the Japanese techniques of preparing sushi are similar to those used in
Mexican ceviche. Also, one of the most important ingredients—cilantro or
Mexican parsley—is equivalent to yuen sai or Chinese parsley and to Portu-
guese coentro. It is thought that the Oriental influence came into the western*

part of Mexico when the Spaniards opened up trade routes between the Philippines and the New World.

If you have never tasted ceviche and are unsure about eating "raw" fish, remember that raw oysters and cherrystone clams on the half shell are typical American appetizers, so eating fish marinated in lime juice is not as shocking as it may first sound.

There are a number of fish which are suited for ceviche. My first experience was with shrimp. Since then we have enjoyed scallops, abalone, mahi mahi (dolphin, called dorado in Baja Mexico), and many more. The Mexicans also use mackerel, red snapper, and corbina, and you may wish to try bass, crab, tuna, oysters, sole, flounder, halibut, shark, pompano, octopus, mussels, or any combination of fish.

The secret of ceviche is in its preparation. It is neither raw nor cooked by heat. Consider it to be pickled or marinated. The citric acid in the juice of the limes make the raw fish opaque and tender. Some Mexican cooks may suggest limones, which are actually limes. Although lemons can be substituted in an emergency, you will not have the same result. Small, tart, juicy Baja limes and Florida Key limes are best.

1 **pound scallops, diced**	½ **cup chopped green pepper**
Juice of 6 limes	½ **cup chopped sweet red**
3 **tablespoons chopped fresh**	**pepper**
cilantro	

Place scallops in a glass or porcelain bowl and marinate with lime juice for approximately two hours in the refrigerator. Drain and add the remaining ingredients, mixing well. Chill at least one additional hour. Serve in bowl.

Variation: For a more elaborate scallop ceviche, substitute two pimientos for the sweet red pepper and add ½ cup chopped red onion, 1 tablespoon tarragon vinegar, ¼ cup cold water, and ¼ teaspoon pepper. The pimientos, green pepper, and onion should be marinated in a separate bowl with the vinegar, water, and pepper. Both the scallops and the vegetables should be marinated for approximately 3 hours. Prior to serving, drain the vegetables and combine with the scallops and the marinade.

ACAPULCO SHRIMP CEVICHE

Mexican   *6 to 10 servings*

This shrimp is "cooked" in lemon juice and then tossed with a colorful combination of aromatic and piquant vegetables and spices.

2 **pounds shelled and**	2 **onions, chopped**
deveined shrimp or firm	8 **medium tomatoes, peeled**
whitefish	**and chopped**
2 **cups lime juice**	

1 cup green olives with pits
  (not black olives)
10 serrano chilies (or to taste),
  seeded and finely chopped
2 cups tomato paste

1 cup olive oil
⅔ cup minced fresh cilantro
  Salt, pepper, and dried leaf
  oregano to taste

Cut shrimp into 1- to 2-inch pieces. Place in a large glass or porcelain bowl with the lime juice and marinate for at least three hours. Drain juice and add onions and tomatoes. Remove pits from olives, chop into small pieces, and add to shrimp, along with remaining ingredients, crumbling oregano through your palms and fingers directly into the bowl. Cover and refrigerate.

Serve as a cocktail snack with fresh tortilla chips or as a first course or luncheon dish.

CEVICHE CON ALCÁPARRAS—CEVICHE WITH CAPERS

Mexican   *4 to 6 servings*

Complement this whitefish ceviche with frothy margaritas for a romantic afternoon snack, Baja style.

1 pound fresh whitefish, cut
  into small pieces
  Juice of 6 limes
1 teaspoon salt
  Dash of freshly ground
  pepper
4 jalapeño peppers, seeded
  and chopped
2 medium tomatoes, peeled
  and chopped

1 large onion, chopped
3 tablespoons capers
¼ cup olive oil
2 tablespoons dry white wine
  or vinegar
2 tablespoons chopped fresh
  cilantro

Garnish

Avocado slices

Place fish in glass or porcelain dish and cover with lime juice. Sprinkle with salt and pepper and allow to marinate in refrigerator for several hours. Drain and add remaining ingredients, except avocado. Mix lightly and chill further.

Serve very cold in shells or cocktail glasses, garnished with avocado slices.

GALATINA—MEXICAN POACHED "PÂTÉ"

Mexican   *2 loaves; 8 to 12 servings*

Similar to a French country pâté, this coarse Mexican meatloaf is ideal for a picnic or al fresco buffet. Pinches of a variety of sweet and aromatic spices gives this galatina a marvelous taste. A similar Argentinian dish, matambre, uses slices of beef wound around the hard-cooked eggs.

2 pounds ground beef	1 clove garlic, minced
Pinch each of ground	¼ cup finely chopped onion
cloves, thyme, marjoram,	½ cup chopped fresh parsley
cinnamon, ginger, nutmeg,	4 hard-cooked eggs, peeled
salt, and pepper	Water
1 egg	½ cup vinegar
2 tablespoons plain bread	½ cup dry white wine
crumbs	1 onion, thinly sliced
2 tablespoons flour	3 bay leaves
1 tomato, finely diced	1 tablespoon cooking oil

In a mixing bowl, combine the meat with the spices, egg, bread crumbs, flour, tomato, garlic, chopped onion, and parsley. Divide meat mixture in half and place the first half in the center of a large double-thick piece of cheesecloth. Slightly flatten meat into a rectangular shape. Place 2 hard-cooked eggs vertically in the center of the meat and form meat into the shape of a loaf, totally encasing the eggs in the center. Roll up meat tightly in the cheesecloth and tie ends close to the meat with kitchen string. (The cheesecloth is to retain the shape of the loaf during the next cooking step.) Repeat process with remaining half.

Place meatloaves in a large pot with water to cover and add vinegar, wine, sliced onion, bay leaves, and cooking oil. Bring to a boil, then reduce to a simmer and cook covered for 1½ hours. Remove meatloaves from liquid and allow to cool thoroughly before removing cheesecloth. Refrigerate for 24 hours.

Serve cold, thinly sliced, accompanied with your favorite salsa.

TEQUILA-MARINATED AVOCADO APPETIZERS

Mexican   *2 to 4 servings*

Simple yet delicious.

1 large avocado	2 tablespoons tequila
1 tablespoon fresh lemon	2 cloves garlic, crushed
juice	⅓ cup olive oil
	Salt to taste
Tequila Marinade (makes	
approximately ½ cup)	
¼ cup cider vinegar	

Using a melon ball kitchen gadget, scoop avocado flesh into balls. Sprinkle with lemon juice to hold the green color. Place avocado in a serving bowl.

To prepare marinade: In a mixing bowl (or in a food processor), whisk together the vinegar and tequila. Add garlic. Slowly dribble in the olive oil. Season to taste with salt.

Pour marinade over avocado, cover, and refrigerate several hours before serving.

LABAN OR MAST—YOGURT

Approximately 1–1½ cups;
Middle Eastern   *4 to 8 servings*

Yogurt has gained tremendous popularity in the United States as a simple breakfast, lunch, or nutritious snack. There are varieties ranging from plain to those pasteurized with fruits, granola, and other additions, including chemical additives. Today there is even frozen yogurt—delicious, but a distant relative of the original yogurt.

Plain yogurt is a very important food item in the Middle East, where it is often served with a garnish of mint, chopped onions, or sometimes other vegetables or fruits, or as the primary ingredient in a sauce or side dish. There is even a cooling yogurt drink called lassi (see Index).

A tangy "cheese," actually yogurt curds (called laban *or* mast*), is yet another use of yogurt in many Middle Eastern countries. It is eaten as a breakfast by the nomadic Bedouin people. In many families it is served as an appetizer to be eaten with bread and a garnish of minced mint and green onions, or as a dessert on top of fresh berries or sliced peaches, when it is like crème fraîche. It is also a welcome side dish to accompany spicy entrees.*

1 **quart plain yogurt**
½ **teaspoon salt**

Place several layers of dampened cheesecloth in a fine-holed strainer or a mold for Coeur à la Crème. (If you use a colander with overly large holes, the yogurt will simply pour through.) Place the strainer (or mold) over a large bowl to catch the drippings.

Mix together the yogurt and salt and pour into the strainer. Carefully bring up sides of cheesecloth and lightly cover with plastic wrap. Refrigerate for at least 8 hours so that the liquid (whey) will drain. Laban can easily be made overnight or even several days in advance.

Though this whey is traditionally discarded, I have on occasion put it to secondary use in making sauces and dressings.

Spoon laban into a bowl and eat as a simple breakfast or appetizer. Serve with garnishes of minced mint and green onions. Or use it on top of a bowl of fresh fruits.

Variation: An Indian sweet "pudding," shrikhanp, is made with laban. Combine laban with 6 tablespoons of sugar and season, if desired, with ¼ teaspoon each ground saffron and cardamom. Blend thoroughly, chill, and garnish with ¼ cup chopped pistachio nuts.

HUMMUS—CHICKPEA-TAHINI SPREAD

Middle Eastern   *8 to 16 servings*

Hummus, a pureed garbanzo-sesame spread, is popular in the Middle East on pita bread or crackers. It reminds me of a peanutty cheese spread or a vegetarian French rillette. Bottled or canned tahini is available at health-food stores and Middle Eastern markets.

1 cup dry garbanzo beans (chickpeas) or 2½ cups canned, drained
½ teaspoon salt
2 large cloves garlic
¾ cup fresh lemon juice
⅓ cup tahini (or more to taste)

¼ cup olive oil
Salt to taste

Garnish

¼ to ⅓ cup minced fresh parsley

Dry garbanzo beans can be soaked overnight and then cooked, or they can be "quick-soaked" just prior to cooking. To use the quick-soak method, rinse the beans and remove any that are badly bruised. Place in a large pot with 3 cups cold water. Bring to a boil and cook uncovered for 2 minutes. Remove from heat and soak for 1 hour. Drain and add 1 quart cold water. Bring to a boil; then slightly lower the heat and cook partially covered for 1 hour, adding more hot water as needed to cover. Add ½ teaspoon salt and continue to cook another 30 minutes or until tender, adding hot water if necessary. Drain and cool. The beans are now ready to use in this recipe or others.

To prepare the spread, place garbanzos and garlic in a food processor and puree. Add lemon juice, tahini, and olive oil and continue to process until well blended. Season to taste with salt. If thinner hummus is preferred, dilute with ½ to 1 cup of the cooking liquid, adding one tablespoon at a time.

Shape mixture into a ball or mound and place on a medium-size platter or in a crock. Allow flavors to mellow several hours before serving.

Hummus can be made a day or more in advance. If so, refrigerate and bring to room temperature before serving.

At serving time, heavily garnish top and sides of hummus with minced parsley. As a party appetizer, spread hummus on pita bread triangles, crackers, raw vegetables, or even apple slices.

Variation: A very simple Middle Eastern snack is made of cooked chickpeas (garbanzo beans) seasoned to taste with salt and pepper. Nahit, the Hebrew word for chickpeas, is traditionally served in Jewish households in this simple manner for such celebrations as a bris, the religious ceremony that accompanies the circumcision of a boy, or at Purim, a holiday honoring Queen Esther (a vegetarian) and her cousin Mordecai, who protected the Jewish people from the wicked Haman.

PICKLED MUSHROOMS

Russian/Polish/Jewish   *4 to 6 servings*

In Russia, a favorite early-morning pastime is walking through the forests stalking wild mushrooms. These prized mushrooms are later cleaned and pickled for several days to be enjoyed with special friends at the zakuska table.

Pickled mushrooms can be found in many European and Middle Eastern cuisines, as well as in the United States as a party hors d'oeuvre. In the United States, most cooks prefer fresh whole button mushrooms. Gourmet produce stands are starting to carry more unusual fresh mushrooms, such as the Oriental shiitake, which has an earthier flavor reminiscent of the Russian wild mushroom.

1 pound small fresh
mushrooms
½ cup red wine vinegar
¾ cup water
3 whole cloves
4 peppercorns
1 small bay leaf

2 whole allspice
1 tablespoon sugar
½ teaspoon salt

Garnish

½ cup chopped onions

Clean the mushrooms with a special mushroom brush or damp paper towels. Do not peel, but trim a thin layer off the stems if they are tough.

In a medium-size pot, combine the vinegar, water, cloves, peppercorns, bay leaf, allspice, sugar, and salt. Bring to a boil, stirring to dissolve the sugar. Add the chopped onions and then reduce heat to a simmer for 5 minutes.

Place mushrooms in a pot of boiling water for 2 to 3 minutes, just until they begin to become tender. Drain and place in a glass jar, ceramic bowl, or plastic container and pour the warm pickling liquid on top. Cover and refrigerate several days before eating. Pickled mushrooms will keep in the refrigerator several weeks. The flavor improves with time.

To serve, drain with a slotted spoon. Serve the mushrooms along with chopped onions as a party hors d'oeuvre.

GRAVLAX WITH MUSTARD-DILL SAUCE

Scandinavian   *8 to 12 servings*

The first time I ever tasted homemade gravlax was about six years ago while summering at the beaches of Oceanside, Oregon, when I was attending a week's cooking classes with James Beard. We prepared dozens of regal whole salmon, from poached to baked. Although all were delicious, my favorite technique was the curing process.

To make gravlax, the most important ingredient is impeccably fresh salmon. Thinly sliced, the fish is properly accompanied with a mustard-dill sauce, finely sliced red onion rings, capers, lemon slices, and black bread. The sauce is also excellent with poached salmon or halibut and cold poached chicken breasts.

1 medium-size fresh salmon (about 5 to 6 pounds), boned, skinned (see Note), and filleted (final weight about 3¼ pounds)

¼ cup kosher or coarse salt (sea salt)

¼ cup granulated or brown sugar

2 teaspoons to 1 tablespoon black peppercorns, coarsely crushed with a mortar and pestle

4 to 6 ounces (3 bunches) baby dill, washed and dried

Mustard-Dill Sauce (makes approximately 1 cup)

½ cup Dijon mustard (a spicy dark variety)

1 tablespoon wine vinegar

¼ cup sugar

½ cup olive oil or ¼ cup each olive and vegetable oil

3 to 4 tablespoons fresh chopped dill

Garnish

Capers

Red onion, thinly sliced

Lemon slices

Carefully remove all bones from the fillets with tweezers.

In a bowl, combine the salt, sugar, and peppercorns. Rub this curing mixture well onto all sides of the salmon.

Cut one large sheet of heavy-duty foil (longer than the fillets) and place a bed of dill on it. Sprinkle the dill with any remaining curing mixture. Put one fillet (slab) of salmon on the dill layer, "skin" side down, and place dill sprigs over salmon; top with the second slab of salmon, "skin" side up, and then dill on top of salmon. Wrap the foil around the fillets, crimping all sides to seal the package well.

Place this foil package in the refrigerator, top with a cutting board, and weight down with a heavy object, such as a brick. Refrigerate salmon for several days. The flavor of the cured fish is best after 3 to 4 days (I've even waited longer), even though some cooks wait only a day. During the curing time, turn the package upside down and reweight so that the juices thoroughly permeate the fish.

To prepare the sauce: Use a food processor (with the metal blade) or an electric mixer to blend the mustard, vinegar, and sugar. Slowly dribble in the oil and stir in the dill. Cover and refrigerate.

At serving time, unwrap the salmon package and pull off all the dill. On a cutting board, slice the salmon very thinly, cutting diagonally at an angle, as is done with smoked salmon or lox. Serve as an appetizer, first course, or luncheon entree with the classic gravlax accompaniments—capers, thinly sliced red onion, lemon slices, sliced black bread, and the mustard-dill sauce.

Variation: For a French version of gravlax, substitute such minced fresh herbs as thyme, tarragon, parsley, and/or rosemary for the dill and, if you wish, splash a little cognac on the fillets before wrapping them in foil.

Note: If desired, the salmon skin can be left on, although I find it is easier both to fillet and serve the fish if the skin is removed before curing. If the salmon is large, use the center-cut portion and prepare remaining fish for another recipe.

ESCABECHE OF POACHED WHITEFISH

International   *8 to 16 servings*

This chilled marinated fish and herb dish makes a remarkable party hors d'oeuvre. Serve it in a large glass bowl so that guests can enjoy the lovely colors. It is also excellent when spooned into the center of a papaya or avocado half and served as a salad entree.

2 pounds firm boned whitefish fillets (such as sheepshead or halibut) or even lobster or crabmeat
Simple court bouillon (see Index)

Escabeche Marinade (makes approximately 4 cups)
1 large red onion, finely chopped

1 bunch cilantro, leaves only, minced
Juice of 3 lemons, 3 limes, and 2 oranges
5 small serrano chiles
2 tablespoons sugar
2 bay leaves, broken
1 large clove garlic, minced
Salt and white pepper to taste

Briefly poach cheesecloth-wrapped fish in court bouillon for about 6 minutes. (Refer to Fish-Poaching Basics—see Index.) Cool in cheese-cloth for 5 minutes, then unwrap, flake into small pieces while still warm, and add to escabeche marinade while still warm so that the marinade easily penetrates the fish.

To made the marinade: It is best to do this while the court bouillon is simmering. In a large container suitable for marinating, combine the onion, cilantro, and juices. Cut the chiles in half, near running water to wash your hands in, and discard the seeds. Finely mince and add to the marinade. Then add sugar, stirring until fully dissolved, bay leaves, garlic, salt, and pepper. Finally, add the warm flaked fish to the marinade. Carefully stir all ingredients, cover, and refrigerate at least 6 hours. Remove bay leaves before serving.

Variation: Escabeche recipes can be found in several Latin American cuisines as well as in Portuguese, Caribbean Island, South African, and Filipino cooking. The whole-fish fillets are often fried in oil, rather than poached in bouillon, cooled, and then flaked. The fish is next marinated in the refrigerator for at least 24 hours, in a sauce made of cooked sliced onions, parsley, garlic, grated carrots, peppercorns, salt, paprika, bay leaf, wine, vinegar, sugar, chopped hot chiles, chopped fresh ginger, and chopped cilantro.

Small squid are fabulous when prepared according to this recipe. Add one tablespoon or more, to taste, of nuoc nam or nam pla (fish sauce) for a Vietnamese or Thai influence.

SALMON MOUSSE IN THE SHAPE OF SALMON

International   *10 to 20 servings*

Ideally, a traditional fish-shaped mold is used to prepare this party hors d'oeuvre. At serving time, unmold the mousse on a bed of unusual greens or soaked dried Japanese seaweed to complete the marine theme. Decorate the platter with thinly sliced cucumbers.

1½ pounds freshly poached boned and skinned salmon fillets (see Note)

1 envelope unflavored gelatin

2 tablespoons chilled lemon juice

2 tablespoons dry vermouth or dry white wine

½ cup boiling chicken broth, strained court bouillon (from the poaching step) or water

½ cup sour cream

¼ cup mayonnaise

2 tablespoons minced fresh dill or 2 teaspoons dried dillweed

1 tablespoon snipped fresh chives

¼ teaspoon freshly grated nutmeg

¼ teaspoon paprika

⅛ teaspoon cayenne pepper

Salt to taste

1 cup heavy cream

Garnish

Pimiento-stuffed olives

Capers

Follow instructions for Fish-Poaching Basics (see Index) to poach the fish. After finely flaking the poached fish, you should have about 2 cups.

In a large bowl, stir gelatin, lemon juice, and vermouth until gelatin is softened, almost dissolved. Add boiling broth and continue to stir until gelatin is fully dissolved. Set aside and allow to cool.

In a smaller bowl, combine the sour cream, mayonnaise, dill, chives, nutmeg, paprika, cayenne pepper, and salt. Taste for seasoning. Whisk creamed mixture into the gelatin, blending thoroughly. Refrigerate 30 minutes.

In another bowl, whip the cream until peaks are glossy and fluffy.

Fold salmon into gelatin mixture and then carefully fold whipped cream in last.

Pour the salmon mixture into a well-oiled 6-cup fish-shape mold. Gently press plastic wrap onto mold to rid any air bubbles. Refrigerate for several hours. This can be made a day in advance.

Unmold at serving time. Place a slice of pimiento-stuffed olive in the eye section. Decorate the "collar" with capers.

Note: It is truly worth your time to use fresh rather than canned salmon in this recipe, as both the pink color and the flavor are more vibrant. However, if really pressed for time, use canned salmon.

GIANT SQUID VINAIGRETTE

International   *8 to 20 servings*

This squid salad is made with the white flesh of the giant squid; we have often fished for this squid in Southern California. It is also occasionally available at the fish markets. Small squid, complete with tentacles, can be substituted for a different yet extremely lovely dish.

3 pounds giant squid, white flesh only	1 tablespoon minced fresh dill or 1 teaspoon dried dillweed
Salt	
¾ cup finely chopped fresh parsley	1½ teaspoons coarsely ground black pepper
4 cloves garlic, finely minced	2 cups olive oil
1 large red onion, chopped	¾ cup red wine vinegar
3 medium green peppers, seeded and sliced into matchstick juliennes	2 large lemons
	1 teaspoon salt
2 tablespoons minced fresh basil or 2 teaspoons dried basil leaves	

Giant squid is handled very differently from small squid. Place white flesh in a pot of salted boiling water and cook until tender, from 30 to 60 minutes. Drain in a colander and allow to cool enough to handle. Cut into ½-inch matchsticklike shreds and place in a large glass or enamel bowl.

If using small squid, refer to Cleaning Small Squid (see Index). Small squid should be immersed in boiling water (or a more flavorsome court bouillon) for only a few minutes until cooked.

Add parsley, garlic, onion, peppers, basil, dill, and black pepper to the squid, tossing to coat well. Add oil and vinegar and toss again. Slice ends off lemons and discard. Thinly slice remaining main sections of lemons, remove seeds, cut each slice into eighths, and add them to squid mixture. Salt to taste and toss everything well. Cover and refrigerate for several hours or days before serving. This dish will keep up to several weeks in the refrigerator.

Serve as a party appetizer or at a luncheon or summer supper.

PICKLED HALIBUT

International   *4 to 10 servings*

Marinated and pickled fish can be found in many cuisines. It is often referred to as escabeche in several Latin American countries and the Philippines. This pickling process differs from the lime-juice marinade for ceviche in that a seasoned liquid with vegetables is simmered and then the fish is briefly poached in it prior to marinating.

1¾ to 2 pounds boneless firm
  fish fillets such as halibut
  or salmon

Pickling Liquid
  1 cup dry white wine
  1 cup water
  ½ cup vinegar (preferably rice
    vinegar)

1 large onion, thinly sliced
2 carrots, cut into thin
  rounds
2 garlic cloves
2 bay leaves
3 tablespoons sugar
2 teaspoons salt
¼ teaspoon whole
  peppercorns

Cut fish into 1- to 1½-inch pieces; set aside.

Place all pickling liquid ingredients in a medium-size saucepan and bring to a boil; then reduce heat to a simmer and cook, partially covered, for 3 to 4 minutes, or until onions begin to soften. Stir pickling liquid, making sure the sugar is fully dissolved. Add fish and carefully stir all ingredients, taking care not to break up fish into small pieces. Partially cover and cook at a gentle simmer another 2 minutes.

Carefully spoon fish, vegetables, and liquid into a glass or porcelain container. Cover and refrigerate several days before serving. The flavor will improve with time, and the dish will keep in your refrigerator for as long as two or three weeks.

To serve, remove fish with vegetables from the liquid. Offer as an appetizer or first course for a dinner or as a luncheon entree on a bed of lettuce.

Variation: For the Israeli pickled fish recipe Dag Kavush, carp or pike is pickled in water and white wine vinegar with chopped onions, bay leaves, cloves, peppercorns, carrots, and salt.

BRANDIED GAME LOAF

International   *3 loaves*

Pâtés and loaves—whether composed of large or small game, beef, fowl, fish, or seafood—originated as hearty feast fare. They could be found on the sideboards and dining-hall tables of nobility and peasant alike. Our modern-day hamburger meatloaf is a direct descendant of these wonderful dishes featuring a variety of coarsely ground meats and fowl. And the fancy chilled fish mousses and pâtés offered in the finest of continental restaurants at exorbitant prices per slice are basically loaves of well-ground and well-seasoned molded meat or fish.

Winter months are an ideal time for what I call fine-food projects, recipes that take a little more time and patience but are well worth the extra effort. If you have any parties coming up, these finished delicacies become excellent appetizers and hostess gifts. During the warmer spring and summer months, you will want to pack your favorite pâté or loaf for an elegant picnic dish.

1 pound venison, beef, or calf's liver, cut into chunks	3 garlic cloves
½ pound duck livers	¼ cup bread crumbs
2 ounces pheasant livers (if unavailable, increase duck livers to 10 ounces)	½ cup brandy
	2 teaspoons Dijon mustard
	2 teaspoons salt
1 pound salt pork, rind removed	1 teaspoon pepper
3 eggs	½ teaspoon each ground thyme and sage
1 pound ground pork	3 to 4 strips extra thick bacon
1 medium onion, quartered	

Using a food processor with the steel chopping blade, puree all livers, ¼ pound salt pork, ground pork, and eggs. Add remaining ingredients (except the remaining salt pork and the bacon). If there is not enough space in your processor for these ingredients, you may have to prepare the meat in several batches and then mix everything together in a large bowl.

Slice remaining salt pork into very thin strips and line a 3-cup terrine with ⅓ of these strips. Spoon approximately ⅓ of the liver mixture into the terrine, place 1½ strips of bacon on top, cover, and bake at 325° for 2½ hours. (It is not necessary to use a hot bath if the terrine has an escape hole.) There is enough mixture for two more terrines. The remaining pâté puree, salt pork, and bacon should be refrigerated during baking time unless you are using three molds.

When done, allow the pâté to cool in the terrine for several hours, thus allowing the fat to harden and encase the meat; then remove from the terrine. The pâté should be completely cooled before eating.

These pâtés can be made a long time in advance. Properly wrapped, they will keep in the refrigerator for several weeks (longer if frozen). The seasonings will mellow with age.

PHEASANT PÂTÉ

International   *4 to 8 servings*

This is a simple pâté that will keep in your refrigerator for several days. The flavor actually improves with time.

2 **tablespoons butter**	¼ **teaspoon dry mustard**
1 **small shallot bulb, minced**	½ **cup pheasant, duck, or**
¼ **teaspoon salt**	**chicken livers**
¼ **teaspoon freshly ground**	2 **tablespoons Marsala wine**
black pepper	1 **egg yolk**

Melt the butter in a skillet. Add the shallot, salt, pepper, and mustard and saute until shallot is soft. Add the livers and Marsala and continue to cook until the livers are done, approximately 3 minutes per side, turning constantly to keep the livers from sticking to the pan.

Place the entire mixture, including pan juices, in a food processor or blender, add the raw egg yolk, and process to puree the mixture. Spoon into a serving bowl and refrigerate. This pâté will keep well in the refrigerator for 3 to 4 days.

Additional Appetizers and Hors d'Oeuvres

Avocado Salsa

Avocado-Tomato-Bacon Salad

California Guacamole with
  Chicken

Caribbean Cold Poached Fish
  with Avocado Sauce

Chilled Poached Albacore with
  Cucumber Sauce

Chirashi-Zushi

Coeur à la Crème (variation)

Cold Poached Salmon in Aspic
  Glaze

Cold Trout in Aspic

Cucumber and Shrimp
  Sunomono

Dill Dip

Green Almond Sauce

Homemade Mayonnaise (aioli)

Italian Roasted Red and Green
  Peppers

Mexicana Guacamole with Homemade Taco Chips

Michael James's Wonderful Quiche

Miso-Grilled Trout

New Orleans Shrimp Remoulade in Cream Puff Basket

Pacific Coast Curry Dip

Salsa Mexicana

Scotch Eggs

Szechwan Chicken Breasts

Tamago

Thai Shrimp Salad

Vietnamese Shrimp and Green Papaya Salad

Dressings, Dips, Sauces, Side Dishes, and Condiments

CUCUMBER-DILL SALAD DRESSING
TANGY YOGURT SAUCE
HONEY-PAPAYA DRESSING
HORSERADISH SAUCE
DILL DIP
MOM HOY'S DRESSING FOR FRUIT SALADS
CALIFORNIA GUACAMOLE WITH CHICKEN
PACIFIC COAST CURRY DIP
LEMONY AVOCADO BUTTER
ROSEMARY VINEGAR
STRAWBERRY-RHUBARB COMPOTE
CRANBERRY-ORANGE DELICIOUS RELISH
FRESH MANGO CHUTNEY CHRISTINA
CARIBBEAN ISLAND HOT PEPPER SAUCE
CRÈME FRAÎCHE
TZATSIKI—GREEK CUCUMBER AND YOGURT DIP
BANANA AND RAISIN RAITA
FRIED PLANTAINS
FRESH TOMATO SAUCE
GREEN SAUCE
PESTO SAUCE
PASSOVER FRUIT AND NUT CHAROSES

AVOCADO SALSA
MEXICANA GUACAMOLE WITH HOMEMADE TACO CHIPS
SALSA MEXICANA
GREEN ALMOND SAUCE
CINNAMON-CLOVE APPLESAUCE
HOMEMADE MAYONNAISE
SHERRIED ONIONS AND ALMONDS
YOGURT CHILE SALAD DRESSING

CUCUMBER-DILL SALAD DRESSING

American   *Approximately ⅔ cup*

This creamy salad dressing is excellent for mixed greens, as an accompaniment for chilled poached chicken or fish, or as a dip for crudités.

¼ cup fresh parsley
2 teaspoons fresh dill (or ¾ teaspoon dried dillweed)
½ cucumber (unwaxed variety), seeded, patted dry, and cut up

¼ cup sour cream
¼ cup mayonnaise
⅛ teaspoon white pepper
Salt (optional)

Place parsley and dill in a blender or a food processor with a metal chopping blade and chop. Add cucumber and coarsely chop. Add sour cream and mayonnaise and process to blend. Season with pepper and salt, if desired. Process quickly to mix thoroughly. Refrigerate until serving time.

TANGY YOGURT SAUCE

American   *Approximately 1½ cups*

A chilled sauce for poached fish or chicken.

1 cup plain yogurt
2 tablespoons cooking oil
2 teaspoons Dijon mustard (preferably a Poupon)
1 teaspoon white wine vinegar

1 teaspoon dried mixed herbs (use your favorites)
Salt to taste
1 tablespoon capers

In a mixing bowl, whisk together the yogurt, oil, mustard, and vinegar. Stir in the herbs and salt. Gently mix in the capers. Refrigerate for a minimum of 1 hour before serving.

HONEY-PAPAYA DRESSING

American   *Approximately 4 cups*

A creamy honeyed dressing is always excellent with a fresh fruit salad or a tossed green salad that includes sliced nectarines, papaya, or oranges along with the lettuce leaves. You'll find this dressing particularly interesting since it makes use of the papaya seeds, which look very much like peppercorns.

Seeds of 1 ripe papaya—approximately ¼ cup (see Note)

2 cups salad oil (I use 1 cup vegetable oil, ½ cup olive oil, and ½ cup peanut oil)

1 cup rice vinegar	1 raw egg yolk
½ cup honey	¾ teaspoon paprika
¼ cup fresh lime juice	Salt to taste
1 tablespoon Dijon mustard	

Clean papaya seeds well of all fruit membrane.

In a food processor or blender, mix the oil, vinegar, honey, lime juice, mustard, egg yolk, and paprika. Process to mix well. Add the seeds and process for several minutes until seeds resemble freshly cracked black pepper.

Pour dressing into a jar or bowl, cover, and chill until needed. Stir or whisk again prior to using. The dressing will keep for several days in the refrigerator.

Pour the desired amount of dressing over a fresh fruit salad or a salad of tossed green to which you've added fresh or canned fruit. One of my favorite salads is butter lettuce, thinly sliced red onion rings, and canned Mandarin oranges.

Note: You can use the peeled fruit in this salad or save for another recipe. Seeds can be reserved in the refrigerator from papaya that has been eaten earlier.

HORSERADISH SAUCE

American   *Approximately 1¼ cups*

A simple horseradish sauce to accompany seafood, fish, and meat dishes.

1 cup sour cream	1 teaspoon capers, with juice
3 tablespoons milk	1 teaspoon dry mustard
1 tablespoon cream-style prepared white horseradish	2 tablespoons chopped fresh parsley
2 tablespoons lemon juice	

Combine sauce ingredients, stirring well. Cover and refrigerate until serving time.

DILL DIP

American   *Approximately 1½ cups*

A good dip to accompany poached fish.

⅔ cup sour cream	1 tablespoon minced fresh parsley
⅔ cup mayonnaise	1 tablespoon chopped scallions
1 tablespoon fresh dillweed or 1 teaspoon dried dillweed	½ dill pickle, finely minced

Combine dip ingredients. Prepare well ahead of time so that the flavors have time to blend; refrigerate.

MOM HOY'S DRESSING FOR FRUIT SALADS

American   *Approximately 1¾ cups*

A compote of fresh seasonal fruits is a delightful and simple side course for a buffet or sit-down dinner. You can dress up your fruits by offering this creamy sauce as an accompaniment.

⅓ cup sugar	¼ cup orange juice
4 teaspoons cornstarch	2 eggs, lightly beaten
¼ teaspoon salt	8 ounces cream cheese at
1 cup pineapple juice	room temperature, cut up

Combine sugar, cornstarch, and salt in the top of a double boiler. Stir in juices and place over second pot of simmering water. Slowly mix in the eggs and bring the mixture to a boil, stirring constantly. Beat in cream cheese. Spoon dressing into a sauce dish and allow to cool.

At serving time, spoon sauce over individual goblets of fruit, or the fruit can be placed in one large attractive bowl and the sauce can be poured on top.

CALIFORNIA GUACAMOLE WITH CHICKEN

American   *6 to 8 servings*

This avocado-chicken dip is also excellent as a sandwich spread, especially inside freshly baked croissants.

2 ripe avocados, mashed	1 medium onion, chopped
1 poached chicken breast, skinned, boned, and finely chopped	1 jalapeño pepper, seeded and chopped
2 teaspoons lemon juice	½ teaspoon cayenne pepper (or to taste)
2 medium tomatoes, chopped	Hot pepper sauce and salt to taste

In a mixing bowl, combine all ingredients, seasoning to taste. Immerse one avocado pit in the center to hold the color. Cover and refrigerate until serving time.

At serving time, discard the pit and place guacamole in a serving bowl.

PACIFIC COAST CURRY DIP

American   *Approximately 1¼ cups*

This outstanding zesty dip was created by Pam Mendelsohn, one of Newport Beach's loveliest hostesses. It is best made several hours in advance of entertaining and served in a crystal bowl surrounded by blanched Oriental peapods—a flowerlike presentation.

2 to 3 teaspoons Dijon
mustard
1 teaspoon dry mustard
2 to 3 teaspoons prepared
white horseradish
1 to 2 teaspoons red wine
vinegar

1 small onion, finely minced
1 to 2 teaspoons curry
powder
1 teaspoon garlic powder
1 cup mayonnaise
Salt to taste

Mix all ingredients together well and refrigerate for several hours or overnight. Spoon into a small serving bowl and place in the center of a larger platter. Surround with blanched Oriental peapods or other favorite crudités.

LEMONY AVOCADO BUTTER

American   *Approximately 4 cups*

Avocado butters are ideal to spread on corn on the cob, grilled meat, fish, fowl, or even toast.

1 avocado, pureed
Juice of 1 lemon

1 pound sweet butter or
margarine, softened

Combine avocado puree and lemon juice. Beat with butter until blended.

Variation: For an herb influence, reduce lemon juice to 2 tablespoons and add 2 tablespoons chopped parsley, ½ teaspoon each dried oregano leaves and ground savory, and ¼ teaspoon dried tarragon.

ROSEMARY VINEGAR

American   *Approximately 4 cups*

Herb and fruit vinegars have become very popular to use in salad dressings and with cooked dishes. They make beautiful hostess and holiday gifts when presented in unusual bottles. A variety of fresh herbs are available year-round, and you can combine them or use them alone with vinegar to obtain a specific flavor. My favorite vinegar is Japanese rice vinegar, as it has a subtle natural sweetness. Other good vinegars are cider, champagne, and white or red wine.

1 bunch fresh rosemary
(between ½ and 1 ounce)

1 quart rice vinegar

Wash rosemary sprigs well and pat dry with paper towels. Place them in a sterile 1- to 1½-quart jar and add vinegar. Cover and keep in a cool, dark place for at least 3 weeks.

To serve, strain and pour into clean decorative jars. If desired, add a fresh sprig of rosemary. Continue to store in a dark, cool place.

Variations: This recipe may be used as a springboard for your favorite herbs. You might also try spearing garlic and/or chiles on long bamboo picks instead of using herbs.

STRAWBERRY-RHUBARB COMPOTE

American   *6 to 8 servings*

Serve this compote chilled or at room temperature as an accompaniment to roasted chicken, lamb, or pork. It is a flavorsome alternative to applesauce.

2 pounds fresh rhubarb,
  ends trimmed, cut into
  2-inch lengths
1 cup sugar
¾ to 1 cup water

¼ teaspoon salt
10 to 15 strawberries, cut up
¼ cup Triple sec or other
  orange-flavored liqueur

In a large saucepan, mix the rhubarb, sugar, water, and salt and heat to a rolling simmer. Cook at a simmer, covered with a slight opening for air to escape, for about 20 minutes, stirring occasionally. When rhubarb has thoroughly stewed, add the strawberries and liqueur. Return to a simmer and cook, uncovered, for another 4 to 6 minutes, stirring occasionally.

CRANBERRY-ORANGE DELICIOUS RELISH

American   *5 to 6 cups*

A native American fruit, cranberries were so called by the Pilgrims because their pink blossoms resembled the heads of cranes—crane berry. Cranberries are well loved by Americans, especially during the Thanksgiving and Christmas holidays. You will find this recipe an excellent addition to your party tables.

2 12-ounce packages fresh
  cranberries
1⅔ cups fresh orange juice
  (with some pulp)
  Rind of 1 orange, coarsely
  chopped

¼ cup orange liqueur
2 cups sugar
2 whole cinnamon sticks

In a medium saucepan, combine the cranberries, juice, rind, orange liqueur, and sugar. Bring to a boil, reduce heat, and add cinnamon sticks. Gently boil for about 8 minutes, stirring often. Cool. Remove cinnamon sticks and store, covered, in the refrigerator until ready to use.

FRESH MANGO CHUTNEY CHRISTINA

Burmese/Indian   *4 to 6 servings*

Many chutneys in India, Sri Lanka, and Burma are made with fresh fruits, whose sweetness provides a welcome contrast to the spicy curries, sambals, and rice dishes they accompany.

3 medium ripe mangoes
¼ cup fresh lime or lemon
  juice
2 tablespoons sugar
1 tablespoon vegetable oil
½ to 1 teaspoon dried red
  pepper flakes

1½ to 2 tablespoons chopped
  fresh mint leaves
2 teaspoons grated lime or
  lemon rind

Peel mangoes and cut flesh away from the center pit into ¾-inch chunks. Place fruit in a nonmetallic bowl and refrigerate. In a small saucepan, combine the juice, sugar, and oil and heat gently, stirring until the sugar has dissolved. Remove from heat, stir in red pepper flakes, and cool mixture to room temperature. Pour sauce over mangoes and toss gently. Sprinkle mint and rind over fruit and chill until serving time. This recipe can be made a day in advance.

Variation: For a Jamaican version of mango chutney, use 2 pounds of unripe mangoes. Peel and remove large pits and cut the meat into small chunks. Place in a pot along with 1 cup vinegar (preferably malt vinegar) and bring to a boil. Cook, stirring, for 10 minutes. Add ½ cup sugar, ¼ cup raisins, ½ teaspoon finely chopped garlic, 3 tablespoons finely chopped fresh ginger, 1 teaspoon finely chopped hot chilies, and 2 teaspoons salt; simmer another 30 minutes. Fruit chutneys are also served as a condiment in South African cuisines. Follow the variation for Jamaican chutney, substituting 1½ cups dried fruits for the unripe mangoes and add ½ cup chopped onions and 2 teaspoons ground coriander with the other ingredients. Simmer until dried fruits and onions are tender.

CARIBBEAN ISLAND HOT PEPPER SAUCE

Caribbean Islands   *Approximately 1½ cups*

Piquant pepper sauces are traditionally served in the Caribbean Islands as an accompaniment to seafood, meat, and poultry dishes. There are hundreds of varieties, all of which have finely chopped fresh hot chiles in common.

¾ cup finely chopped fresh hot chiles, seeded (use a variety of colors and types)
⅓ cup finely chopped onion
2 large cloves garlic, finely chopped
⅓ cup fresh lime juice or malt vinegar
½ teaspoon minced fresh ginger
1 teaspoon salt

Combine the chiles, onion, garlic, lime juice, ginger, and salt in a small stainless steel or enamel saucepan. At a high temperature, bring liquid to a boil, stirring constantly, and boil for 2 minutes. Cool to room temperature before serving.

Variation: This is a fairly simple version of a Caribbean pepper sauce. Other ingredients can be added to make it more elaborate, including 1 to 2 tablespoons finely chopped unripe papaya, ¼ cup finely chopped shallots, ½ teaspoon ground turmeric. Olive oil can be floated on the top. This sauce can also be pureed to a smooth consistency, though I prefer the textured sauce.

CRÈME FRAÎCHE

French

If you are not familiar with crème fraîche, it is a thick cream, originally from France, that is both sweet and tart. If you have never had the pleasure of making it at home, there are three versions. They will keep several days, even up to a week, covered in your refrigerator—that is, if you don't eat them with a spoon as I do.

Crème fraîche can be used with desserts such as fresh fruits, pies, and tarts, and it can also be used in soups and sauces.

Crème Fraîche I (makes 2 cups)
1 cup sour cream
1 cup heavy cream

Spoon sour cream into a large glass measuring cup, glass bowl, or jar. With a wire whisk, gradually stir in the cream. Lightly cover with plastic wrap and leave at room temperature 8 to 10 hours. Whisk again and store in the refrigerator. Some cooks suggest that you pour the crème fraîche through a filter, such as a paper drip-coffee filter, and discard the liquid, reserving the thicker cream.

Crème fraîche is best allowed to mellow in the refrigerator for 24 to 36 hours before using.

Crème Fraîche II (makes 1½ cups)

Some people prefer their crème fraîche sweeter, as in this version.

½ cup sour cream
1 cup heavy cream

Follow directions for Crème Fraîche I.

Crème Fraîche III (makes 1 cup)

In this thinner version, buttermilk somewhat "sours" the cream.

1 cup heavy cream   1 tablespoon buttermilk

Follow directions for Crème Fraîche I.

TZATSIKI—GREEK CUCUMBER AND YOGURT DIP

Greek/Turkish/Indian

*Approximately 4 cups;
6 to 10 servings*

Serve this refreshing dip in a large chilled bowl as an appetizer with triangles of pita bread or crudités or in small individual bowls to accompany an entree with piquant seasonings, such as an Indian curry. In Middle Eastern cuisine this is also enjoyed as a cold soup (cacik), garnished with an ice cube to ensure its iciness.

3 medium cucumbers, peeled and finely chopped
3 cups plain yogurt
2 large cloves garlic, finely minced
2 tablespoons lemon juice or vinegar
1 tablespoon olive oil

Salt and white pepper to taste
A hint of dried oregano (optional)

Garnish

Fresh mint leaves, chopped
Fresh chives, snipped

Combine the cucumbers and yogurt in a large, deep mixing bowl. Stir in the lemon juice, olive oil, and seasonings. Cover and refrigerate several hours, preferably 24, for flavors to fully mingle.

At serving time, garnish with a sprinkling of mint and chives.

Variation: To serve as a Turkish cacik or Bulgarian tarator (cold soup), add ¼ cup crushed ice to each of four soup bowls filled with the cucumber and yogurt mixture. The Bulgarian recipe often includes 4 to 5 tablespoons finely chopped walnuts.

BANANA AND RAISIN RAITA

Indian

4 servings

A raita is a traditional Indian yogurt dish used as an accompaniment to an often spicy main dish. The creamy texture of the yogurt is a soothing contrast to such piquant dishes. The main ingredient of a raita is the plain yogurt, which is mixed with an endless combination of vegetables and/or fruits. In this version, the bananas and raisins are a sweet contrast to the somewhat pungent but not spicy cumin and cilantro.

1 cup yogurt	1 tablespoon finely chopped
1 medium to large banana, thinly sliced	fresh cilantro
	½ teaspoon ground cumin
3 tablespoons raisins, steeped in boiling water 10 minutes and drained well	**Garnish**
	A few whole cilantro leaves

In a serving bowl, gently stir together yogurt, bananas, raisins, cumin, and chopped cilantro, taking care to mix ingredients well but not to mash bananas. Cover and refrigerate several hours to chill. Garnish at serving time with whole cilantro leaves.

FRIED PLANTAINS

Indonesian   *2 to 6 servings*

Cooked bananas of several varieties are popular in Indonesian cuisine, served as a side dish, snack, or dessert course. The plantain, a member of the banana family, resembles the more common fruit, but it is about double in size and is too starchy to eat raw. Cooked, it takes on a mellow flavor. It is ready for cooking when the outer skin is black.

Plantains can be sliced and pan-fried in hot oil, which is done in Guatemala and other Latin American countries. Or, like an American fritter, it can be dipped in a sweetened batter and deep-fried, to be eaten at room temperature.

1 plantain (about 12 ounces), very thinly sliced on the diagonal (see Note)	½ teaspoon cinnamon
	3 to 4 tablespoons cold water
Flour for dusting	1 egg
	Cooking oil for deep-frying, heated
Batter	
½ cup flour	
1 tablespoon brown sugar	

Lightly dust plantain slices with flour so that the batter will adhere.

In a mixing bowl, combine the batter ingredients, but do not over-mix; the batter should be somewhat lumpy. Dip plantain slices in batter. Fry about 5 slices at a time in hot oil (around 350°) about 2 minutes, until lightly browned on both sides. Remove with a slotted spoon to a rack to drain off excess oil. Continue process until all slices are fried.

Line a basket or serving bowl with paper towels and place plantain in the basket. Serve at room temperature.

Note: To ensure that the plantain slices will be tender, you might try the Latin American culinary trick of pounding the slices with the bottom of a glass.

FRESH TOMATO SAUCE

Italian   *Approximately 2½ cups*

When I visited Rome, I fell in love with a fresh tomato sauce served with fish and pasta. You might try this as a dipping sauce or condiment for chilled poached fish or chicken breasts.

3 cups chopped fresh tomatoes	1 tablespoon chopped fresh mint
2 cloves garlic	¼ cup olive oil
¼ cup fresh parsley	Salt and pepper to taste

Place all ingredients in a food processor or electric blender and puree.

GREEN SAUCE

Italian   *Approximately 2 cups*

Pesto sauce is often referred to as green sauce, and sometimes walnuts are used instead of pine nuts. This unusual version also replaces the basil with spinach leaves. Serve this sauce as an accompaniment to chicken, fish, or seafood, or toss with your favorite pasta or vegetables. For a classic pesto sauce recipe, refer to Minestra di Verdura (see Index).

2 cups firmly packed spinach leaves	½ cup olive oil
½ cup firmly packed chopped fresh parsley	2 tablespoons butter
2 cloves garlic	½ cup freshly grated Parmesan cheese
¼ cup chopped walnuts	1 teaspoon salt
	¼ teaspoon pepper

Combine all ingredients in a food processor with a steel blade and process to make a paste.

If you are using this sauce for pasta, you may wish to slightly thin it with a little liquid from the boiling pot. This recipe makes enough sauce to toss with 1¼ to 1½ pounds of pasta.

Variation: For a Southwest American recipe, substitute cilantro leaves for the spinach.

PESTO SAUCE

Italian   *Approximately 2 cups*

A fragrant sauce made of fresh basil, pine nuts, olive oil, and seasonings, pesto is delightful with a chilled minestrone style soup or as a sauce for pasta or salad vegetables.

¼ pound Parmesan cheese, cut into small pieces
4 cloves garlic
¼ teaspoon pepper
2 cups loosely packed fresh basil leaves, carefully torn

by hand so as not to bruise the leaves (see Note)
½ cup pine nuts
1 teaspoon salt
¼ teaspoon white pepper
¾ to 1 cup olive oil

To make the sauce using a food processor fitted with a steel blade, add one ingredient at a time and process for about 2 to 3 minutes at each step. Set sauce aside until ready for use. If using a mortar and pestle, it is best to grate the Parmesan cheese instead of cutting it into small pieces. The garlic should be chopped. Then, pound and grind the basil and garlic together and add the remaining ingredients, one at a time, until each is fully absorbed into the paste.

Note: If fresh basil is not available, you can use the dried leaves and soak them in olive oil. Although this makes a tasty sauce, it really doesn't compare to the fresh, but it's better than no pesto. Fresh parsley leaves can also be substituted for the basil, if necessary. In this case, some olive oil–soaked dried basil should definitely be added to the parsley pesto.

PASSOVER FRUIT AND NUT CHAROSES

Jewish   *Approximately 2 cups*

During the Passover Seder ceremony, charoses—a delicious mixture of apples (and occasionally other fruits), nuts, cinnamon, and wine—is served to symbolize the mortar used in brickbuilding by the Jewish people when they were slaves in Egypt. This recipe for fruit and nut charoses is so good that you'll want to make plenty for dinner. If you have any leftovers, you can add it to another recipe, such as matzo meal muffins or cake.

2 red apples, finely chopped, cored, and seeded but unpeeled
½ lemon
½ lemon rind, finely grated
1 cup chopped walnuts

¼ cup raisins, chopped
2 teaspoons honey
1 teaspoon cinnamon
1 teaspoon sweet red kosher wine

Place chopped apples in a bowl and squeeze in the juice of the lemon. Add the grated lemon rind, nuts, raisins, honey, cinnamon, and wine. Stir all ingredients together, cover, and refrigerate until serving time. Serve with matzos.

AVOCADO SALSA

Mexican *Approximately 5 cups*

Mexican salsas or sauces can be used for numerous purposes. You can serve them as a party hors d'oeuvre with homemade chips or crudités, or they're excellent as a filling or topping for omelets and crepes, and a spoonful is wonderful in many soup recipes. I'm fond of salsa as a side dish to accompany practically any traditional Mexican dish or a simple broiled or barbecued entrée.

- 2 ripe avocados, sliced
- 2 large tomatoes, peeled, chopped, and seeded
- 1 medium red onion, chopped
- 1 green pepper, seeded and chopped
- 1 jalapeño pepper, seeded and chopped
- 2 tablespoons fresh lemon juice
- 1 teaspoon salt
  Dash pepper

Toss all ingredients gently so as not to break up the avocado too much (as you would for a guacamole).

MEXICANA GUACAMOLE WITH HOMEMADE TACO CHIPS

Mexican *6 to 8 servings*

I first enjoyed this version of guacamole, containing tomatoes and the small, fiery green serrano chile, in the provincial town of León, the "shoe capital" of Mexico. To retain the luscious green color of your guacamole while it is being refrigerated, hide an avocado pit in the center.

- 3 avocados
- 2 tomatoes
- 1 medium onion
- 1 serrano chile
- 1 tablespoon minced fresh cilantro
- 2 tablespoons salad oil
- 1 tablespoon lemon juice
  Salt to taste
  Corn tortillas

Finely chop the avocados, tomatoes, and onion. Cut the chili in half and remove seeds, taking care not to rub your eyes, as this serrano is very spicy. (Some cooks prefer to wear rubber gloves when working with chiles. I find it easiest to slice and seed them near running cold water; then as I slice them, I can immediately rinse away the seeds.) Finely chop the chiles and add to vegetables. Mix in cilantro, oil, and lemon juice, and salt to taste.

Place an avocaco pit in the center, cover, and refrigerate until ready to use.

To make homemade taco chips: Cut desired amount of corn tortillas into pie wedges (about 8 per tortilla) and deep-fry a few at a time in hot oil, about 375°, until golden on both sides; drain. Continue frying process until all chips are finished. Place in a bowl lined with paper towels to drain off excess cooking oil. Salt to taste. Taco chips can be made in advance and stored lightly covered at room temperature.

Serve guacamole as an appetizer with crudités or taco chips or as a sauce to accompany other Mexican recipes.

Variation: Four thinly sliced radishes may be added.

SALSA MEXICANA

Mexican   *Approximately ½ to ¾ cup*

This red sauce is an excellent accompaniment to most Mexican dishes. It is also a good base for guacamole—simply add diced or mashed avocados.

1 **large tomato**	1 **to 2 tablespoons minced**
2 **serrano chiles, seeded**	**fresh cilantro (optional)**
2 **cloves garlic**	**Salt and pepper to taste**
½ **medium onion**	
2 **tablespoons fresh lemon**	
juice	

Finely chop tomato, chiles, garlic, and onion and mix together in a serving bowl. Add lemon juice, cilantro (if desired), salt, and pepper. Mix well and allow to sit for a few minutes. Stir and serve.

GREEN ALMOND SAUCE

Mexican   *Approximately 1 cup*

The concept of pureeing nuts with herbs can be found throughout the world, and this Mexican parsley and almond sauce is quite similar to Italian pesto.

This sauce can be used as an accompaniment to simple fried fish or fowl or as a dipping sauce for crudités.

¼ cup blanched almonds (see Note)
5 tablespoons chopped fresh parsley or cilantro
1 clove garlic
3 hard-cooked egg yolks
½ cup cooking oil (preferably peanut oil)
¼ cup vinegar
Salt and pepper to taste

Using a food processor or blender, combine all sauce ingredients and puree until well blended and smooth.

Note: If almonds are not blanched, soak in hot water to loosen skin and peel.

CINNAMON-CLOVE APPLESAUCE

International   *6 to 8 servings*

All over the world you will find applesauce served as an accompaniment to fowl, lamb, and pork. You can vary this basic recipe with your choice of spices and cooking liquid. For an adult version, use wine or champagne instead of water or juice.

8 apples (if possible, use two different kinds, such as 4 Pippins and 4 Red Delicious), quartered, unpeeled (see Note)
Juice of 1 lemon
1 cup water
5 cloves
1 teaspoon cinnamon
1 tablespoon sugar (optional)

Place apples in a saucepan with the lemon juice, water, cloves, cinnamon, and sugar. (Some cooks prefer to add sugar after the sauce is finished, so that they can taste the sauce to see if sugar is needed.) Cover pan and simmer until apples are tender, about 20 minutes. Put apples through a food mill and then discard the apple skins.

Serve slightly cooled, chilled, or at room temperature.

Note: If you do not own a food mill, you will need to peel and core apples before making the sauce. However, it is far better to cook the apples unpeeled, as doing so adds a beautiful color as well as more nutrition.

HOMEMADE MAYONNAISE

International   *Approximately 2 cups*

Those cooks who have never prepared homemade mayonnaise, whether by hand or machine, may approach this recipe with some trepidation. Fear not, as mayonnaise is one of the simplest, most basic of recipes: eggs (some recipes call for yolks only, others for the addition of a whole egg), oil (generally olive oil, but sometimes other vegetable oils or a combination), and seasonings (mustard, salt, pepper, and lemon juice or vinegar). From a basic mayonnaise, you can create other dressings and sauces, such as aioli (French garlic mayonnaise), allioli (Spanish garlic mayonnaise), herb mayonnaise, Thousand Island dressing, Russian dressing, horseradish mayonnaise, and fruit dressing.

There are certain basic tricks to making mayonnaise. Every ingredient must be at room temperature. All utensils and equipment must be immaculately clean (wash with warm water and dry thoroughly). The oil must be added to the eggs very, very slowly, especially at first. To aid in adding droplets of oil, you may wish to use a small pouring can, an eye dropper, or a measuring cup and the tip of a teaspoon.

The beginner should start with about ½ cup oil per egg yolk. As you become more experienced with how much oil the eggs can handle, increase the amount of oil. When preparing the mayonnaise, listen for the sounds it makes. If it begins to "crackle" as you add the oil, take this as a signal that it has pretty much reached its limit for holding oil. Be careful, or the mayonnaise may separate. To help stabilize the finished mayonnaise, add 1 to 2 teaspoons of boiling water to the completed recipe and stir thoroughly. Cover and store in the refrigerator; it will keep very nicely for 1 to 2 weeks.

What do you do if your mayonnaise separates? Separation usually occurs if you did not follow one of the preceding tips, particularly if you added the oil too fast, not allowing the eggs to absorb it completely before the next addition. If your mayonnaise separates, start with another room-temperature egg yolk. Stir it up in clean equipment and very slowly, drop by drop, add the separated mixture. If you become frustrated and wish to start from scratch, do not toss out this "curdled" sauce. Store it in the refrigerator to use when pan-frying vegetables and other foods. What you have is seasoned oil with a little egg.

As you become more experienced, you will find yourself making a batch of homemade mayonnaise practically every week. Once you taste this thick, shiny, luscious, pale yellow sauce, you'll find that commercial varieties simply do not compare.

2 egg yolks at room temperature	¼ teaspoon salt (or more to taste)
1 whole egg at room temperature	White pepper to taste
	1 teaspoon Dijon-style

mustard at room
temperature, or ½
teaspoon dry mustard
1 teaspoon fresh lemon juice
or vinegar at room
temperature (or more to
taste)

1½ to 2 cups olive oil or half
olive oil and vegetable oil
(or as much oil as the
mayonnaise will hold)
1 teaspoon boiling water

Using a large bowl and a wire whisk or an electric beater, a food processor, or a blender, vigorously beat eggs with salt, pepper, mustard, and lemon juice until the mixture is well blended. Beating constantly, add oil, drop by drop, in a very slow and steady stream, making sure all the oil is absorbed before adding the next drops. There should be no trace of oil on the top of the sauce when adding more oil. After the first ½ cup of oil, the mixture will begin to emulsify and the oil can be added in a slightly faster stream. If using an electric mixer or blender, increase the speed at this step.

When the eggs have absorbed the oil, the mayonnaise is ready for tasting. Adjust seasonings to taste. Stir in boiling water. Store, covered, in the refrigerator until needed.

Variations

Aioli/allioli (garlic mayonnaise): Garlic mayonnaise should be made entirely with olive oil. Proceed with your favorite technique to make mayonnaise, adding 8 pureed extra-large garlic cloves to the first step when mixing the eggs with the seasonings. If desired, use 4 egg yolks instead of 2 yolks and 1 whole egg. Increase the lemon juice to about 1 tablespoon. Aioli can be used as a spread for crusty French bread and as a delicious garlicky sauce for chilled or room-temperature boiled or steamed vegetables (potatoes, artichokes, carrots, zucchini, broccoli), eggs, beans, poached or boiled fish, seafood, meat, or fowl. Makes approximately 2 cups.

Russian dressing/Thousand Island dressing: Add ½ cup catsup, ½ cup minced green pepper, ¼ cup minced onion, and 1 teaspoon minced pimiento to the completed mayonnaise recipe. For a spicier sauce, substitute part of the catsup with bottled chili sauce. Serve as a dressing for salads and sandwiches. Makes approximately 3 cups.

Herb mayonnaise: Add ½ cup sour cream, 6 tablespoons minced fresh herbs (use a variety, such as basil, chervil, parsley, chives), and 1 large pureed garlic clove to complete mayonnaise recipe. Serve as a dressing for poached or steamed fowl, fish, seafood, or vegetables. Makes approximately 2¾ cups.

Fruit dressing: Combine 2 cups plain yogurt with completed mayonnaise and sweeten to taste with fruit juice. Serve as a dressing for fruit salads and gelatin molds. Makes approximately 4 cups.

Horseradish mayonnaise: Add 2 tablespoons (or more, to taste) prepared horseradish, 1 tablespoon minced fresh dill, and grated rind of 1 small lemon to completed mayonnaise. Serve as a dressing for cooked seafood, fish, fowl, or meat. Makes approximately 2 cups.

SHERRIED ONIONS AND ALMONDS

International   *6 to 8 servings*

Petits oignons (tiny French onions) and almonds make a lovely condiment to serve alongside chicken and beef. You can make this recipe several days in advance, but do allow time for the delicately sweet and sour sauce to "soften" at room temperature, as the caramelized sugar tends to harden in the refrigerator.

2 10-ounce containers fresh small pearl onions (see Note)
3 tablespoons butter
1 tablespoon olive oil
½ cup whole blanched almonds (optional)
1 tablespoon brown sugar

Few gratings of whole nutmeg
Cayenne pepper and salt to taste
3 tablespoons dry sherry
1 tablespoon vinegar (preferably rice vinegar)

Drop whole unpeeled onions in a saucepan of boiling water and cook for 3 minutes. Drain and rinse with cold water. Cut off the root end with a paring knife and, with your fingers, carefully peel off the outer brown tissuelike skin.

Melt butter with olive oil in a large skillet over low heat. Add almonds, if desired, and stir to coat. Sprinkle brown sugar, nutmeg, cayenne pepper, and salt over nuts. Continue to cook, stirring continuously, over low heat. The sugar will melt and begin to caramelize. Add onions to the skillet, stirring gently to coat them with the sauce. Pour in sherry and vinegar and again gently stir to coat. Reduce heat to very low, cover, and let onions cook about 45 to 50 minutes, stirring occasionally.

Allow onion mixture to cool and serve at room temperature. If made in advance, refrigerate, but remember to bring the dish to room temperature before serving.

Note: If tiny fresh onions are not available, substitute frozen. Simply defrost them—do not parboil.

YOGURT CHILE SALAD DRESSING

International   *Approximately 1⅔ cups*

A simple salad dressing to toss with your favorite greens.

¼ cup diced green chiles
3 tablespoons mayonnaise
Juice of ½ lime
1 teaspoon sugar

½ teaspoon salt
1 garlic clove, finely minced
1 cup plain yogurt

Combine chiles, mayonnaise, lime juice, sugar, salt, and garlic in a food processor or blender and process until smooth. Remove to a mixing bowl and stir in yogurt.

Additional Dressings, Dips, Sauces, Side Dishes, and Condiments Included with Other Recipes

African Brown Lentil Salad (Ethiopian Dressing)

African Fish Cone (African Dilled Dressing)

Asparagus Vinaigrette

Atjar (Indonesian Vegetable Sauce)

Baby Artichokes and Tomatoes in an Herb Vinaigrette

Cabbage Slaw with Garden Vegetables (Cabbage Slaw Dressing)

Cacumbar—Indian Tomato-Cucumber-Onion Salad (Indian Masala Dressing)

Cambodian Chicken and Tofu Salad (Cambodian Dressing)

Caribbean Cold Poached Fish with Avocado Sauce

Cherry Tomatoes in a Basil Vinaigrette

Chilled Noodles with Cucumbers and Mushrooms (Summer Salad Dressing)

Chilled Poached Albacore with Cucumber Sauce

Chinese Chicken and Vegetable Salad (Chinese Chicken Salad Dressing)

Chinese Radish Cucumber Salad (Oriental Salad Dressing)

Chinese Spareribs with Sweet-Tart Marinade

Cold Poached Salmon in Aspic Glaze

Cucumber in Dilled Cream

Escabeche of Poached Whitefish (Escabeche Marinade)

Farmer Salad (Simple Oil and Vinegar Dressing)

Fettucini with Marinated Tomato, Olives, and Peppers (Oil and Vinegar Dressing)

French White Bean Salad (Herb and Lemon Dressing)

Gravlax with Mustard-Dill Sauce

Greek Salad (Greek Salad Dressing)

Honey-Soy Marinated Chicken Legs

Indonesian Gado Gado (Gado Gado Peanut Dressing)

Indonesian Mixed Salad (Indonesian Dressing)

Italian Roasted Red and Green Peppers (Parsley Vinaigrette)

Japanese Eggplants in Miso Dressing

Japanese Pork Loin Roast/Teriyaki Marinated Steak Slices (Ponzu Sauce)

Lobio-Russian String Beans with Herb Vinaigrette

Maifun with Chicken Salad (Soy-Vinegar Oil Dressing)

Marino Marinated Mushroom Salad with Maui Dressing

Mediterranean Marinated Tomato Salad (Mediterranean Dressing)

Mezedaki (Greek Marinade)

Mom's Apricot Glazed Ham

Moroccan String Bean and Cilantro (Moroccan Spicy Tomato Dressing)

Mother's Chicken Salad Hawaiian (Hawaiian Salad Dressing)

New Orleans Shrimp Remoulade in Cream Puff Basket (Remoulade Sauce)

Opihi (Coconut Cream Sauce)

Orange-Avocado Salad (Creamy Vinaigrette Dressing)

Oriental Asparagus with Sesame Seed Sauce

Pancit Salad (Filipino Pancit Dressing)

Parisian Carottes Râpées (Parisian Salad Dressing)

Pennsylvania Dutch Beet, Apple, and Egg Salad (Cooked White Salad Dressing)

Pennsylvania Dutch Pickled Beets and Eggs (Pennsylvania Dutch Pickling Liquid)

Persian Cucumber Dressing (Middle Eastern Yogurt and Herb Dressing)

Pesto Sauce

Pickled Cooked Vegetables and Tofu with Goma Dressing

Poached Chicken Breasts with Plum Sauce (Tkemali Sauce)

Potato and Roasted Green Pepper Salad with Mustard Vinaigrette

Potato Salad with Tangy Blue Cheese Dressing

Romaine Salad with Roquefort Dressing

Russian Bean Salad with Walnut Sauce (Satsivi Sauce)

Salad Nicoise (Nicoise Dressing)

Seafood Pancit Salad (Pancit Dressing)

Spinach-Mushroom Salad with French Dressing

Spinach with Sesame Dressing

Szechwan Chicken Breasts (Szechwan Pepper Sauce)

Szechwan Chicken, Vegetable, and Noodle Salad (Szechwan Salad Dressing)

Tapenade

Teriyaki Marinated Steak Slices

Trout Party Dip (Cocktail Sauce)

Turkey Salad with a Hint of Orient (Hint of Orient Dressing)

Vietnamese Chicken
   Salad/Vietnamese Shrimp
   and Green Papaya Salad
   (Vietnamese Dressing)
Vitello Tonnato (Tonnato Sauce)

Watercress and Mushroom Salad
   with Walnut Oil Dressing
Watercress and Walnut Salad
   (French Dressing with
   Mustard)

Desserts

Cheesecake Sauce for Fresh Fruits
Sweet Potato and Almond Halva

Stewed Rhubarb
Oasis Fruits

Soups and Beverages

AFRICAN TOMATO-AVOCADO-BUTTERMILK SOUP
GREENGROCER'S ZUCCHINI SOUP
VICHYSSOISE—CHILLED POTATO AND LEEK SOUP
SOUTHWEST AMERICAN TOMATO-CILANTRO SORBET
PAPAYA-ORANGE SOUP
KAERNEMAELKSKODSKAAL—SCANDINAVIAN
BUTTERMILK SOUP
COLD AVGOLEMONO—GREEK EGG AND LEMON SOUP
LASSI
MINESTRA DI VERDURA WITH PESTO SAUCE
BORSCHT—BEET SOUP
SANGRIA PUNCH
CHILLED AVOCADO SOUP WITH TEQUILA
MARTHA JEAN'S SOUR CHERRY SOUP
BLUEBERRY SOUP
COLD ALMOND AND GARLIC SOUP
SENEGALESE SOUP
CARROT-ORANGE SOUP
PEAR, APPLE, AND CUCUMBER SOUP

CUCUMBER REFRESHER
TURNIP GAZPACHO
TOMATO AND SPLIT PEA SOUP
SUSAN'S LEMON SQUASH SOUP
MINTED FRESH PEA SOUP

AFRICAN TOMATO-AVOCADO-BUTTERMILK SOUP

African   *8 to 10 servings*

The natural sweet taste of pureed ripe tomatoes is outstanding in this soup. The final dish, garnished with diced cucumbers and sour cream, reminds me of a Spanish gazpacho.

3 pounds tomatoes (8 medium-size), peeled and seeded
2 tablespoons tomato paste
1 cup buttermilk
1 tablespoon olive oil
1 avocado, mashed to a puree
Juice of 1 lemon
2 tablespoons finely minced fresh parsley

Salt and pepper to taste
Hot pepper sauce

Garnish

1 cucumber, peeled, seeded, and diced
Sour cream, plain yogurt, or crème fraîche

Puree tomatoes in a food processor or food mill, and then press through a sieve to remove seeds. In a large mixing bowl, beat the pureed tomatoes, tomato paste, buttermilk, and oil. Toss pureed avocado with 1 tablespoon of lemon juice to hold the color. Add the avocado, remaining lemon juice, and parsley to the tomato mixture; stir to mix well. Season to taste with salt, pepper, and a generous number of drops of hot pepper sauce. Refrigerate several hours before serving.

At serving time, taste soup for seasonings. Ladle into individual chilled bowls and have guests garnish their portions with cucumber and sour cream. Pass hot pepper sauce around to add more piquancy.

GREENGROCER'S ZUCCHINI SOUP

American   *6 to 10 servings*

Zucchini is a greengrocer's delight, a handsome, healthy vegetable that can be used from soups to sweets. You'll enjoy this light and cool meal opener.

1½ pounds zucchini, washed
5 to 6 green onions
1 medium onion
¼ cup butter
Salt and pepper to taste
Dash of dry ginger

4 cups chicken broth
½ cup half-and-half

Garnish

Sour cream or plain yogurt

By hand or using a food processor fitted with a shredding blade, shred the zucchini and scallions. Finely chop the onions.

Place the zucchini, scallions, and onion in a large soup pot and saute in butter until they are soft and tender, about 5 minutes, stirring often so that the vegetables do not burn. Season with salt, pepper, and ginger. Stir in the chicken broth and continue to cook over medium heat for another 15 minutes.

Return the soup to the food processor, fitted with the chopping blade—or use a food mill or sieve—and puree, adding the cream. Place soup in a large bowl, cover, and refrigerate for several hours or overnight until thoroughly chilled.

Serve in chilled bowls garnished with a dollop of sour cream or yogurt.

VICHYSSOISE—CHILLED POTATO AND LEEK SOUP

American   *6 servings*

Although many people think vichyssoise is a French soup, it is actually American, created by Louis Diat when he was chef at New York's Ritz Carlton. The French version, Potage Parmentier, is traditionally not chilled.

2 large leeks (about 1 pound)	1 cup half-and-half
3 tablespoons butter	½ cup heavy cream
1 medium onion	Salt and white pepper to taste
2 medium potatoes (preferably red rose), peeled and sliced	**Garnish**
1 quart chicken broth, heated	Snipped fresh chives or scallion tops
Sprinkling of dried dillweed	Thinly sliced cucumber
	Caviar

Trim and discard root ends of leeks, keeping the firm green part but not the softer leaves. Slit leeks open lengthwise with a sharp paring knife and wash out all sand and dirt. Coarsely chop the white and firm green parts.

Place both varieties of onions in soup pot with butter and saute over low heat about 15 minutes, occasionally stirring, until soft, not browned. Add potatoes, stirring to coat with onions, for 1 minute. Stir in broth. Bring to a boil and then reduce to a simmer. Sprinkle with a hint of dill and continue to cook at a simmer until potatoes are tender, about 15 minutes.

Press through a sieve or food mill, or use a food processor, taking care when processing not to totally puree and thus lose all texture. Stir in the two creams. Season generously with salt and pepper. Pour into a glass or porcelain bowl, cover, and refrigerate several hours or, better yet, overnight.

To serve, ladle into chilled bowls and garnish with chives, cucumber, and/or caviar.

Variation: Between ½ and ¾ cup dry vermouth can be added to the soup during the last 5 minutes of simmering the vegetables. For an outstanding chilled potato, leek, and pear soup, add 3 ripe pears that have been peeled, cored, and cubed when pressing soup through a sieve or processing it in a food processor.

A South African version of a chilled potato and onion soup includes cucumber, pickles, and mint. Add 1 peeled and seeded cucumber when processing the soup mixture. Stir in 1 finely chopped sweet gherkin and 2 teaspoons finely chopped mint leaves, and proceed with recipe according to above instructions. When serving, garnish with additional chopped gherkin and minced green onions.

SOUTHWEST AMERICAN TOMATO-CILANTRO SORBET

American   *4 servings*

A sorbet is usually considered a dessert, but I find this recipe for frozen cilantro-seasoned pureed tomatoes to be more like an icy soup. Follow a scoop of this with a wonderful chicken or pasta salad.

6 very large tomatoes, peeled and seeded	1 lime, thinly sliced
2 to 3 tablespoons finely chopped fresh cilantro	1½ tablespoons brown sugar (or more to taste)

Puree tomatoes in a food processor or food mill, and then press through a sieve to remove all seeds. Place tomatoes in a saucepan along with 1 tablespoon chopped cilantro, the lime slices, and the brown sugar. Heat to a simmer and cook for a few minutes to allow the lime to slightly flavor the tomatoes. Remove and discard the lime slices.

Allow mixture to cool, stir in remaining cilantro, spoon mixture into an electric ice cream maker, if you have one, and process according to manufacturer's directions. This sorbet can also be made in the freezer in ice cube trays. Refer to Watermelon Ice and Ginger-Melon Ice (see Index) for further freezing instructions.

To serve, bring to room temperature for about 5 minutes to soften slightly. Spoon into stemmed goblets and garnish with an additional cilantro leaf or twist of lime.

Variation: Either fresh mint or basil can be substituted for the cilantro.

PAPAYA-ORANGE SOUP

Caribbean Islands   *6 servings*

The color of this lovely soup is as glorious as an island sunset. The hint of spice from the cumin is a beautiful mate to the sweet fruits.

2 cups cold chicken broth
1 envelope plain gelatin
1 egg white at room temperature
1 cup fresh orange juice, strained
1 papaya, seeded and mashed

Salt and ground cumin to taste

Garnish (optional)
Crème fraîche (see Index)
Finely chopped almonds
Grated coconut

Pour broth into a soup pot, sprinkle gelatin over top, and set aside to soften for 5 minutes. In a small bowl, beat the egg white until frothy. Add egg white to soup mixture and bring to a boil, whisking constantly until gelatin is fully dissolved and soup is frothy. Remove from heat and allow to cool 10 minutes.

Pour soup into a food processor or blender, adding the orange juice and papaya, and process to a puree. Season soup to taste with salt and ground cumin. Refrigerate several hours or overnight.

At serving time, taste for seasonings. Pour soup into individual chilled soup bowls and cups. Garnish as desired.

KAERNEMAELKSKODSKAAL— SCANDINAVIAN BUTTERMILK SOUP

Danish   *6 servings*

Although considered a sweet soup for dessert or luncheon, this creamy liquid reminds me of a sweet milk sauce. The taste is almost like a liquid cheesecake. Try it in a chilled wine goblet over fruit, or in a chilled soup bowl. My favorite fruits to accompany it are fresh blueberries or sliced peaches.

2 eggs
¼ cup sugar
1 teaspoon lemon juice
1 lemon rind, grated
1 teaspoon vanilla extract

1 quart buttermilk
1 pint fresh blueberries

Garnish (optional)
Whipped cream

In a large bowl, beat eggs with a wire whisk. Slowly whisk in the sugar, continuing to beat until the mixture forms "threads." Beat in the lemon juice, rind, and vanilla. Slowly whisk in the buttermilk. Refrigerate several hours to chill thoroughly.

To serve, place fruit in the bottom of chilled goblets or bowls, spoon liquid over top, and serve immediately. If desired, top with a dollop of whipped cream.

COLD AVGOLEMONO—GREEK EGG AND LEMON SOUP

Greek   *4 to 6 servings*

This classic Greek cold egg and lemon soup is very creamy, almost custardy. The tart lemony taste, heightened by the mint garnish, is very refreshing for a lunch or dinner dish on a blistery hot day. Although it isn't sweet, my husband prefers to sip this soup as a final, dessertlike course.

2 cups chicken stock

2 teaspoons cornstarch diluted in 2 tablespoons water

4 egg yolks

½ cup fresh lemon juice, strained

1 cup heavy cream at room temperature

Salt and white pepper to taste

Garnish

2 tablespoons minced fresh mint leaves

Pour chicken stock into a soup pot and bring to a boil. Add diluted cornstarch, stirring, and reduce heat to a simmer for 5 minutes to thicken slightly. Place egg yolks in a medium-size bowl and, with a wire whisk, beat until light and slightly thickened. Beat in lemon juice and cream. Add about ¼ cup simmering broth to the yolk mixture to lighten, then slowly pour egg mixture into the soup, whisking constantly. Cook over low heat 3 to 5 minutes; do not boil. Season with salt and white pepper. Cool and then chill well for several hours or overnight.

At serving time, spoon into chilled soup bowls and garnish with mint.

LASSI

Indian   *4 servings*

Lassi, a very popular Indian refreshment, is yogurt thinned with water and seasoned with spices and sugar.

1 cup plain yogurt

3 cups ice water

1 teaspoon ground cumin

1 teaspoon salt

½ to 2 teaspoons sugar (optional)

Garnish

Sprinkling of ground hot red pepper and/or mint leaves

A quick method of preparing lassi is to place the yogurt, ice water, cumin, and salt in a food processor or blender and process until smooth. Sweeten to taste with sugar, if desired. Refrigerate until serving time.

Serve in chilled glasses and garnish each portion with a sprinkling of hot red pepper and/or a sprig of mint leaves.

Variation: To make the Iranian yogurt drink dugh, reduce the ice water to 1½ cups and substitute ¼ teaspoon each ground celery seeds, ground dry mint, and ground savory for the cumin and optional sugar. Serve in glasses over ice. Sprinkle powdered rose petals on top as a garnish, if desired.

MINESTRA DI VERDURA WITH PESTO SAUCE

Italian   *6 servings*

Featuring fresh seasonal vegetables, Minestra di Verdura is particularly delicious when served Genovese style with a topping of pesto sauce.

1 medium onion, chopped	1 cup shredded cabbage
1 leek, well cleaned and diced (firm parts only)	Salt to taste
1 clove garlic, minced	2 quarts boiling beef stock
½ cup olive oil	1 cup shell-shaped pasta, cooked and drained
½ cup chopped carrots	6 to 12 tablespoons pesto sauce (see Index)
½ cup chopped celery	
1 cup chopped zucchini	
1 cup chopped green beans	
1 8-ounce can peeled whole Italian tomatoes with the liquid, chopped	

In a large soup pot over medium heat, saute the onion, leek, and garlic in olive oil until soft and golden. Add the carrots and saute for 2 minutes, stirring occasionally. Add the other vegetables, one at a time, sauteeing each for a few minutes before adding the next. Season with salt and add the boiling stock, stirring to mix well. Cover the pot and continue to simmer for 2 hours. Add the pasta and cook another 10 minutes. Allow soup to cool then chill overnight or for 24 hours.

At serving time, place soup in individual large chilled soup bowls. Swirl one or two tablespoons of pesto sauce into each bowl and accompany with plenty of crusty Italian bread.

BORSCHT—BEET SOUP

Jewish   *8 servings*

A perfect hot summer soup. I remember my Buba serving this at supper time to cool the adults. We grandchildren never liked it, but as I grew up I began to crave a big bowl of chilled sweet-sour borscht with a hot boiled potato and lots of sour cream.

You'll find this recipe a little unusual as it not only uses the beets, but also includes some of their nutritious stems and leaves, an excellent source of vitamin A and B. I also first cook the beets in their skins to retain these vitamins.

8 medium-size beets (about 2½ pounds), including leaves and stems
2½ quarts water
1 large onion, grated
3 tablespoons brown sugar
Juice of 1 large lemon
1 tablespoon salt (or more to taste)

2 eggs at room temperature
6 medium-size red new potatoes or white potatoes

Garnish

1 cup sour cream
1 cucumber, peeled, seeded, and diced

Cut beets off their stems, reserving the fresh, unbruised leaves and firm stems. Scrub beets well and put in soup pot with water. Bring water to a boil, reduce heat to a simmer, cover, and continue to cook 25 to 30 minutes, or until beets are tender. Meanwhile, wash reserved stems and leaves and finely chop.

Remove beets from their liquid with a slotted spoon. Place chopped leaves and stems and grated onion in liquid and continue to simmer. Allow beets to cool enough to handle before peeling and grating them, using a food processor if you have one.

Return grated beets to their liquid and stir well. Simmer soup another 20 minutes. As "shum," a foamy substance, rises, remove with a slotted spoon and discard. Add sugar, lemon juice, and salt. Stir well and simmer another 30 minutes. Remove from heat.

Beat the eggs in a medium-size bowl. Gradually whisk 1 cup of soup liquid into the eggs to prevent curdling. Then slowly whisk egg mixture into soup pot.

Allow soup to cool slightly at room temperature, about 30 minutes. Then cover and refrigerate for several hours before serving.

Prior to serving, boil potatoes until barely tender; peel.

To serve, ladle into individual chilled bowls. Add hot boiled potato, a dollop of sour cream, and garnish with chopped cucumber.

SANGRIA PUNCH

Mexican   *Approximately 2½ gallons*

A Mexican fiesta is not a fiesta without sangria to drink with the appetizers.

2 gallons dry red wine
1 pint tequila
1 cup sugar

3 large oranges, sliced
3 lemons, sliced
3 limes, sliced

Pour the burgundy and tequila into a big pot. Add the sugar and stir until it is fully dissolved. You may find it simpler to first dissolve the sugar in a little hot water and then add the sweet "syrup" to the wine-tequila. Add the sliced fruits and refrigerate several hours so that the fruit juices will mix with the punch. When serving, add ice cubes to keep the sangria cold.

CHILLED AVOCADO SOUP WITH TEQUILA

Mexican   *4 servings*

Served in chilled bowls, this creamy pale green soup is an excellent first-course alternative to the well-known guacamole dip and chips.

2 ripe avocados, sliced
1 cup chicken broth
1 tablespoon fresh lemon juice
2 tablespoons tequila or dry white wine

1 cup heavy cream
Salt, white pepper, and cayenne pepper to taste

Garnish

Cilantro leaves

Place avocados in a food processor or blender with chicken broth, lemon juice, and tequila. If quantity is too much for your machine, do in two batches. Process, slowly adding the cream. Season to taste with salt, pepper, and cayenne pepper. Transfer mixture to a glass or porcelain bowl.

Cover and refrigerate several hours or, better yet, 24 hours to allow flavors to mellow.

At serving time, ladle into chilled soup bowls. Garnish with a generous amount of cilantro leaves. If cilantro is not available, sprinkle with minced parsley, chives, or another favorite fresh herb.

Variation: Another version of this soup can be made by pureeing 4 medium avocados, ½ medium onion, 1 tablespoon cilantro, and salt and pepper to taste. Add 2 quarts chicken stock and chill well for 24 hours. Garnish with finely chopped chile peppers.

SCANDINAVIAN SOUR CHERRY SOUP

Scandinavian   *6 to 8 servings*

Chilled fruit soups to be served as a first course or an unusual dessert are favorite dishes throughout most of Europe. This sour cherry soup with its Scandinavian tracings was created by Martha Jean Rutherford, a very grand friend and cook extraordinaire, from her childhood taste recollections.

2 cups chicken broth, preferably homemade and unsalted

4 cups pitted sour cherries, pureed
2 tablespoons sugar

½ teaspoon ground cumin
   (or more to taste)
Dash ground white pepper

1 cup dry white wine
Crème fraîche and mint
sprigs, for garnishes

Place all ingredients, except garnishes, in a soup pot or large sauce-pan and simmer until reduced and thickened slightly. Chill overnight or preferably two days. Ladle into chilled bowls and serve with a dollop of crème fraîche and a sprig of fresh mint.

BLUEBERRY SOUP

Scandinavian   *4 servings*

Although classified as a soup, I consider this more as a thick but liquid heavenly fruit dessert. On a warm summer day, you could even serve this as a first course for your patio brunch or luncheon menu. The color is startlingly bright, as is the taste.

1 pint blueberries, washed
1½ cups water
⅓ cup sugar
½ teaspoon cinnamon
4 whole cloves
2 tablespoons lemon juice
2 tablespoons cornstarch

¼ cup dry white wine

Garnish

Grated lemon rind
Crème fraîche or sour
creme (optional)

Place blueberries, water, sugar, cinnamon, and cloves in a soup pot. Bring to a boil, partially cover, and reduce heat. Occasionally stir the mixture with a wooden spoon, crushing blueberries against the side of the pot with the back of the spoon. Simmer until blueberries are tender, about 10 minutes. Stir in lemon juice.

In a small cup, mix the cornstarch with the wine to dissolve; stir into soup. Return soup to a boil, stirring constantly, for 1 minute.

Chill soup and serve in chilled bowls or wine goblets. Garnish with grated lemon rind and, if desired, a swirl of crème fraîche or sour cream.

COLD ALMOND AND GARLIC SOUP

Spanish   *4 to 6 servings*

This classic icy-cold Spanish soup, similar to gazpacho blanco (a "white" gaz-pacho) has a rich nutty garlic taste, complemented well by the fruity last-minute addition of white grapes. Serve it as a first course to be followed by a Mediterranean-style tomato and pepper salad, herb-roasted chicken or lamb, and steamed seasonal vegetables dressed with olive oil and lemon juice.

⅓ cup olive oil
4 slices French or white bread, crusts removed, cut up
3 to 4 cloves garlic, crushed
¾ cup blanched almonds, chopped

4 cups chicken broth
3 tablespoons white wine
1 cup seedless white grapes, halved lengthwise (or more to taste)

Heat olive oil in a skillet and saute the bread and garlic until they begin to brown lightly. Add almonds, stirring well to coat with the seasoned oil; do not let the garlic burn. Place mixture in a food processor and puree. Add chicken broth and white wine. Chill several hours or overnight. At serving time, pour soup into individual bowls and add grapes and an ice cube to each bowl. There should be enough grapes so that every spoonful will have the sweet taste.

Variation: To make gazpacho blanco, use ice water instead of chicken broth, vinegar instead of wine. Traditionally, the ingredients are combined with the use of a mortar and pestle, but a food processor or blender saves considerable time and energy. No prior sauteeing is necessary; simply puree all ingredients, except the grapes, and refrigerate.

SENEGALESE SOUP

International   *6 servings*

The classical Senegalese soup is an English chicken soup with a generous amount of curry powder for seasoning and color. I have added a tropical touch with a combination of fruits and vegetables.

1 medium onion, chopped
½ cup diced celery
2 medium tart green apples, peeled, cored, and diced
3 tablespoons butter
1 tablespoon curry powder
Dash cayenne pepper
1 tablespoon flour

4 cups chicken broth
Salt to taste
1 cup half-and-half

Garnish

1 avocado, thinly sliced
1 small banana, thinly sliced

In a soup pot, cook onion, celery, and apples in butter over medium heat for about 10 minutes, until onions are soft, not browned. Sprinkle curry powder over mixture, stirring to coat everything evenly. Sprinkle with cayenne. Add flour and stir to coat everything well. Slowly add the broth, stirring with each addition, to blend liquid into curried mixture. Simmer soup about 5 more minutes until vegetables and apples are tender. Season to taste with salt.

Pour mixture into a food processor or blender and puree until smooth, and then slowly add cream. Refrigerate for several hours.

At serving time, ladle into chilled bowls. Garnish each bowl with avocado and banana slices.

Variation: Avocado can be added to the soup during the pureeing stage, if desired, to incorporate its flavor. Garnish soup with only sliced bananas or slivers of poached chicken.

CARROT-ORANGE SOUP

International   *4 servings*

This exotic carrot-orange soup with Arabian influences is fruity, fragrant, and slightly spicy. Its color is a sensational orange blush.

1 pound carrots, scraped and sliced
¼ cup chopped onion
2 tablespoons butter
2 cups chicken broth
Juice of 2 oranges, strained (¾ cup)
Grated rind of 1 orange

Juice of 1 lemon
¼ teaspoon ground cardamon
Salt, white pepper, and freshly grated nutmeg to taste

Garnish

Chopped dried dates

Place carrots, onion, and butter in a heavy soup pot and saute over low heat for 5 to 7 minutes, stirring occasionally until onion is wilted and butter is absorbed by vegetables. Add chicken broth, stirring thoroughly, slightly increase heat, and cook until vegetables are tender, about 18 to 20 minutes.

Puree soup in a food processor or blender, processing for a few seconds to one minute, leaving a little texture. Return soup to pot, add orange juice, rind, lemon juice, and cardamon. Season generously with salt, pepper, and nutmeg and simmer another 1 to 2 minutes.

Cool to room temperature and then chill several hours or overnight. Garnish individual servings with chopped dates.

PEAR, APPLE, AND CUCUMBER SOUP

International   *4 servings*

Chilled fruit soups, which have been popular in Europe for many years, are made with seasonal berries, cherries, plums, nectarines, peaches, pears, and apples—as in this recipe. When serving, be imaginative and bring out your prettiest crystal goblets, brandy snifters, or punch bowl and cup sets. The following soup reminds me of a sophisticated applesauce. Although you probably won't be able to detect the cucumber, I find it adds a "clean" taste as well as color to the final soup.

2 ripe pears, peeled, cored, and chopped
2 large tart green apples, peeled, cored, and chopped
Juice of 1 lemon
1 medium cucumber, peeled, seeded, and cut up

½ cup dry white wine or champagne

Garnish

Sour cream
Roquefort or other blue cheese, crumbled

Place pears and apples in a heavy saucepan with the lemon juice (to hold the color of the fruit) and simmer, stirring often, 8 to 10 minutes, until fruit is tender. Spoon fruit into a food processor or blender and process a few seconds. Add cucumber and continue to process until everything is pureed. Add the wine and process quickly to mix. Chill the mixture for several hours or overnight.

At serving time, swirl sour cream into individual servings and garnish tops with Roquefort cheese for a final tang.

CUCUMBER REFRESHER

International   *4 to 8 servings*

Cucumber, a very cool vegetable, is refreshing to eat or drink in a soup. This recipe is somewhere between a beverage and a chilled soup.

1 large cucumber (about 8 ounces), peeled and sliced thinly
1 large hothouse cucumber (about ¾ pound), partially peeled (see Note) and sliced thinly
Salt

2 cups plain yogurt
1 cup buttermilk
¼ cup chopped fresh cilantro
White pepper to taste

Garnish

Additional cucumber "fingers"

Place cucumbers on paper towels and salt them. Cover with additional paper towels and allow the cucumbers to sit from 5 to 30 minutes so that excess liquid is drained off. (If you are pressed for time you can use the cucumbers immediately, but your soup will be a little watery.)

In a blender or food processor, combine the yogurt and buttermilk; process to mix. Add the cucumber and cilantro and quickly process again until well blended. Season to taste with pepper. Thoroughly chill before serving.

At serving time, pour chilled soup into chilled glass mugs or giant wine/beer glasses and garnish with cucumber "fingers."

Note: You can leave most of the skin on hothouse cucumbers, as they are not waxed. The skin is very tender as well as colorful.

TURNIP GAZPACHO

International   *6 to 10 servings*

I created this unusual gazpacho, based on the Spanish cold tomato and vegetable soup, one afternoon when my cooking friend and fellow author Richard Nelson challenged me to create a unique recipe utilizing an abundance of turnips we had on hand in the refrigerator. The experiment was so successful that I have made this many times since.

For a buffet, place this gazpacho in a large bowl nestled in an even larger bowl filled with crushed ice, which will keep the soup completely chilled. Serve with homemade taco chips (see Index), as you would a Mexican salsa, or with homemade garlic-flavored croutons, as you would a more traditional Spanish gazpacho.

4 medium-size turnips, peeled and diced
2 very large tomatoes (see Note)
1 medium-size green pepper
4 jalapeño peppers
10 medium-size green onions, including firm green tops, chopped
3 cloves garlic, finely minced

Juice of 3 limes
⅓ cup olive oil
1 tablespoon dried leaf oregano
2 teaspoons salt
1 teaspoon cracked black pepper
¼ teaspoon cayenne pepper (or more to taste)

In a medium-size pot, boil turnips for about 5 minutes; immediately refresh in cold water with ice to help set the texture and color. Place tomatoes in boiling water for a few seconds and then rub under cold water; the skin should come off easily. Roast peppers under the broiler, place in a plastic bag, refrigerate to sweat for about 20 minutes, and then peel off black skin. The peppers will now be very sweet.

Place the turnips in a medium-to-large-size serving bowl. Finely chop the peeled tomatoes and place with their juice in the bowl with the turnips. Remove seeds from the peeled peppers and finely chop. Add to the bowl of vegetables, along with green onions and garlic. Mix vegetables together by tossing with your fingers. Add lime juice and olive oil. With your hands, crush oregano directly into the bowl and season with salt and pepper. Again, toss all ingredients thoroughly with your hands. Place bowl in the refrigerator for gazpacho to thoroughly chill.

Note: If a thinner gazpacho is preferred, tomato juice can also be added, to taste, until desired consistency is reached.

TOMATO AND SPLIT PEA SOUP

International   *4 to 6 servings*

A mixture of fresh and dried vegetables stars in this sophisticated yet hearty chilled soup. The chiles add a touch of fire.

1 large onion, chopped
2 strips bacon, cut into
    1-inch lengths
1 cup dried green split peas,
    well washed and picked
    over
2 stalks celery, chopped
3 carrots, scraped and
    chopped
1 28-ounce can peeled whole
    Italian tomatoes, with
    liquid, mashed with a
    wooden spoon
1½ tablespoons chopped fresh
    parsley
1 small green pepper, seeded
    and chopped

2 small yellow chiles, seeded
    and chopped
¼ teaspoon dried thyme
¼ teaspoon dried sweet basil
1 clove garlic, pureed
    Salt and pepper to taste
    Dash cumin
1 bay leaf
3 cups chicken broth
2 cups water

Garnish

Heavy cream or sour
cream

In a large soup pot, saute the onion and bacon over low heat for 10 minutes or until onion is soft. Add the vegetables, one at a time, stirring constantly. Add the spices and seasonings, stirring to blend the flavors. Add the chicken broth and water; stir to mix well. Bring soup to a boil; cover, reduce heat to the lowest possible simmer, and cook for 3 hours. Remove the bay leaf and, in several batches, force soup through a sieve or puree in a food processor. Check for seasoning and chill overnight or for 24 hours.

Serve soup as a main dish in chilled soup bowls, garnishing each bowl with heavy cream or sour cream.

SUSAN'S LEMON SQUASH SOUP

International   *4 to 6 servings*

My close friend and fellow food writer Susan Slack created this delightful chilled summer squash soup. The curry powder adds piquancy.

4 or 5 small crookneck
    squash (summer squash),
    sliced
2 tablespoons butter
2 green onions, chopped

½ teaspoon curry powder, or
    more to taste (optional)
2 cups chicken stock
1 teaspoon sugar

½ teaspoon salt, or to taste
1 tablespoon fresh lemon
juice
½ cup heavy cream

Garnish

Crème fraîche or sour
cream
Minced chives

Saute squash in butter with scallions about 5 minutes or just until vegetables are tender. Sprinkle curry powder over vegetables while they are being sauteed. Put vegetables into blender or processor and blend until mixture is smooth. A little stock can be added if necessary. Cool mixture to room temperature and then add the stock, sugar, salt, lemon juice, and cream.

Chill until serving time. Serve with a dollop of crème fraîche and a sprinkling of chives.

MINTED FRESH PEA SOUP

International   *6 to 8 servings*

The concept of this rich, minty green pea and Oriental pea pod soup has South African origins. I have also enjoyed a similar soup, created one summer's afternoon by James Beard and his students; fresh green peas (with their shells), along with the defrosted variety, were cooked in a seasoned broth, pureed, and then yogurt was added.

5 cups chicken broth
2 cups frozen green peas,
defrosted
1 pound Oriental pea pods,
flowery ends and strings
removed
1 medium onion, studded
with 4 cloves
2 tablespoons chopped fresh
mint
1 teaspoon sugar

3 tablespoons butter
3 tablespoons flour
1½ cups milk, at room
temperature
Salt and white pepper to
taste

Garnish

Additional chopped fresh
mint leaves

Pour chicken broth into a heavy soup pot and bring to a boil. Add the two varieties of peas, onion, and mint. Add sugar and stir thoroughly. Return broth to a boil and then reduce to a simmer; cook 20 to 30 minutes, stirring occasionally, until peas are very tender. Remove onion and discard.

Puree soup—in batches, if necessary—in a food processor, blender, food mill, or sieve, allowing some texture.

Melt butter in a heavy saucepan or pot (it's best to clean and reuse the first pot) over low heat. Add flour and cook the mixture to make a roux, being careful not to burn the butter or flour. Add the pea puree and the milk, stirring constantly. Continue cooking over low heat, stirring constantly, for about 5 minutes, until soup is well blended and slightly thickened. Do not let soup come to a boil. Cool at room temperature and then refrigerate several hours or overnight.

At serving time, garnish individual portions with additional mint.

Variation: For a lighter, thinner version of this soup, 3 cups milk, rather than 1½ cups, can be added. For a richer version, cream can be substituted for the milk.

Additional Soups and Beverages

Tzatsiki—Greek Cucumber and
    Yogurt Dip

Light Salads and Vegetable Dishes

MOROCCAN STRING BEANS AND CILANTRO
AFRICAN BROWN LENTIL SALAD
SPINACH-MUSHROOM SALAD WITH FRENCH DRESSING
PEAS AND ONION SALAD
MARINATED ARTICHOKE HEART AND RICE SALAD
APPLE WALNUT SALAD
RED AND GREEN PEPPERY COLE SLAW
CABBAGE SLAW WITH GARDEN VEGETABLES
SEVEN LAYER SALAD
FARMER SALAD
PENNSYLVANIA DUTCH PICKLED BEETS AND EGGS
MACARONI AND EGG SALAD WITH
SOUR CREAM DRESSING
POTATO SALAD WITH TANGY BLUE CHEESE DRESSING
GRANDMA FISHER'S POTATO SALAD
MARINO MARINATED MUSHROOM SALAD
WITH MAUI MUSTARD
ARMENIAN POTATO SALAD WITH RED ONIONS AND
GREEN PEPPER
CHINESE RADISH-CUCUMBER SALAD
ORIENTAL CELERY SALAD WITH SESAME OIL
RODKAAL—EVY'S DANISH RED CABBAGE
PEELED ASPARAGUS WITH LEMON JUICE AND OLIVE OIL
BEET RÂPÉ
PARISIAN CAROTTES RÂPÉES
STRING BEANS AND TOMATOES PROVENÇALE

WATERCRESS AND WALNUT SALAD

WATERCRESS AND MUSHROOM SALAD WITH WALNUT
OIL DRESSING

CUCUMBER IN DILLED CREAM

GERMAN BEET SALAD WITH SOUR CREAM

GERMAN PICKLED RADISH SALAD INGE

GREEK BAKED AND MARINATED SPRING
GARDEN VEGETABLES

PEPINO ENSALADA—GUATEMALAN CUCUMBER SALAD

ROSA'S RADISH SALAD

GUATEMALAN POTATO AND VEGETABLE SALAD

CACUMBAR—INDIAN TOMATO-CUCUMBER-ONION
SALAD

INDONESIAN MIXED SALAD

ATJAR—INDONESIAN PICKLED VEGETABLES

IRANIAN CUCUMBER, ONION, AND YOGURT SALAD
WITH RAISINS

MEDITERRANEAN MARINATED TOMATO SALAD

ITALIAN ROASTED RED AND GREEN PEPPERS

GREEN PEPPER AND TOMATO SALAD

TOMATO-MOZZARELLA-BASIL SALAD

SIMPLE SALT-PICKLED SALAD VEGETABLES

SPINACH WITH SESAME DRESSING

JAPANESE EGGPLANTS IN MISO DRESSING

PICKLED COOKED VEGETABLES AND TOFU WITH GOMA
DRESSING NAMASU

CUCUMBER AND SHRIMP SUNOMONO

KIMPIRA GOBO, CARROT, AND CELERY

CANDIED SWEET POTATOES

CHILLED NOODLES WITH CUCUMBERS
AND MUSHROOMS

BUBA'S FRUIT KUGEL

SUSAN'S KOREAN MARINATED SPINACH

SUKI'S KIM CHEE

AVOCADO-TOMATO SALAD

LEÓN JÍCAMA SALAD

ENSALADA DE NOPALES—CACTUS LEAF SALAD

CUCUMBER-RADISH SALAD

YUCATECAN PICKLED ONIONS
PERSIAN CUCUMBER SALAD
TABBOULEH—BULGUR SALAD
TOMATOES AND CUCUMBERS WITH LABAN
ORANGE, RED ONION, AND RADISH SALAD
RUSSIAN CUCUMBERS WITH CREAMY DRESSING
LOBIO—RUSSIAN STRING BEANS WITH
HERB VINAIGRETTE
RUSSIAN BEAN SALAD WITH SATSIVI (WALNUT) SAUCE
MARINATED BRAISED LEEKS
ORANGE-AVOCADO SALAD
AVOCADO-ARTICHOKE SALAD
AVOCADO-TOMATO-BACON SALAD
POTATO AND ROASTED GREEN PEPPER SALAD WITH
MUSTARD VINAIGRETTE
ROMAINE SALAD WITH ROQUEFORT DRESSING
BABY ARTICHOKES AND TOMATOES IN A
HERB VINAIGRETTE
CHERRY TOMATOES IN A BASIL VINAIGRETTE
MARINADE
GARDEN FAR EAST SALAD
ASPARAGUS VINAIGRETTE

MOROCCAN STRING BEANS AND CILANTRO

African   *6 to 8 servings*

This highly seasoned tomato-based dressing is equally good with string beans or other vegetables, such as eggplant, broccoli, zucchini, carrots, or peas.

1 pound string beans, ends trimmed

Moroccan Spicy Tomato Dressing (makes approximately ¼ cup)

    4 teaspoons tomato paste
    2 tablespoons lemon juice or vinegar
    1 large clove garlic, finely minced

1 teaspoon cayenne pepper
1 teaspoon cumin
½ teaspoon paprika
1 tablespoon olive oil, peanut oil, or other cooking oil
Salt and pepper to taste

3 tablespoons chopped cilantro

Thinly slice string beans into juliennes about 2 inches in length. (String beans should resemble the French bean cut.) Boil in water to cover until barely tender, about 4 to 5 minutes, drain, and rinse with cold water and ice cubes to set the color.

To make the dressing: Put tomato paste in a small bowl and mix with lemon juice. Add garlic, cayenne, cumin, and paprika, stirring to blend well. Slowly mix in the olive oil. Season to taste with salt and pepper.

Place string beans in a serving bowl and toss with cilantro. Add dressing and toss well. Let sit at room temperature several hours to allow flavors to mingle. This can be made a day in advance and refrigerated. Bring to room temperature before serving.

AFRICAN BROWN LENTIL SALAD

African   *4 to 6 servings*

From Ethiopia comes this flavorful hearty lentil salad.

1 cup brown lentils
4 cups chicken broth or water
½ onion, studded with 2 whole cloves
1 bay leaf

Ethiopian Dressing (makes approximately 1¾ cups)

    1 large leek (about 8 ounces), including firm

green parts, well cleaned, or 6 to 8 shallots, peeled (see Note)
3 cloves garlic
3 serrano chiles
1 jalapeño chile
2 tablespoons vinegar
1½ tablespoons cooking oil
Salt and pepper to taste

Soak lentils in water to cover for 2 hours; drain. Place in a pot with the chicken broth, onion, and bay leaf. (I find the chicken broth gives a wonderfully full-bodied taste to the lentils.) Bring to a boil and then reduce heat to a simmer. Partially cover and cook about 20 minutes or until tender but not mushy; drain.

To make the dressing: In a food processor, coarsely chop leek with garlic. Near running water, to rinse your hands as often as necessary, carefully slit open and seed the serrano and jalapeño chiles. Add both to the food processor with the leek and garlic and process for a few seconds, but do not puree. Mix in the vinegar and oil and season to taste with salt and pepper.

Toss dressing with lentils. Allow to sit at room temperature at least 1 hour, occasionally tossing.

Note: The original salad is made with shallots, which are not always easily available and are often expensive. I have found leeks to be a most suitable substitute.

SPINACH-MUSHROOM SALAD
WITH FRENCH DRESSING

American   *6 servings*

A crisp spinach salad with raw mushrooms and snappy watercress is a light opening course for a hearty dinner.

2 bunches fresh spinach
½ pound very large fresh
   mushrooms
1 bunch watercress

French Dressing (makes approximately 1 cup)

½ cup salad oil
2 tablespoons olive oil

½ cup vinegar (preferably rice vinegar)
½ teaspoon salt
   Dash freshly ground black pepper
3 tablespoons freshly grated Parmesan cheese

Clean spinach by carefully removing the stems from all the large leaves and breaking the stems off at the bottoms of the small, tender leaves. Wash well to remove all dirt and sand; pat dry with paper towels. Wrap spinach in paper towels and place in refrigerator to recrisp. Wipe mushrooms clean with a damp mushroom brush or paper towels. Cut off the very bottom part of the stems and slice mushrooms as thinly as possible. Wrap in paper towels and refrigerate. Wash and dry watercress, discard tough stems, and cut watercress into small branchlike flowers. Wrap in paper towels and refrigerate.

To make the dressing: Combine the oils in a bowl or measuring cup and whisk in the vinegar, salt, and pepper. The Parmesan cheese can either be whisked into the dressing or tossed separately with the salad.

In a large salad bowl, combine the spinach, mushrooms, watercress, and Parmesan cheese (if it has not been added to the dressing) and toss with the dressing. Divide among salad plates.

PEAS AND ONION SALAD

American   *6 to 10 servings*

I could not begin to count the number of times I have made this salad for small dinners as well as large buffets. As your party increases, simply increase the proportions. You, too, will love this salad.

2 16-ounce bags frozen baby peas, defrosted (see Note)
1 medium onion, thinly sliced
¼ cup chopped fresh mint, *not* dried

3 tablespoons salad oil
2 tablespoons honey
Salt to taste
½ cup sour cream
1½ tablespoons vinegar (preferably rice vinegar)

Mix peas with onion and mint, tossing well. Add oil, honey, and salt, mixing well. Refrigerate overnight. Prior to serving, mix the sour cream and vinegar and pour into salad. Toss well.

Note: If using fresh peas, shell and boil until barely tender and rinse with cold water. You need 2 generous cups of peas.

MARINATED ARTICHOKE HEART AND RICE SALAD

American   *10 to 14 servings*

A superb salad for a buffet or elegant picnic.

2 cups long-grain brown rice, cooked in chicken broth
3 6-ounce jars marinated artichoke hearts, drained (with liquid reserved) and chopped
¼ cup minced green onions

½ cup chopped fresh parsley
4 medium tomatoes, chopped
⅓ cup freshly grated Parmesan cheese
1 cup mayonnaise
Salt and pepper to taste

Allow cooked rice to cool. In a large bowl, combine the rice with the artichoke hearts, green onions, parsley, tomatoes, and Parmesan cheese. In a small bowl, thoroughly combine the mayonnaise with the marinade from 2 jars of the artichoke hearts. (You will not need the liquid from the third jar, so save it for another recipe.) Season the dressing to taste with salt and pepper. Pour dressing over rice salad and toss well. Cover and refrigerate until serving time.

Variation: If you wish to expand this recipe, you might try adding flaked tuna, sliced cooked sausage, and/or chopped hard-cooked eggs.

APPLE WALNUT SALAD

American   *6 servings*

A variation on the classic Waldorf Salad, using yogurt as the base of the dressing and adding a favorite Swiss cheese, Jarlsberg.

2 tart green apples, cored, diced, and unpeeled
1 lemon, cut in half
½ cup diced celery
¼ cup coarsely chopped walnuts
3 ounces Jarlsberg cheese or other favorite Swiss cheese, sliced into matchstick juliennes

Dressing (makes approximately 1 cup)

1 cup plain yogurt or mayonnaise
1 teaspoon Dijon mustard (preferably Poupon or another seedless variety)

In a salad bowl, toss the diced apple with the juice of ½ lemon to hold the color; reserve remaining half for the dressing. Add the celery, walnuts, and cheese and toss well.

To make the dressing: Whisk together the yogurt, juice of remaining lemon, and mustard in a small bowl.

Pour dressing over apple mixture and toss well to coat all ingredients. Cover and refrigerate until serving time.

RED AND GREEN PEPPERY COLE SLAW

American   *6 to 10 servings*

One of my favorite family cole slaws—dressy enough for company—is this easy-to-make red and green salad composed of green cabbage, sweet red pepper, and sweet red onion. The mayonnaise and sour cream dressing, zipped with vinegar and cayenne pepper, perks up the cabbage.

1 medium head cabbage, cored and shredded
1 large sweet red pepper, seeded and finely chopped
1 large red onion, finely chopped

Cole Slaw Dressing I (makes approximately 1 cup)

⅔ cup mayonnaise
⅓ cup sour cream
2 tablespoons vinegar (preferably rice vinegar)
1 teaspoon sugar
Cayenne pepper to taste
Salt to taste (optional)

Vegetables can be shredded and cut by hand or with a food processor, using the fine slicing blade for cabbage and the chopping blade for the red pepper and onion. In a large bowl, combine the cabbage, red pepper, and onion.

To make the dressing: In a small bowl, mix all ingredients and stir to make sure sugar is dissolved. Taste for seasoning.

Pour dressing over cabbage mixture, toss well, cover, and refrigerate until serving time.

CABBAGE SLAW WITH GARDEN VEGETABLES

American   *6 to 12 servings*

This is one of the best cole slaws you will ever taste. It's crunchy and fresh, and the dressing is not too heavy. Whenever I have a craving for cole slaw, this is the one I make. It's excellent for backyard picnics, as well as elegant buffet dining.

If you own a food processor, you will find the time is cut down tremendously.

1 large head cabbage, cored	Cabbage Slaw Dressing II
½ medium green pepper, seeded	(makes approximately 1⅓ cups)
10 radishes	¼ cup vinegar
4 carrots	2 tablespoons sugar
1 medium onion	2 teaspoons salt
	½ teaspoon pepper
	2 teaspoons Dijon mustard
	1 cup mayonnaise

Using a food processor, slice cabbage, green pepper, and radishes with the thin slicing blade. Shred carrots with the medium shredding blade, and finely chop onions with the metal chopping blade. If preparing without a processor, shred cabbage and carrots, thinly slice radishes, cut thin juliennes of green pepper, and finely chop onion. Combine vegetables in a large bowl, tossing to mix well.

To make the dressing: In a medium-size bowl or large measuring cup, combine the vinegar with the sugar, salt, and pepper, stirring to dissolve sugar. Stir in mustard and blend in mayonnaise, mixing thoroughly.

Pour dressing over vegetables and toss. Cover and refrigerate several hours, during which time the vegetable juices will thin the dressing. Toss again before serving.

SEVEN LAYER SALAD

American   *6 to 8 servings*

A favorite American salad concept is the layered salad. Practically every cook has a version of layering fresh vegetables (sometimes the frozen variety), top-

ping them with a mayonnaise-based dressing, and then refrigerating the dish for several hours to allow the flavors to mellow. These salads are ideal for picnics, pot lucks, and busy household dinners. Remember, do not toss until serving time.

This particular layered salad is the creation of my late mother-in-law, Anabel Hoy.

1 small head lettuce, torn into bite-size pieces
½ cup diced green pepper
½ cup diced celery
1 onion, diced
1½ cups fresh peas, cooked, or 1 10-ounce package frozen peas, defrosted and drained

2 cups mayonnaise or 1 cup each sour cream and mayonnaise
2 teaspoons sugar
1 cup shredded cheddar cheese
8 slices bacon, fried crisp and crumbled

In a large salad bowl, preferably glass so that you can see the layers, place the lettuce, green pepper, celery, onion, and peas. Sweeten the mayonnaise with the sugar and spread over the peas. Sprinkle cheese and bacon over the top. Cover bowl and refrigerate overnight. Toss prior to serving.

Variation: Crumbled blue cheese can be substituted for the cheddar cheese. Strips of poached or roasted chicken can be substituted for the bacon.

FARMER SALAD

American   *4 to 6 servings*

One of my childhood food memories is of a salad my grandmother called Farmer Salad—a combination of all the salad vegetables she had on hand.

3 large tomatoes, peeled (if desired) and cut into wedges
½ to 1 green pepper, seeded and cut into rings
1 large or 2 medium cucumbers, peeled, thinly sliced, and drained on paper towels about 10 minutes
2 green onions, including firm green tops, thinly sliced
¼ cup chopped red onion
8 radishes, thinly sliced

2 tablespoons minced fresh parsley

Simple Oil and Vinegar Dressing (makes approximately 1 cup)

⅓ cup red wine vinegar
1 teaspoon minced fresh herbs on hand, such as parsley or thyme
½ teaspoon Dijon mustard
Pinch of sugar
⅔ cup salad oil
Salt and pepper to taste

Combine salad vegetables in a large bowl.

To make the dressing: In a small bowl, combine the vinegar, herbs, mustard, and sugar. Slowly whisk in salad oil and season to taste with salt and pepper and additional sugar, if desired. This dressing is excellent with other salads, particularly firm vegetable mixtures.

Pour dressing over vegetables and toss. Cover and refrigerate at least an hour before serving. Toss and serve.

Variation: Other vegetables or foods can be added or substituted, such as zucchini slices, olives, or even hard-cooked egg halves.

PENNSYLVANIA DUTCH PICKLED BEETS AND EGGS

American   *8 servings*

Whether you're cooking dishes for a big family reunion or simply like to have some Americana recipes on hand when friends stop by, you'll love this one for pickled beets and purple eggs. As a child growing up in Pennsylvania, I often enjoyed this as a side dish with fried chicken or baked ham. The Danes make a similar pickled beet recipe without the eggs.

8 small to medium beets
  (about 1¼ pounds),
  trimmed (don't cut off the
  roots or top ½ inch)

**Pennsylvania Dutch Pickling
Liquid**

  2 cups cider vinegar
  1 cup water

1 cup packed brown sugar
1 teaspoon salt
6 whole cloves
4 whole allspice
1 cinnamon stick

8 hard-cooked eggs, peeled
  (see Note)

Boil or bake beets until tender. Drain, rinse with cold water, and peel off skins with your fingers. Trim off root ends and cut into thick slices.

While beets are cooking, combine the pickling liquid in a saucepan, stirring all ingredients. Bring liquid to a boil and boil for 8 minutes. Cool slightly.

Place beets and eggs in a large crock or glass bowl. Pour warm pickling liquid over them, cover, and refrigerate for several days. Occasionally spoon liquid over eggs.

Note: This recipe can be made with beets alone. If so, use 10 to 12 beets.

MACARONI AND EGG SALAD WITH SOUR CREAM DRESSING

American   *6 to 10 servings*

When I think of macaroni and egg salads, this creamy recipe comes to mind. Bring it to room temperature before serving so that the sour cream dressing has the proper consistency.

1 8-ounce package elbow macaroni, cooked, drained, rinsed with cold water, and drained again
1 cup sour cream
2 hard-cooked eggs, coarsely chopped
½ cup chopped celery
⅓ cup chopped dill pickle

½ cup chopped onion
1 pimiento, chopped
½ cup peeled, seeded, and chopped cucumber
2 tablespoons white wine vinegar
1 teaspoon salt
¼ teaspoon pepper
Hot pepper sauce to taste

Place cooked macaroni in a large salad bowl and add remaining ingredients, carefully tossing to combine flavorings. Refrigerate for a minimum of 1 hour; then let stand at room temperature for about 30 minutes before serving.

POTATO SALAD WITH TANGY BLUE CHEESE DRESSING

American   *4 servings*

Potato salads are classic American picnic and family get-together fare. Recently there has been a move away from the traditional mayonnaise-based dressing to dressings featuring yogurt, crème fraîche, or oil and vinegar. This yogurt–blue cheese dressing delicately colored and seasoned with sweet paprika is a tangy sauce for the humble potato. It is also excellent with tossed greens and pasta salads.

1½ pounds light-skinned potatoes
3 hard-cooked eggs, cut up

Yogurt-Blue Cheese Dressing
(makes approximately 1¼ cups)

¾ cup plain yogurt
¼ cup mayonnaise
2 teaspoons vinegar (preferably rice vinegar)

¼ cup crumbled blue cheese
½ teaspoon paprika
½ teaspoon salt
¼ teaspoon white pepper

Garnish (optional)

1 tablespoon minced chives or green onion stems

Boil potatoes in their skins until barely fork tender; do not overcook. Drain and rinse with cold water. When potatoes are cool enough to handle, peel them with your fingers and cut into bite-size chunks. Place potatoes in a salad bowl and add eggs.

To make the dressing: Combine ingredients for dressing and toss with potatoes and eggs. This dressing can be made in advance and refrigerated until needed. Cover salad and refrigerate until serving time.

To serve, carefully toss again and garnish top with minced chives or green onion stems.

Note: This potato salad can be extended by adding other vegetables, such as chopped celery, chopped green onions, sliced cucumber, and/or sliced radishes.

GRANDMA FISHER'S POTATO SALAD

American   *8 to 10 servings*

What makes a unique potato salad? In this one, a couple of special steps add to its great taste, especially when it is still a little warm.

- 5 pounds small red-skinned potatoes
- 2 tablespoons plus ½ teaspoon salt
- 4 stalks celery, diced
- ½ large red onion, diced
- 1 cup vinegar
- ⅓ teaspoon dry mustard
- 1 cup plus 1 tablespoon mayonnaise
- ½ cup sour cream

Wash potatoes in cold water to remove excess red color. Place in a large pot, cover with cold water, and bring to a boil. Add 2 tablespoons of salt, cover pot, and cook over medium heat until done. Fork test in 20 minutes for doneness; don't let potatoes become mushy.

Place celery and red onion in a bowl and cover with vinegar.

Drain water from cooked potatoes, allow them to cool enough to handle, and remove skins. Cut peeled potatoes into medium-size chunks and sprinkle them with the remaining ½ teaspoon of salt.

Drain vinegar from celery and onion (reserve vinegar). Add celery and onions to potatoes. Add dry mustard and 1 cup mayonnaise to vegetables and mix thoroughly. Combine the remaining 1 tablespoon mayonnaise with 1 tablespoon of reserved vinegar, add to the sour cream, and toss mixture with the potatoes, celery, and onion. Add more salt to taste. Cover and refrigerate until needed.

MARINO MARINATED MUSHROOM SALAD
WITH MAUI MUSTARD

American   *4 to 6 servings*

Maui mustard is a particularly piquant variety from Hawaii, available at many fine gourmet shops. When I cook with it, I often sneak a teaspoonful to taste. You'll enjoy this marinated mushroom dish as a first-course dish or an unusual alternative to tossed greens.

1 pound mushrooms, wiped clean and sliced

Maui Mustard Dressing (makes approximately 1¼ cups)

  ¼ cup Maui or Dijon mustard

  4 to 5 tablespoons strawberry or raspberry vinegar

½ teaspoon ground oregano
½ teaspoon ground tarragon
¼ teaspoon freshly ground pepper
¾ cup hazelnut oil or olive oil

Garnish

  Minced fresh parsley

Place mushrooms in a bowl suitable for marinating.

To make the dressing: Combine the mustard, vinegar, and seasonings in a small bowl. Slowly whisk in the oil.

Pour over mushrooms and toss well. Cover and refrigerate 24 hours. Remove from refrigerator 1 hour before serving. Place on individual salad plates and garnish with minced parsley.

ARMENIAN POTATO SALAD WITH RED ONIONS AND GREEN PEPPER

Armenian   *8 to 12 servings*

You will want to accompany roasted lamb or chicken and simple fish recipes with this mellow potato salad.

3 pounds red-skinned potatoes
1 medium red onion, thinly sliced and separated into rings
1 green pepper, seeded and finely chopped

3 tablespoons minced fresh parsley
Juice of ½ lemon
⅓ cup olive oil
Salt, pepper, and cayenne pepper to taste

Boil potatoes in their jackets until barely tender. Cool enough to handle, cut into generous bite-size pieces while still warm. Place potatoes in a large salad bowl along with onion rings and green pepper; mix well. (I have found it easiest to mix salads like this with my hands rather than with spoons.) Add parsley and lemon juice; carefully toss again. Dribble oil over the vegetables and season to taste with salt, pepper, and cayenne pepper; toss and set aside several hours for salad ingredients to mellow. If refrigerated, bring to room temperature before serving.

Variation: For an Italian main-dish salad, add one 7-ounce can tuna (drained) to potato salad mixture.

CHINESE RADISH-CUCUMBER SALAD

Chinese *4 servings*

This easy-to-prepare dish can be served as either a simple salad or a condiment with an Oriental feast.

1 bunch radishes, coarsely chopped

1 cucumber, cut in half, peeled, drained on paper towels about 15 minutes, and coarsely chopped

Oriental Salad Dressing (makes approximately 2 tablespoons)

1 tablespoon rice vinegar
2 teaspoons soy sauce
½ teaspoon sugar
1 teaspoon sesame oil

2 cups coarsely shredded cabbage, kept refrigerated until serving

In a medium-size bowl, combine the radishes and cucumber.

To make the dressing: In a small bowl, mix together the vinegar and soy sauce. Add sugar, stirring to dissolve.

Pour dressing over vegetables, toss thoroughly, and refrigerate until serving time.

At serving time, place chilled cabbage on a serving dish. Toss vegetables again with dressing and spoon on top of cabbage. Serve immediately.

ORIENTAL CELERY SALAD WITH SESAME OIL

Chinese *4 servings*

A delicate, tasty salad to add to your array of Chinese dishes for a traditional Oriental banquet.

6 large stalks celery
4 teaspoons soy sauce

1 teaspoon sugar
2 teaspoons sesame oil

Slice celery into 1½-inch lengths and then slice into matchstick juliennes. Parboil celery for a few seconds; immediately drain and add cold water with ice cubes to stop the cooking and set the color. Dry thoroughly and refrigerate.

In a small bowl, mix the soy sauce, sugar, and sesame oil, stirring until sugar is dissolved; refrigerate dressing. To serve, toss celery with dressing. This can be done several hours in advance and kept in the refrigerator.

Variation: Sliced asparagus or cabbage can be substituted for the celery.

RODKAAL—EVY'S DANISH RED CABBAGE

Danish   *6 to 10 servings*

In the Scandinavian countries, Christmas Eve is traditionally a night of great family feasting. A smorgasbord is set out with pickled fish, pâtés, pork, sausages, salads, and breads. One of the favorite dishes is this classic red cabbage salad.

1 large head red cabbage (approximately 3 pounds)
3 tablespoons butter
2 tablespoons sugar
1 tablespoon white vinegar
1 tablespoon fresh lemon juice

2 tablespoons water
1 to 1½ cups currant jelly, depending upon desired sweetness, at room temperature

After removing the hard center core of the cabbage and any bruised or limp outer leaves, shred the head of cabbage. In a medium-size skillet, melt the butter and slowly sprinkle the sugar over it, stirring continuously. Add the cabbage, vinegar, lemon juice, and water. Cover and simmer 2 to 3 hours, occasionally stirring, until cabbage is very tender. Add the currant jelly and stir until the jelly is melted and the cabbage is coated. Taste for seasonings, adjusting the sugar or vinegar as desired. Allow to cool to room temperature or refrigerate to chill before serving.

PEELED ASPARAGUS WITH LEMON JUICE AND OLIVE OIL

French   *4 servings*

A favorite French first course to serve rather than a salad.

1 to 2 pounds asparagus, peeled (see Note)
1 to 2 lemons

½ cup light olive oil
Salt and freshly ground pepper

Place asparagus flat in a large skillet with salted water to cover and gently boil until tender, about 5 to 7 minutes, depending on thickness. Arrange asparagus spears on four individual salad plates and cool to room temperature.

To serve, squeeze lemon juice directly onto asparagus. Carefully pour olive oil over top and add freshly ground salt and pepper.

Note: To peel asparagus, carefully hold a stalk in one hand and, with a potato peeler or sharp knife in your other hand, remove the tough skin. You should peel deeper at the thick end and quite sparingly at the top end, near the tip.

BEET RÂPÉ

French   *4 to 8 servings*

A French grated salad is a râpé. Small beets are excellent eaten raw in this simple salad.

3 or 4 beets (¾ pound), peeled and grated
1 tablespoon grated onion
2 tablespoons cooking oil
Juice of 1 lemon

Salt and pepper to taste

Garnish

2 teaspoons minced fresh parsley

Place beets in a mixing bowl along with the onion, oil, and lemon juice and toss. Season to taste with salt and pepper. Cover and refrigerate until serving time. Spoon into serving bowl and garnish with parsley.

PARISIAN CAROTTES RÂPÉES

French   *6 to 8 servings*

The color of this French grated-carrot dish is beautiful and the taste is simple and good. It can also be served as a Moroccan appetizer.

1 pound carrots, peeled, trimmed, and coarsely shredded (approximately 3 cups)

Parisian Salad Dressing (makes approximately ½ cup)

3 tablespoons olive oil
3 tablespoons salad oil
Splash walnut oil (optional—but it adds a lovely hint of walnuts)

1 to 2 tablespoons lemon juice
1 teaspoon Dijon mustard (Poupon or other seedless variety)
Salt and pepper to taste

Garnish

2 tablespoons minced fresh parsley

Place carrots in a serving bowl.

To make dressing: In a medium-size bowl, combine the oils and 1 tablespoon lemon juice, whisking well. Whisk in the mustard and season to taste with salt and pepper; add additional lemon juice to taste.

Pour dressing over carrots and toss well. Cover and refrigerate until serving time. (This salad can be made several hours in advance.) Prior to serving, garnish with minced parsley.

Variation: Substitute finely chopped walnuts for the parsley as a garnish. This same salad can be transformed into a Moroccan appetizer by eliminating the mustard and parsley and adding 2 cloves finely minced garlic and 4 teaspoons vinegar.

STRING BEANS AND TOMATOES
PROVENÇALE

French   4 to 6 servings

In this country French string bean and tomato side dish, the oils and tomatoes become a "sauce" during the cooking.

3 tablespoons olive oil
5 tablespoons cooking oil
(see Note)
1 large onion, chopped
1 to 1½ pounds fresh string
beans, ends trimmed

1 beefsteak tomato or 3
smaller tomatoes, chopped
(about 1 cup)
Salt and pepper to taste

In a large skillet, heat the olive oil with 2 tablespoons of the cooking oil. Add onion and cook over medium heat until lightly wilted. Add string beans and the remaining oil, cover, and cook at medium heat for 10 minutes, stirring occasionally. Add tomatoes, season with salt and pepper, and continue cooking for another 3 to 5 minutes. Check seasoning. Allow to cool and then refrigerate. Serve chilled as a salad, side dish, or hors d'oeuvre.

Note: This may seem like a lot of oil, but when cooked with the tomatoes and onions the oil becomes a fresh tomato sauce.

WATERCRESS AND WALNUT SALAD

French   6 servings

This salad is proof that an elegant dish does not have to involve lengthy preparation.

1 bunch watercress, torn
into pieces, stems removed
1 head butter or bibb
lettuce, torn into pieces
1 bunch chives, snipped
¼ cup chopped walnuts

French Salad Dressing with
Mustard (makes approximately
1 cup)

⅔ cup olive oil
⅓ cup red wine vinegar
1 teaspoon Dijon mustard
Salt and pepper to taste

In a salad bowl, combine the watercress, lettuce, chives, and walnuts.
To make the dressing: Combine the oil, vinegar, mustard, salt, and pepper in a jar and shake for 30 seconds. The dressing can also be made in a food processor by processing the vinegar and mustard and then slowly adding the oil. Season to taste. Refrigerate dressing until needed. This dressing is excellent with other salads.

Shake dressing again and pour over greens. Toss salad and serve immediately.

WATERCRESS AND MUSHROOM SALAD WITH WALNUT OIL DRESSING

French   *2 to 4 servings*

This walnut oil-based dressing will soon be one of your favorites.

1 bunch of watercress
8 large mushrooms

Walnut Oil Dressing (makes approximately 1 cup)

2 tablespoons fresh lemon juice
⅓ cup vinegar (preferably rice vinegar)

2 cloves garlic, crushed in a garlic press
1 tablespoon Dijon mustard (Poupon is excellent)
2 tablespoons peanut oil
½ cup walnut oil
Salt to taste

Tear watercress leaves off stems. Mince the top and sweet part of the stems; discard the thicker, bitter stems. Place in salad bowl. Wipe mushrooms clean with damp paper towels or mushroom brush, removing the bottom part of the stems. Thinly slice and add to watercress.

To make the dressing: In a small bowl, whisk together the lemon juice, vinegar, garlic, and mustard. Add oil slowly in a stream, whisking constantly and season to taste with salt.

To serve, toss watercress and mushrooms with dressing and serve immediately.

CUCUMBER IN DILLED CREAM

German/Danish/Polish   *6 to 8 servings*

Cucumber salads are found in most cuisines of the world. This is a favorite.

3 medium cucumbers, peeled, thinly sliced, and placed on paper towels for 10 minutes to drain (see Note)

Dilled Cream Dressing (makes approximately 1 cup)

¾ cup sour cream
2½ tablespoons vinegar (preferably rice vinegar;

other choices might include cider, champagne, or some other white vinegar)
1 tablespoon snipped chives
2 teaspoons minced fresh dill or ¾ teaspoon dried dillweed
Salt and white pepper to taste

Place cucumbers in a salad bowl; glass is most attractive for this recipe.

To make dressing: In a medium-size bowl, whisk together the dressing ingredients and pour over cucumbers. Toss cucumbers and dressing until well blended.

Cover and refrigerate for several hours before serving.

Note: If you use the European hothouse variety of cucumbers, it is not necessary to peel them.

GERMAN BEET SALAD WITH SOUR CREAM

German   *4 to 8 servings*

Similar to a French râpé, this German beet salad is tossed with a sour cream–based dressing instead of a light French dressing.

3 to 4 beets (¾ pound), peeled and grated	1 tablespoon mayonnaise
3 to 4 tablespoons grated onion	2 tablespoons lemon juice
	1 to 2 teaspoons sugar
	Salt and pepper to taste

Sour Cream Dressing (makes approximately ¾ cup)

½ cup sour cream

Garnish

2 teaspoons chopped fresh dill

Place beets and onion in a bowl.

To make dressing: In a small bowl, whisk together the sour cream, lemon juice, and sugar until smooth. Season to taste with salt and pepper. Pour dressing over beets and toss. Cover and refrigerate until serving time.

To serve, spoon beets into a serving bowl and garnish with dill.

Variation: Other vegetables can be substituted for the beets, such as sliced cucumbers or mushrooms.

GERMAN PICKLED RADISH SALAD INGE

German   *8 servings*

This zesty radish salad can be made with your choice of radish, although it is traditionally prepared with a long white radish similar to the Japanese daikon. In Germany there is a red radish, similar in size to the white icicle and very hot, that is also excellent for this recipe.

This salad can be served as an accompaniment to a light meal of cold cuts, sliced tomatoes, and a tossed green salad or as a condiment with pork roast or prime rib of beef. An unusual hors d'oeuvre called a German War Sandwich calls for spooning this radish salad on top of buttered cocktail-size rye bread.

1 medium-size daikon (about 1 pound), peeled and coarsely grated

1 medium onion, finely chopped

1 cup vinegar (preferably cider)

½ cup water

3 tablespoons cooking oil

Salt and pepper to taste

Garnish (optional)

Minced parsley

Combine radish and onion in a large bowl. Thin vinegar with water, pour over radish mixture, and toss. Add oil and season to taste with salt and pepper. Toss and let sit at room temperature for 1 to 2 hours. Pickling liquid should be fairly vinegary, not oily.

Serve with a slotted spoon. If desired, garnish with minced parsley.

Note: This salad/condiment will keep for several days in the refrigerator, becoming more pungent.

GREEK BAKED AND MARINATED SPRING GARDEN VEGETABLES

Greek   *6 to 8 servings*

When this layered casserole of spring vegetables comes out of the oven, you'll be tempted to sit down and eat it warm, but do wait and savor it chilled. It is a wonderful medley of gently cooked garden vegetables marinated in a sauce made of broth, olive oil, and herbs.

1 pound zucchini, cut into thin slices

1 large onion, thinly sliced and separated into rings

¾ pound green beans, ends trimmed, cut into 2- to 3-inch lengths

1 pound cherry tomatoes, cut in half

1 pound red-skinned potatoes, unpeeled, thinly sliced

¼ cup minced fresh parsley

1 tablespoon minced fresh oregano

Marinade (makes approximately 2 cups)

1 cup olive oil

½ cup chicken broth

½ cup dry white wine

2 tablespoons white vinegar or lemon juice

1 tablespoon honey

Salt and pepper to taste

In a large oven-to-table casserole (preferably glass so that you can see the layers), place the zucchini, slightly overlapping. Next, place a layer of onions, of string beans, of tomatoes (seed side down), and, finally of potatoes. Sprinkle parsley and oregano over the top.

To make the marinade: In a large measuring cup, mix the olive oil, chicken broth, wine, vinegar, honey, salt, and pepper, stirring to dissolve the honey. Pour liquid over the vegetables.

Lightly cover the casserole with aluminum foil and bake at 350° for 2 hours.

Allow to cool at room temperature for about 30 minutes. With a bulblike turkey baster, squeeze some of the juices from the bottom of the casserole on top of the vegetables. Refrigerate, covered, for several hours before serving.

Variation: A wide variety of vegetables can be added or substituted, including eggplant, green peppers, squash, mushrooms, carrots, celery hearts, and leeks.

This dish is quite similar to Rumanian ghivetch (gavetich), which my great-grandmother often made. Start the casserole with a layer of melted butter and a whole carp (white fish) and then add more butter and layers of such seasonal vegetables as peas, carrots, and string beans, along with canned stewed tomatoes (with the juice) and 1 cup precooked white rice. Lightly cover and bake at 350° about 1 hour, until the fish and vegetables are tender. Cool at room temperature and then refrigerate until well chilled. At serving time, season to taste with salt and pepper.

PEPINO ENSALADA—GUATEMALAN CUCUMBER SALAD

Guatemalan   *4 to 6 servings*

This Latin American cucumber salad is one of the simplest yet most delightful I have ever tasted. The lemon juice and salt combine to make a zippy dressing to pour over the cucumber and onion.

2 **medium cucumbers**   2 **ounces fresh lemon juice**
½ **medium onion, thinly**   1 **tablespoon salt**
   sliced and separated into
   rings

Slice off the tip ends of each cucumber and rub the ends with the cut pieces—a culinary trick that helps to eliminate the bitter liquid from the cucumbers. Peel cucumbers and then score vertically with the tines of a fork to create a design. Thinly slice cucumbers and arrange on a platter. Place onion rings on top.

Mix together the lemon juice and salt in a small bowl or cup, stirring to dissolve the salt. Pour over salad and refrigerate until serving time.

Variation: For a South African version of this cucumber salad, substitute red wine vinegar for the lemon juice, add ½ teaspoon sugar, stirring to dissolve, and 2 to 3 teaspoons finely minced hot chilies.

ROSA'S RADISH SALAD

Guatemalan   *4 servings*

A Guatemalan woman who lived with our family for a few months made this tasty salad as an accompaniment to fried chicken or bistec.

2 bunches radishes (about ¾ pound or 24 radishes), minced	1 tablespoon minced onion
	1 tablespoon lemon juice
3 tablespoons minced fresh mint	1 tablespoon salt (or to taste)

Toss all ingredients in a salad bowl and refrigerate until serving time.

GUATEMALAN POTATO AND VEGETABLE SALAD

Guatemalan   *4 to 6 servings*

An excellent Latin American potato salad.

2 medium russet potatoes, peeled and diced	½ pound string beans, diced
Salt	½ cup mayonnaise
2 large carrots, diced	1 to 2 tablespoons chopped onions

Boil potatoes in salted water for about 15 to 20 minutes, or until tender; drain. Boil carrots and string beans together in salted water for about 8 to 10 minutes, or until tender; drain. Combine vegetables in a serving bowl, add mayonnaise and onion, and stir well but gently to mix thoroughly. Allow flavors to mellow at least 30 minutes. Refrigerate until serving time.

Note: If desired, a little lemon juice or vinegar can be added after tossing with mayonnaise. Toss again.

CACHUMBAR—INDIAN TOMATO-CUCUMBER-ONION SALAD (Indian Masala Dressing)

Indian   *4 to 8 servings*

The combination of fresh chiles, ginger, garlic, cilantro, and lemon or lime juice makes a light Indian dressing, referred to as "masala," for garden vegetables. In this salad, the "wet" masala dressing incorporates only fresh ingredients. Some Indian masalas, of which there are countless varieties, use only dry seasonings, others a mixture of dry or whole spices. Masalas, which vary in spiciness from mild to hot, are a vital part of Indian cooking, often added just prior to eating to retain their aroma.

I find this salad more intriguing than the simple "salat" of sliced vegetables used as a bed for Indian-style tandoori (barbecued) meats and fowl.

1 large beefsteak tomato or 2 to 3 medium tomatoes, cut into wedges

1 large cucumber, peeled and thinly sliced

1 medium onion, thinly sliced and separated into rings

Indian Masala Dressing (makes approximately ¾ cup)

1 to 2 teaspoons minced fresh ginger

2 tablespoons minced fresh cilantro

1 clove garlic, minced

2 small green serrano chiles, seeded and finely chopped

Juice of 2 lemons or limes

Combine the tomato, cucumber, and onion in a serving bowl. Combine dressing ingredients in a small bowl, and gently toss with salad vegetables. Refrigerate for several hours.

Variation: This salad can easily be transformed into an Indonesian chunky-style sambal to be used as a relish or to accompany an Indian curry. In this case, the tomatoes, cucumber, and onion should be diced but the seasonings remain the same. Or the condiment can be made more elaborate and fiery by adding ground turmeric, cumin, chiles, saffron, cloves, cardamom, cinnamon, fennel, nutmeg, and/or mace. A little coconut milk and trassi (shrimp paste) can also be mixed in.

INDONESIAN MIXED SALAD

Indonesian   *3 to 6 servings*

This simple mixed salad, a variation on the traditional gado gado, exemplifies the Indonesian mix of vegetables and textures. It is excellent for any vegetarian menu since the tofu adds protein. Also, there is no oil in the dressing, thus making it a good choice for the diet-conscious. The addition of cayenne pepper gives the salad its zing.

6 to 8 ounces tofu, drained

½ pound fresh bean sprouts

1 medium cucumber, peeled and thinly sliced

1 cup finely shredded cabbage

Indonesian Vegetable Dressing (makes approximately ⅓ cup)

⅓ cup fresh lemon juice

1 teaspoon brown sugar

⅛ teaspoon cayenne pepper (or more to taste)

Salt to taste

Garnish

¼ cup chopped unsalted raw peanuts (see Note)

Cut tofu into 1- to 2-inch cubes and wrap in paper towels to drain for about 20 minutes. Place bean sprouts in a bowl and cover with boiling water; soak 30 to 60 seconds and then drain. Place cucumber slices between paper towels to drain for about 10 minutes. Combine drained vegetables and cabbage in a bowl, mixing well.

To make the dressing: Combine ingredients in a small bowl or measuring cup and blend well. Pour on top of salad and toss.

The salad can sit at room temperature about 30 minutes, or it can be refrigerated for later use.

Before serving, toss again and garnish with nuts.

Note: Roast peanuts by placing them in a single layer in a baking tin and baking in a hot oven (about 450°) for about 5 minutes, shaking or stirring occasionally. Be careful not to let them burn. Cool.

ATJAR—INDONESIAN PICKLED VEGETABLES

Indonesian   *4 to 6 servings*

An atjar can be as simple as sliced cucumber and onion that has soaked in a dressing of vinegar, sugar, and garlic, or as elaborate as a combination of colorful vegetables with a spicy, peanutty dressing. Although this is considered "pickled" according to Indonesian cuisine, the vegetables do not soak in a liquid dressing but are marinated in a fairly thick sweet-piquant sauce. It can also be used as a seasoning base for a number of other vegetable, meat, chicken, and fish dishes.

1 medium cucumber, peeled and seeded
2 medium carrots, scraped
1 medium green pepper, seeded
1 medium sweet red pepper, seeded
4 green onions, including firm green tops
1 tablespoon cooking oil

Indonesian Vegetable Sauce (makes approximately ½ cup)

2 cloves garlic

2 teaspoons chopped fresh ginger
¼ teaspoon cumin (or more to taste)
¼ teaspoon cayenne pepper
1½ tablespoons brown sugar
1 teaspoon salt
¾ teaspoon turmeric
2 tablespoons unsalted roasted peanuts
½ cup vinegar (preferably rice vinegar)
¼ cup water

Slice the cucumber, carrots, green and red pepper, and green onions into thin 2-inch-long juliennes and stir-fry in a wok or large skillet with the cooking oil for 1 minute. Spoon vegetables into a large bowl.

To make the sauce: Place the garlic, ginger, cumin, cayenne, sugar, salt, and turmeric in a food processor or blender and process a few seconds until everything is well blended. Add peanuts and process until the mixture is almost pastelike. Place the mixture in a saucepan with the vinegar and water and bring to a boil; reduce heat to a simmer and cook about 3 minutes until the sauce has thickened.

Toss sauce with vegetables until everything is well coated. Cover and refrigerate until serving time. This is best made at least 8 hours in advance.

IRANIAN CUCUMBER, ONION, AND YOGURT SALAD WITH RAISINS

Iranian   *4 to 8 servings*

The basic idea for this salad was given to me by an Iranian friend of my husband's. I serve this dish to my family practically every week, as it is a favorite with adults and children alike.

2 cucumbers, peeled and
  thinly sliced
Salt
1 cup plain yogurt
½ cup sliced green onions,
  including firm green tops

Crushed black pepper to
  taste
¼ cup raisins

In a colander, mix cucumbers and salt with your hands to distribute the salt. Let the cucumbers drain for about 10 minutes, and then rinse them with water, drain again, and pat dry with paper towels.

Place cucumbers in a medium-size salad bowl (preferably glass so you can see all the colors). Add green onions, separating them as much as possible with your fingers, and stir in the yogurt. Season with salt and pepper.

The salad can be made several hours in advance and refrigerated, covered. At serving time, stir in the raisins.

MEDITERRANEAN MARINATED TOMATO SALAD

Italian   *6 to 8 servings*

This is a handsome tomato salad to delight a buffet. The dressing—featuring an unusual combination of anchovies and marjoram—is tantalizing; even those who don't care for anchovies will remark on its tastiness. Serve this salad with crusty bread chunks to dip up all the dressing.

3 extra-large beefsteak
  tomatoes (2 to 2½
  pounds)

Mediterranean Dressing (makes
approximately 1 cup)

3 oil-packed anchovies,
  drained and patted dry
Juice of 1 lemon
1 large clove garlic, minced
1 tablespoon finely chopped
  fresh marjoram, oregano,

or rosemary, or 1 teaspoon	½ cup olive oil
crushed dry marjoram	Salt and pepper to taste
leaves	

Cut tomatoes crosswise into ¼-inch thick slices and arrange on a large platter, overlapping slightly.

To make the dressing: Mash anchovies, using the tines of a fork, and put them in a mixing bowl with the lemon juice, garlic, and marjoram. Slowly whisk in the olive oil. Season to taste with salt and pepper. The dressing can be made ahead of time and refrigerated, covered, but it should be brought to room temperature before adding to the tomatoes.

Make the tomato salad at least 30 minutes in advance of serving time so that the tomatoes will be permeated with the dressing. Serve at room temperature.

ITALIAN ROASTED RED AND GREEN PEPPERS

Italian   *6 to 10 servings*

Roasted sweet red and green bell peppers, lightly dressed with a parsley vinaigrette, are an unusual first-course vegetable to serve in place of a salad.

6 large green peppers (see Note)	Pepper juices
4 to 6 large red peppers	Salt and pepper to taste
	Garnish
Parsley Vinaigrette	Small black Nicoise olives
¼ cup minced parsley	Capers
2 cloves garlic	Chopped hard-cooked eggs
1 tablespoon rice vinegar or	Minced anchovies
fresh lemon juice	(optional)
5 tablespoons olive oil	

Place peppers on a tray under broiler and roast, turning often, until skins are totally blistered and blackened. Wrap peppers in kitchen tea towels or put in a plastic bag and place in refrigerator to cool for about 15 to 30 minutes. The peppers will steam and sweat, making the skins easy to remove.

Working over a bowl to capture the pepper juices, peel off blistered skins. Slit peppers in halves or thirds; remove and discard the seeds, stems, and ribs, but reserve the juice. Arrange peppers decoratively on a serving platter.

To make the vinaigrette: In a food processor or blender, process the parsley, garlic, vinegar, olive oil, and reserved pepper juice until well-blended. Season to taste with salt and pepper. Spoon dressing over peppers and allow peppers to marinate several hours at room temperature, occasionally spooning dressing over top.

This dish can be made 1 or 2 days in advance and then covered and refrigerated. Bring to room temperature before serving.

Prior to serving, decorate, if desired, with your choice of garnish. Serve with crusty Italian bread to soak up the fabulous dressing.

Note: If yellow bell peppers are available, you may wish to substitute some for the green, thus introducing a third color.

GREEN PEPPER AND TOMATO SALAD

Italian   *2 to 3 servings*

A simple salad for broiled and roasted foods.

1 large beefsteak tomato,
  thinly sliced
1 green pepper, roasted
2 tablespoons olive oil
  Salt and pepper to taste

Garnish (optional)
  Minced parsley (preferably
  Italian flat-leaf parsley)

Place tomato on a serving platter. Peel the roasted pepper with your fingers, cut it in half, and remove seeds. Cut into julienne slices and arrange on top of tomatoes.

Drizzle olive oil over pepper and tomato. Season with salt and pepper. Garnish, if desired, with minced Italian parsley.

Note: I sometimes like to sprinkle Italian dried red pepper flakes on top of this salad.

TOMATO-MOZZARELLA-BASIL SALAD

Italian   *8 servings*

During the summer and early fall months when tomatoes are at the height of their season, this is a fragrant and colorful salad. Assembled on one large platter, it is a most impressive dish.

4 large beefsteak tomatoes,
  sliced and peeled, if desired
½ pound Mozzarella cheese
  (preferably the Buffalo
  variety), thinly sliced

8 anchovy fillets, drained and
  patted dry (optional)
½ cup minced fresh basil
  Olive oil
  Salt and pepper to taste

Arrange tomatoes and cheese in alternating slices on a platter or on individual serving plates. Place anchovy fillets on top, if desired, and sprinkle with minced basil. Splash with olive oil and season to taste with salt and freshly ground pepper.

Variation: Although the wonderfully aromatic basil is classically served with this salad, it is not always easy to obtain. I have also made a similar delicious salad with minced fresh cilantro, watercress, or parsley. Another attractive salad can be made by using red, green, and yellow tomatoes.

SIMPLE SALT-PICKLED SALAD VEGETABLES

Japanese   *4 servings*

A simple salt-pickled vegetable medley can be ready to eat after half an hour, or, if time allows, the vegetables can pickle for several hours to let the flavors mingle even more. It can be served as either a condiment or a side dish. Other vegetables can be processed in a similar way; in fact, this is an excellent method to use with greens and cabbage.

10 red radishes (approximately ½ pound), trimmed, with some leaves left on
1 large turnip (approximately ½ pound), peeled

1 4- to 5-inch chunk of daikon (approximately ½ pound), peeled
1 cucumber
2 tablespoons salt (or to taste)

Coarsely chop radishes and finely chop their leaves. Slice turnip and daikon into thin circles, and then cut into quarters. If using European-style hothouse cucumbers, slice and quarter like the turnip; other cucumbers must be peeled and seeded.

Combine all vegetables in a large, fairly low glass, porcelain, or plastic container. Sprinkle with salt and, with your hands, massage salt into the vegetables and set aside. In 30 minutes, drain off all the water that rises.

The vegetables can be served immediately or allowed to pickle further. If you use them later, place a sheet of wax paper on top of the vegetables and weight them down. Keep at room temperature for several hours, checking liquid as it rises, occasionally draining it off.

You can enjoy these salt-pickled vegetables as they are, or, if you find them too salty, rinse them in cold water, drain them, and dry them with paper towels.

SPINACH WITH SESAME DRESSING

Japanese   *4 to 8 servings*

Sesame seeds mixed with soy sauce, mirin, and dashi make a wonderful dressing for any vegetable—most traditionally, spinach, cucumbers, and green beans.

2 bunches spinach (about
1¾ to 2 pounds), washed
and trimmed
1 tablespoon rice vinegar

**Sesame Dressing (makes
approximately ⅔ cup)**

3 tablespoons sesame seeds,
toasted

¼ cup soy sauce
2 tablespoons mirin
2 tablespoons dashi
(Japanese fish stock) or
chicken stock
Sugar (optional)

Bring a large pot of water to a rapid boil and stir in the spinach and vinegar. Cook for only a few seconds; then remove and drain thoroughly.

To make the dressing: Place toasted sesame seeds in a suribachi (Japanese mortar), a food processor, or a blender and grind to open the seeds but not enough to make a paste. Mix the seeds with soy sauce, mirin, dashi, and sugar, if desired, to taste.

Place drained spinach on a serving platter. Top with sesame sauce and let the dish sit at room temperature for flavors to mellow before serving.

JAPANESE EGGPLANTS IN MISO DRESSING

Japanese   *8 to 10 servings*

Miso and toasted sesame seeds ground together make a basic aemono dressing (aemono means "dressed things") for practically any cooked vegetable. In this recipe, I've used the small Japanese eggplant. Serve as a condiment or as an accompaniment to other dishes.

2 to 3 pounds Japanese
eggplants, unpeeled and
sliced into fingers
Salt
Cooking oil

**Miso-Sesame Seed Dressing
(makes approximately 1 cup)**

⅓ cup light miso
⅓ cup sesame seeds, toasted
3 tablespoons mirin
1 tablespoon rice vinegar

Place eggplant fingers on paper towels and salt them. Set aside for 10 to 20 minutes to drain off excess liquid, then wipe off excess salt. Brush eggplants with oil and broil for 4 to 6 minutes, turning, or until all sides are wrinkled. Remove eggplants from broiler and keep warm until serving time.

To make the dressing: Using a food processor, blender, or suribachi (Japanese mortar), grind together and blend the miso, sesame seeds, mirin, and vinegar.

To serve, either top eggplants with sauce or toss them together. Serve at room temperature.

PICKLED COOKED VEGETABLES AND TOFU WITH GOMA DRESSING NAMASU

Japanese *8 to 10 servings*

A sesame seed–based dressing is tossed with several cooked vegetables and tofu pockets for this excellent salad. Serve small portions as an accompaniment to your meal.

3 age (tofu pockets or pouches), cut in half horizontally

2 pounds daikon, peeled and shredded

2 medium (½ pound) carrots, peeled and shredded

2 green onions, white part only, sliced into matchstick juliennes

¼ cup reconstituted wakame, thinly sliced (see Note)

Namasu Goma Dressing (makes approximately 1½ cups)

½ cup sesame seeds, toasted
⅔ cup sugar (or more to taste)
½ cup rice vinegar
1 tablespoon salt

Place sliced tofu pockets in a pot of boiling water and cook for 3 minutes to drain off excess oil. Keep pressing the tofu under the water and against the sides of the pot. Drain and cool. Slice tofu into thin shreds and then squeeze dry through the palms of your hands.

Combine daikon, carrot, green onion, tofu, and wakame in a large dry skillet—in two batches, if necessary. Cook over high heat for about 2 minutes, stirring constantly, until vegetables are wilted. Place vegetables in a colander to cool and drain.

When vegetables are cool enough to handle, take small amounts at a time in your hands and squeeze out excess liquid. Place vegetables in a bowl.

To make the dressing: In a suribachi (Japanese mortar), food processor, or blender, grind the toasted sesame seeds, taking care not to overgrind them; the paste should have texture. Blend in the sugar, vinegar, and salt. Place this mixture in a saucepan and bring to a boil.

Pour sesame dressing over vegetables and toss. Cover and refrigerate. Serve the salad chilled or at room temperature. It will keep for several days, or even weeks, covered, in the refrigerator.

Note: To reconstitute dried wakame (seaweed), soak it in water for 15 to 60 minutes, drain, and remove the hard portions.

CUCUMBER AND SHRIMP SUNOMONO

Japanese *6 servings*

Sunomono—literally, "vinegared things"—is similar to salad and is composed of raw or cooked ingredients. Popular items include cucumber, cabbage, let-

tuce, daikon, carrots, onions, mushrooms, spinach, string beans, pea pods, cauliflower, broccoli, celery, seaweed, seafood, fish, and occasionally fowl, meat, and/or fruit. The common ingredient in all cases is vinegar. Generally the dressing is sweetened with sugar and flavored with mirin (sweet sake), soy sauce, lemon juice, sesame seeds or oil, salt, and/or wasabi. Small portions of sunomono can be offered to start a meal instead of a zensai, or appetizer, or to complement an entree.

1 **large hothouse cucumber (about 10 ounces) or 2 to 3 regular cucumbers**

Su-Soy Dressing (makes approximately ¼ cup)

1 **tablespoon rice vinegar**

1 **to 2 tablespoons soy sauce**

1 **teaspoon sugar**

½ **teaspoon salt (optional)**

¼ **teaspoon sesame oil**

4 **ounces cooked baby shrimp**

If using a European-style hothouse cucumber, you do not need to peel; waxed cucumbers should be peeled. Slice cucumber(s) thinly and wrap in paper towels for 5 to 30 minutes to drain off excess liquid.

To make the dressing: Combine the dressing ingredients in a measuring cup, stirring to dissolve the sugar. This dressing is excellent with other salads.

To serve, place cucumber and shrimp in a serving bowl, pour dressing over them, and toss well.

KIMPIRA GOBO, CARROT, AND CELERY

Japanese   *4 servings*

An excellent vegetable dish is this combination of woodsy burdock root (gobo), carrots, and celery. Serve with a traditional Japanese dinner or as an accompaniment to another cuisine. It's excellent with roasted chicken or poached fish.

3 **medium stalks burdock root (6 ounces)**

2 **tablespoons rice vinegar**

1 **large carrot**

2 **stalks celery**

1 **tablespoon cooking oil**

2 **tablespoons soy sauce**

2 **tablespoons mirin**

1 **tablespoon sugar**

Cayenne or chili powder to taste

Scrub burdock very well and immediately place in a bowl of cold water. Take 1 stalk at a time and slice into matchstick juliennes 2 to 3 inches long. Return juliennes to water and repeat process until all burdock is properly sliced. Drain and add fresh water. Pour in 1 tablespoon vinegar. Repeat process in about 15 minutes. Soak burdock for ½ hour. (This process helps retain the white color of the burdock as well as tenderize it.)

Peel or scrub carrot and slice into matchstick juliennes. Wash celery and slice in the same manner.

Drain burdock and combine with the carrots and celery.

Heat oil in a large skillet. Add the vegetables, stirring to coat with the oil. Stir in the soy sauce, mirin, and sugar and simmer about 5 minutes, or until vegetables are tender but still crisp. For a spicy touch, season to taste with cayenne or chili powder.

Serve either at room temperature or chilled.

CANDIED SWEET POTATOES

Japanese   *4 to 8 servings*

On the outside, Japanese sweet potatoes (yams) look very much like American sweet potatoes. But on the inside they're much lighter in color, resembling yams. Handle them as you would an American yam. Sweetened, they are popular as a New Year's Day buffet recipe, and are also traditionally served for special celebrations and birthdays. You might even serve them for a sweet snack or dessert.

1 pound Japanese sweet potatoes or American yams Salt	Garnish (optional) Black sesame seeds

Sugary Syrup

½ cup sugar
½ cup water

Peel potatoes and slice them into large chunks. Soak in salted cold water for several hours (or a minimum of 30 minutes), changing the salt water several times. Place in boiling salted water and cook until tender, about 10 minutes; drain.

In a saucepan, make a sugary syrup by bringing the sugar and water to a boil. Reduce the heat to a simmer and cook until golden, about 7 minutes. Stir the cooked potatoes into the syrup.

Place in a serving bowl and garnish, if desired, with black sesame seeds. These potatoes can be made in advance and served either at room temperature or chilled.

CHILLED NOODLES WITH CUCUMBERS AND MUSHROOMS

Japanese   *4 to 6 servings*

In summer, the Japanese enjoy cold dishes, especially those made with noodles. To serve this as a main dish, add slices of cooked omelet (tamago), pork, seafood, or chicken.

½ pound soba or somen (noodles), cooked, drained, rinsed, and chilled
2 large cucumbers
Salt
4 large shiitake, soaked for several hours, drained, and sliced into matchstick juliennes
¼ cup beef broth or dashi
2 tablespoons soy sauce
2 tablespoons sugar

Summer Salad Dressing (makes approximately 1⅓ cups)
½ cup rice vinegar
1 teaspoon cooking oil
½ cup soy sauce
¼ cup beef broth or dashi
2 tablespoons sugar

Garnish
2 scallions, chopped

Keep noodles refrigerated, in a large serving bowl, until ready to serve.

Peel cucumbers. Slice in half lengthwise and remove seeds. Lightly sprinkle with salt and let drain for a few minutes on paper towels. Rinse and pat dry. Cut into 3-inch lengths and then slice into matchstick juliennes.

Place sliced mushrooms in a saucepan with ¼ cup broth, soy sauce, and sugar. Heat the liquid, stirring for 3 minutes. Remove the mushrooms and set aside. Reserve the liquid to add to the dressing.

To make the dressing: Combine the vinegar, oil, soy sauce, ¼ cup broth, and sugar in a saucepan and simmer for 5 minutes. Add the reserved mushroom cooking liquid, cool at room temperature, and then chill.

To serve, arrange cucumbers and mushrooms attractively on top of noodles and pour sauce over both vegetables and noodles. Garnish center of platter with chopped scallions.

BUBA'S FRUIT KUGEL

Jewish   *6 to 8 servings*

Kugels (noodle casseroles) are always popular during the Jewish holidays. Served at room temperature, this makes an excellent side dish or an unusual dessert. Serve the chilled leftovers with sour cream—if you're lucky enough to have any leftovers.

¼ pound mixed dried fruits
1 large apple, peeled, cored, and cut into chunks
1 tablespoon sugar
½ teaspoon cinnamon
2 tablespoons cooking oil
8 ounces medium egg noodles, cooked and drained

2 tablespoons butter
3 eggs, separated
3 tablespoons apricot-pineapple preserves
½ teaspoon salt

Cut the dried fruit into medium-size pieces and scald them in a small pot of boiling water; keep the fruit in the water for a few minutes to soften.

Combine the apple, sugar, and cinnamon, tossing well. Drain the dried fruits and add to the apple mixture.

Put the oil in an oven-proof casserole (8½ inches square and 2 inches deep), and place casserole dish in a preheated 350° oven. (This is to heat the oil.)

In a large bowl, toss the warm noodles with butter, allowing noodles to cool. Beat the egg yolks and add them to the noodles, mixing thoroughly. Add the fruits, preserves, and salt and toss again. Beat the egg whites until stiff and fold them into the noodle mixture.

Remove the heated casserole from the oven and spoon in the noodle mixture, making sure all the fruits are covered by the noodles. Tilt the casserole, one side at a time, so that the oil in the bottom rises at the side, and spoon it over the top of the noodle mixture. (See Note.) Bake the kugel at 350° for 1 to 1½ hours, or until the top is golden brown. Cool and serve at room temperature.

Note: The two unusual steps of heating the oil and tilting the casserole with it, as well as separating the eggs, were my grandmother's (Buba's) tricks for ensuring a moist, fluffy kugel.

SUSAN'S KOREAN MARINATED SPINACH

Korean   *4 servings*

Serve small dishes of this Korean spinach salad as a side dish to accompany a multicourse Oriental dinner.

1 **pound fresh spinach, washed, with large stems removed**

Korean Marinade

1 **teaspoon soy sauce**
1 **tablespoon rice vinegar**
½ **teaspoon salt**
2 **teaspoons sesame seed oil**

2 **large cloves garlic, minced**
2 **green onions, minced**
1 **tablespoon toasted sesame seeds**
¼ **to ½ teaspoon kochu (Korean red pepper powder)**
1 **teaspoon sugar**

Drop spinach into 2 quarts of boiling water. As soon as the spinach has wilted, immediately drain and rinse with cool water. Squeeze excess water from spinach, and then chop 5 or 6 times into smaller pieces.

Combine the remaining ingredients and add to the spinach, blending well. Refrigerate until serving time.

Note: I find this powder more pungent than cayenne pepper. If substituting cayenne, increase to taste.

SUKI'S KIM CHEE

Korean   *6 to 8 servings*

Bottled kim chee is often available in jars in the refrigerated section of most major supermarkets, along with pickles. But wait until you taste the homemade version. This kim chee recipe features pickled cabbage along with oysters; the zip comes from the powdered red pepper.

1 large head cabbage	2 small raw oysters, finely
1 to 2 tablespoons salt	chopped (optional)
2 cloves garlic, crushed	3 tablespoons powdered red
1 teaspoon finely chopped	pepper (or to taste)
fresh ginger	Additional salt
2 green onions, finely	
chopped	

Wash cabbage head, discarding hard center core, and cut into 2- to 4-inch pieces. Place in a large bowl with 1 to 2 tablespoons of salt for 1 hour, turning cabbage after 30 minutes. Wash cabbage again and drain thoroughly.

Return cabbage to bowl and add garlic, ginger, green onions, oysters, and red pepper. Salt to taste. Chill and serve.

AVOCADO-TOMATO SALAD

Mexican   *2 servings*

This simple salad is excellent with barbecued or broiled meats.

1 large tomato, thickly sliced	1 teaspoon olive oil
1 avocado, thinly sliced	1 teaspoon fresh cilantro
¾ teaspoon salt	leaves
1 teaspoon freshly ground	
pepper	

Arrange tomato on a serving platter. Top slices with avocado and sprinkle with salt, pepper, and cilantro. Drizzle olive oil over top.

Variation: Lemon or lime juice may also be sprinkled on top.

LEÓN JÍCAMA SALAD

Mexican   *4 to 8 servings*

A lovely salad from the provincial Mexican town of León. Jícama is a brown potato-looking root vegetable. When peeled, it is white and its crunchy texture resembles raw potato, radish, and water chestnut. Don't be fooled by its starchy appearance, however, as jícama has an unusual sweet quality. In Mexico, it is often peeled, sliced into thin strips, and sprinkled with fresh lime juice and chili powder, to be eaten as a snack. It also makes an excellent low-calorie substitute for potato chips to dunk in a dip. You might even add a few slices to a family-style tossed salad.

1½ pounds jícama, peeled and coarsely diced
Juice of 2 limes or lemons
½ teaspoon salt
¼ teaspoon chili powder (or more to taste)

4 ounces grated Mexican white cheese or Monterey Jack cheese

Garnish

Cilantro leaves

Toss jícama in a bowl with the lime juice, salt, and chili powder. Add cheese and toss again. Cover and refrigerate for several hours to let flavors mellow.

At serving time, spoon on to a platter and garnish with cilantro leaves. Serve as an appetizer or salad course.

ENSALADA DE NOPALES—CACTUS LEAF SALAD

Mexican   *6 to 8 servings*

Nopales, flat cactus leaves, are available at many produce stands that cater to Mexican customers. Having traveled extensively throughout the West and having hiked many cacti fields, I find it amusing to cook and eat the "dangerous" pricklers.

15 nopales
Salt
1 teaspoon baking soda (see Note)
2 large onions, thinly sliced and separated into rings
1 to 2 avocados, sliced
2 large tomatoes, sliced
5 serrano chiles, seeded and diced (optional)

¼ to ½ cup grated Parmesan cheese
2 to 4 tablespoons dried leaf oregano
3 tablespoons minced fresh cilantro
3 tablespoons vinegar
¼ cup olive oil

Peel nopales, taking care to remove the "eyes," or spikes, and cut into long strips somewhat resembling string beans. Place in a saucepan (traditionally a copper pot) with water, a pinch of salt, and the baking soda. Bring water to a boil and cook for 15 to 20 minutes, or until tender. Drain and rinse with cold water.

Place in a large serving bowl and add the onion, avocados, tomatoes, chiles and Parmesan cheese. Crumble oregano through the palms of your hands directly into the salad. Add cilantro and toss all vegetables. Add vinegar and oil and toss again. Season to taste with salt.

Serve immediately or cover and refrigerate until later. This salad is best served at room temperature.

Note: In Mexico, a red hot copper coin is used instead of the baking soda. This keeps the nopales a dark green color and prevents them from becoming slimy.

CUCUMBER-RADISH SALAD

Mexican   *2 to 4 servings*

I prefer to use a European or hothouse variety of cucumber in this recipe because its unwaxed skin need not be peeled. The color and crispness of the skin make an attractive and tasty addition to the salad.

1 medium hothouse cucumber, thinly sliced
8 medium radishes, coarsely chopped
2 tablespoons minced fresh mint
2 tablespoons salad oil
Juice of 1 lemon

Salt to taste
Dash hot pepper sauce
2 teaspoons dried leaf oregano
2 tablespoons grated Mexican white cheese or Monterey Jack cheese

Mix cucumber, radishes, and mint in a salad bowl. Add the salad oil and toss. Squeeze lemon juice directly into bowl and toss. Season with salt and hot pepper sauce. Rub oregano through the palms of your hands directly into the bowl. Add cheese and toss well. Cover and refrigerate several hours before serving.

YUCATECAN PICKLED ONIONS

Mexican   *4 to 10 servings*

These pickled onions are traditionally used as a garnish for simple fried fish, tacos, enchiladas, or your favorite Mexican recipe.

4 large red onions, sliced into rings
½ cup vinegar

6 tablespoons cooking oil
4 black peppercorns
Salt to taste

Place onions in a saucepan with vinegar, cooking oil, peppercorns, and salt. Bring to a boil, reduce heat to a simmer, and cook about 20 minutes, or until onions appear translucent. Cover and refrigerate for several hours.

At serving time, drain and use as a garnish for fried fish fillets or other favorite Mexican recipes.

PERSIAN CUCUMBER SALAD WITH YOGURT AND HERB DRESSING

Middle Eastern   *6 to 8 servings*

Cucumbers respond well to this aromatic Middle Eastern dressing.

2 medium to large cucumbers, peeled

Middle Eastern Yogurt and Herb Dressing (makes approximately 1¾ cups)

1½ cups plain yogurt
2 tablespoons vinegar (preferably rice vinegar)
1 tablespoon sugar

2 teaspoons minced fresh mint
1 tablespoon snipped fresh dill
1 teaspoon sesame seeds, toasted
½ teaspoon salt
Dash white pepper

Thinly slice cucumbers and place on paper towels to drain excess liquid.

To make the dressing: In a mixing bowl, whisk together the yogurt, vinegar, and sugar until sugar is dissolved. Stir in the mint, dill, sesame seeds, salt, and pepper.

Place cucumber slices in a serving bowl and add dressing. Cover and refrigerate several hours before serving.

TABBOULEH—BULGUR SALAD

Middle Eastern   *8 to 12 servings*

This Syrian tabbouleh can be served as a party appetizer, a salad course, or a vegetarian main dish. Originally it was served with grape leaves to scoop up the salad. You can use the crisp center leaves of Romaine lettuce or wedges of pita bread for this same purpose. The main ingredients in a tabbouleh are bulgur (cracked wheat), parsley, mint, tomatoes, green onions, and green pepper, dressed with lemon juice and olive oil.

1 cup fine bulgur
2 cups minced fresh parsley
¾ cup minced fresh mint
3 tablespoons minced fresh
   cilantro
1 green pepper, seeded and
   finely chopped
½ cup very thinly sliced green
   onions, including firm
   green tops

2 large beefsteak tomatoes,
   seeded, chopped (about 1
   cup), and peeled, if desired
Juice of 2 lemons
⅔ to ¾ cup olive oil
Salt, pepper, and cayenne
   pepper to taste

Soak bulgur in cold water to cover for 30 to 60 minutes. It will greatly expand. Drain through a sieve, pressing against the side of the sieve with a wooden spoon. Place bulgur on a clean kitchen towel and squeeze out all remaining excess water.

Put bulgur in a large salad bowl with the parsley, mint, cilantro, green pepper, green onions, and tomatoes and toss with your hands. Pour lemon juice over the mixture and toss again. Slowly pour olive oil over the mixture and again toss. Season to taste with salt, pepper, and cayenne pepper.

Refrigerate until needed, but serve at room temperature. This salad can be made several hours to a day in advance.

Variation: You can use other ingredients, as you wish—diced cucumbers, olives, fruit, cooked seafood, lamb.

TOMATOES AND CUCUMBERS WITH LABAN

Middle Eastern   *4 to 5 servings*

Laban—a thickened, almost cheeselike yogurt that is popular in Syria and several other Middle Eastern countries—makes an excellent tangy dressing base for these colorful vegetables.

2 beefsteak tomatoes, thinly
   sliced
1 cucumber, peeled, thinly
   sliced, and drained on
   paper towels
½ cup laban (see Index)
4 to 6 tablespoons fresh
   cilantro leaves

2 tablespoons olive oil
1 to 3 tablespoons ground
   cumin
Freshly ground black
   pepper

Alternate tomato and cucumber slices on a serving platter. Spoon laban over top and sprinkle with cilantro. Dribble olive oil over all, and add cumin and pepper to taste—as spicy as you can handle.

Variation: If you have not made laban, you can substitute plain yogurt, but the dressing will be considerably thinner. Sour cream or crème fraîche are other substitutions.

ORANGE, RED ONION, AND RADISH SALAD

Moroccan   *4 to 5 servings*

Bright orange and red, this is an ideal salad for a buffet.

6 naval oranges
1 large red onion, thinly sliced and separated into rings
8 radishes, thinly sliced
Juice of 1 lemon

¼ teaspoon ground cumin
Dash of cayenne pepper (or more to taste)
½ cup olive oil
2 tablespoons minced fresh parsley or cilantro

Peel oranges, cutting off all outer white membrane. Cut oranges crosswise into ¼-inch thick slices. Remove all seeds. Reserve any juice that may run out during this step.

In a serving dish, preferably glass, place the onions, separating all slices, and top with oranges and then radishes.

Pour reserved orange juice into a bowl with the lemon juice. Mix in the cumin and cayenne pepper. Slowly pour in olive oil, whisking constantly. Pour dressing over salad. Garnish with parsley or cilantro. Cover and refrigerate until serving time.

Prior to serving, tilt the dish to get dressing and spoon on top.

RUSSIAN CUCUMBERS WITH CREAMY DRESSING

Russian   *4 to 6 servings*

A simple cucumber dish with a creamy herb dressing, this is excellent for a zakuska appetizer table. You might also try this dressing with tossed greens.

2 medium cucumbers, peeled and thinly sliced
Salt

Russian Cream Dressing
(makes approximately ½ cup)

¼ cup sour cream
½ teaspoon Dijon mustard
1½ teaspoons vinegar
2 hard-cooked eggs

1 teaspoon minced fresh cilantro
1 teaspoon minced fresh tarragon or basil
1 teaspoon minced fresh parsley
Salt and white pepper

Garnish

Fresh herb leaves

Place cucumbers in a colander, salt them, and allow to drain for 15 minutes. Rinse and dry thoroughly with paper towels.

To make the dressing: In a medium-size bowl, mix the sour cream, mustard, and vinegar. Separate the eggs, reserving the whites. Mash egg yolks with the tines of a fork and add to the dressing. Mix well, seasoning with the minced herbs, salt, and pepper.

Place cucumbers in a salad bowl and toss with the dressing. Finely chop hard-cooked egg whites to resemble caviar and sprinkle on top of cucumbers (see Note). Garnish center with a few fresh herb leaves. Cover and refrigerate several hours.

Note: If using dressing for tossed greens, cut the egg whites into larger slices, not small gratings.

LOBIO—RUSSIAN STRING BEANS WITH HERB VINAIGRETTE

Russian   *4 servings*

Lobio, a Russian bean dish, can be done equally well with string beans or with red kidney beans. The vinaigrette dressing illustrates the French influence on Russian cuisine. The color of the beans dressed with this vinaigrette is a velvety deep green.

¾ pound green beans, ends trimmed

Lobio Vinaigrette Dressing (makes approximately ½ cup)

¼ cup finely chopped fresh parsley
2 tablespoons chopped onions

2 tablespoons chopped fresh cilantro
1 clove garlic, minced
1 tablespoon vinegar
2 tablespoons salad oil
Salt, pepper, and cayenne pepper to taste

Cut beans into 2-inch lengths and boil in salted water until barely tender, about 5 to 6 minutes. Immediately drain and rinse with cold water and ice cubes to set the color; drain.

To make the dressing: In a small bowl, combine the parsley, onions, cilantro, garlic, and vinegar. Slowly whisk in the oil; season to taste.

Place string beans in a salad bowl and toss with the dressing. Allow to sit at room temperature at least an hour for flavors to mingle. If made early in the day, refrigerate and bring to room temperature before serving.

Variation: A Russian version of a pesto sauce, satsivi sauce (see the following recipe) can be added to this vinaigrette, resulting in a most unusual and delicious dressing.

RUSSIAN BEAN SALAD WITH SATSIVI (WALNUT) SAUCE

Russian   *6 to 8 servings*

The technique of making satsivi, a Russian walnut sauce, is quite similar to the Italian pesto sauce (see Index). Ground walnuts, rather than pine nuts, are mixed with garlic and herbs to form a paste. The sauce is then thinned with vinegar and chicken broth or water instead of olive oil. This walnut sauce is traditionally tossed with beans or vegetables and served as a side dish or salad; it can also be tossed with pasta.

½ **pound dried red kidney beans or 2 cups canned (see Note)**

Satsivi Sauce (makes approximately ¾ cup)

   ½ **cup walnuts, ground**
   1 **clove garlic, finely minced**
   4 **teaspoons minced fresh parsley**

2 **teaspoons minced fresh cilantro**
1½ **tablespoons finely chopped onion**
1 **tablespoon red wine vinegar**
¼ **cup chicken broth**
   Salt, pepper, cayenne pepper, and paprika to taste

Kidney beans can be prepared in one of the following methods. (1) Wash and soak in cold water 6 to 8 hours. (Soaking too long will cause beans to begin to open.) Drain and place in a pot with cold water to cover. Bring to a boil, remove any "shum" that rises, reduce heat to a simmer, and lightly cover. Continue to cook until tender, about 1 to 1½ hours, stirring occasionally and checking the water level. (2) Wash beans and place them in a pot with water to cover. Slowly bring to a boil and then remove from heat. Allow beans to soak in the hot water for 1 hour; drain. Refill the pot with cold water to cover and proceed as in the first cooking technique, simmering until tender; drain.

To make the sauce: Prepare a paste of the walnuts and garlic, using a food processor, blender, or mortar and pestle (the traditional method). Add the parsley, cilantro, onion, and vinegar, and quickly process. Slowly add the broth, mixing well. Season to taste with salt, pepper, cayenne pepper, and paprika.

Place beans in a large salad bowl. Toss with the satsivi sauce and leave at room temperature for at least an hour for flavors to mellow, occasionally tossing the beans with the sauce. If made further in advance, cover and refrigerate; bring to room temperature before serving.

Note: Canned beans can be substituted though the taste will not be the same.

MARINATED BRAISED LEEKS

Turkish *6 to 10 servings*

This Turkish vegetable dish, also found in Greece, is excellent as a side course with roasted fowl or lamb.

6 to 8 leeks (2 pounds)
½ cup olive oil
½ cup chopped onion
1 large clove garlic, minced
2 teaspoons fresh thyme or
  ¾ teaspoon dried thyme
½ teaspoon fennel seeds

Salt and white pepper to taste
1 cup chicken broth or water

Garnish

Lemon wedges

Trim off the root tip and soft green leaves of leeks and carefully open leaves a little to wash away all dirt—leeks are very sandy. Cut leeks crosswise into 1½- to 2-inch lengths. Again check for dirt; set aside.

Heat oil in a heavy, deep skillet or soup pot. Add the chopped onion, garlic, thyme, and fennel. Cover and saute over low heat for 5 minutes, until onion is tender. Add leeks, spooning the oil mixture over them, along with salt, pepper, and broth. Lightly cover and simmer for 25 to 30 minutes, until leeks are tender and much of the cooking liquid is absorbed.

Cover and refrigerate the leeks, allowing flavors to mellow for at least a day. (This dish will keep well for 1 week.)

To serve, bring to room temperature and garnish with lemon wedges.

Variation: Other vegetables such as mushrooms or string beans can be prepared in a similar manner.

ORANGE-AVOCADO SALAD

International *4 servings*

This colorful orange and avocado salad, tossed with a creamy-style vinaigrette dressing, is an excellent first course with a spicy or tomatoey main dish.

**Creamy Vinaigrette Dressing
(makes approximately ¾ cup)**

- ½ cup salad oil
- 2 tablespoon wine vinegar
- ¼ cup mayonnaise
- 1 teaspoon mixed dried herbs (see Note)

- 2 large oranges, peeled and sectioned
- 1 large avocado, cut into chunks
- 1 head butter or Boston lettuce, torn into bite-size pieces

To make the dressing: Combine ingredients in a glass jar and shake well. Refrigerate for several hours so that ingredients have time to mellow. Prior to tossing with salad, bring dressing to room temperature.

At serving time, place orange sections, avocado chunks, and lettuce in a salad bowl, toss with dressing, and serve immediately.

Note: If fresh herbs are available, use 1 tablespoon minced fresh herbs of your choice.

AVOCADO-ARTICHOKE SALAD

International   *4 to 6 servings*

This simple salad can be expanded by using the recipe as a base and adding bite-size pieces of bibb lettuce. For the dressing, use the marinade, adding fresh lemon juice to taste.

- 1 avocado, diced
- 1 6-ounce jar marinated artichoke hearts, drained (reserve marinade for another recipe)
- 2 green onions, coarsely chopped

Salt and pepper to taste

Garnish

Cilantro leaves

Place avocado in a salad bowl. Coarsely dice artichokes and add, along with the green onions. Season with salt and pepper and toss to mix well. Spoon onto serving plates and garnish with cilantro.

AVOCADO-TOMATO-BACON SALAD

International   *4 servings*

This is one of my family's favorite salads, almost a salsa. I refer to it as Cal-Mex cuisine.

8 strips bacon, cut into
1½-inch lengths

2 ripe but still firm
avocados, cut into ¼-inch
cubes
Juice of 1 lemon

2 beefsteak tomatoes or 4
medium tomatoes, cut into
¼-inch cubes

6 green onions, including
firm green tops, thinly
sliced

1 tablespoon olive oil
Salt and pepper to taste

Garnish

Cilantro leaves

Fry bacon until crisp but not black; drain on paper towels and set aside. Sprinkle avocados with 1 tablespoon lemon juice to hold the color. Combine avocados, tomatoes, green onions, and bacon in a mixing bowl. Add the remaining lemon juice and olive oil and carefully toss. Do not allow the avocados to become mushy. Season to taste with salt and pepper.

Spoon salad onto individual plates and garnish the tops of each with cilantro leaves.

Variation: To expand this to a salsa, add chopped peppers, chiles, onions, and dried leaf oregano to taste.

POTATO AND ROASTED GREEN PEPPER SALAD WITH MUSTARD VINAIGRETTE

International   *6 to 8 servings*

The secret of most potato salads is to carefully toss the cooked potatoes while still warm with the dressing so that the potatoes absorb the flavors. In this potato and roasted pepper salad, the dressing is one of my favorite thick oil and vinegar sauces, seasoned well with Dijon mustard. The vinaigrette goes quite well with other vegetable salads, simple greens, and as a sauce for chilled sliced meats.

2 pounds light-skinned
potatoes, boiled, partially
peeled, and cut into large
pieces

2 medium green peppers,
roasted, peeled, and cut
into thin strips

¼ cup minced fresh parsley

Mustard Vinaigrette (makes
approximately ½ cup)

1 tablespoon vinegar
(preferably rice vinegar)

1 tablespoon Dijon mustard

3 tablespoons olive oil

3 tablespoons cooking oil (or
increase olive oil)
Salt and pepper to taste

In a salad bowl, mix the potatoes, peppers, and parsley, carefully tossing by hand so as not to break up the potatoes.

To make the dressing: Whisk the vinegar and mustard together in a small bowl. Whisk in the oil very slowly, as when making mayonnaise, so that the dressing becomes thick. Season to taste with salt and pepper. Dressing can be made several days in advance and kept, covered, in the refrigerator. Bring to room temperature for about 30 minutes before adding to salad.

Pour dressing over the warm potatoes and peppers and carefully toss. Cover and allow flavors to mellow for several hours.

Serve the salad in a glass bowl or a lettuce-lined salad bowl.

ROMAINE SALAD WITH ROQUEFORT DRESSING

International   *4 servings*

You'll find this Roquefort dressing to be one of the best ever. Other hearty greens can be used, but do keep the salad simple so that the dressing plays the starring role.

1 large head Romaine lettuce, washed and crisped

Roquefort Dressing (makes approximately 1¼ cups)

3 tablespoons red wine vinegar

1½ teaspoons Dijon mustard (Poupon is excellent)

⅔ cup salad oil

4 ounces Roquefort or blue cheese, crumbled

Salt and pepper to taste

Place lettuce in a large salad bowl.

To make the dressing: In a mixing bowl, combine the vinegar and mustard. slowly whisk in the oil. Stir in the crumbled cheese and season to taste with salt and pepper. The dressing can be made in advance and refrigerated. Stir to combine ingredients again before tossing with salad.

Toss lettuce with dressing and serve.

BABY ARTICHOKES AND TOMATOES IN AN HERB VINAIGRETTE

International   *4 to 8 servings*

Baby artichokes, which are about the size of an egg, are one of the prize offerings of a fine produce stand. They are very tasty and tender when cooked;

practically the entire artichoke is edible. Here artichokes and cherry tomatoes are marinated in an Italian-French vinaigrette fragrant with fresh basil, oregano, and parsley.

9 or 10 baby artichokes
(about 1 pound)
1 lemon, cut in half
1 clove garlic
4 peppercorns
1 bay leaf
Salt
12 cherry tomatoes

Herb Vinaigrette (makes approximately ¾ cup)

¼ cup lemon juice
1 clove garlic, finely minced

1 tablespoon minced fresh basil
1 tablespoon minced fresh oregano
1 tablespoon minced fresh parsley (preferably the Italian flat-leaf variety)
½ cup olive oil
Salt and pepper to taste

To prepare the baby artichokes, pull off and discard the outer 2 to 4 layers of leaves until you reach the tender, light green leaves. Trim the stems and tops; it is not necessary to remove the center thistlelike choke. Rub all cut parts with half a lemon.

Bring a medium-size pot of water to a boil and add the remaining lemon half, the garlic, peppercorns, bay leaf, and salt and bring to a boil. Place the artichokes in the boiling liquid, cover, and cook 15 to 20 minutes, or until tender. Remove artichokes and place upside down in a colander to drain.

With a toothpick, generously pierce little holes all over the cherry tomatoes so that they will absorb the vinaigrette.

To make the dressing: In a medium-size bowl, combine the lemon juice, garlic, and herbs and stir well. Slowly dribble in the olive oil, whisking constantly. Season to taste with salt and pepper. This dressing is excellent with other salads, particularly those for marinated cooked vegetables.

While the artichokes are still warm, place in a salad bowl, add tomatoes, pour dressing over top, and toss well to coat. Cover and refrigerate for several hours, occasionally spooning vinaigrette over the artichokes and tomatoes. Bring to room temperature before serving.

Variation: If you wish to prepare this dish with only artichokes, the dressing is sufficient for 1½ pounds (about 12 to 13). For another color and an interesting taste, add pitted ripe black olives. In the fall and winter, brussels sprouts are a traditional holiday favorite, and they can be substituted for the baby artichokes.

CHERRY TOMATOES IN A BASIL VINAIGRETTE MARINADE

International   *6 to 10 servings*

Although this aromatic basil marinade is magnificent with the cherry tomatoes, you might try it with other seasonal garden vegetables.

2 pints cherry tomatoes, cut in half

Basil Vinaigrette Marinade
(makes approximately 1 cup)

½ cup lemon juice

3 tablespoons finely minced fresh basil

1 large clove garlic, finely minced

½ cup olive oil

Salt and pepper to taste

Place tomatoes in a bowl suitable for marinating.

To make the dressing: In a small bowl, combine the lemon juice, basil, and garlic. Slowly dribble in the olive oil, whisking constantly. Season to taste with salt and pepper.

Pour marinade over tomatoes, cover, and place in refrigerator for several hours, occasionally spooning marinade over tomatoes. Bring to room temperature before serving.

GARDEN FAR EAST SALAD

International   *2 to 4 servings*

This salad originated one summer day from a collection of vegetables I was growing in our garden. You can vary the vegetables according to your tastes and your garden's success.

1 clove garlic, cut in half

¼ cup of your favorite vinaigrette dressing (refer to Index)

10 leaves Romaine lettuce, washed and crisped

2 cups cauliflower flowerets

5 green onions, chopped

¼ cup chopped fresh parsley

¼ cup raisins

⅛ teaspoon dry mustard

¼ teaspoon powdered ginger

⅛ teaspoon salt

Rub a large wooden salad bowl with garlic and then discard. Pour salad dressing into the bowl and swirl it around to coat the bowl. Add lettuce, cauliflower, onions, parsley, and raisins and toss well. Season with mustard, ginger, and salt. Toss again to coat all vegetables.

ASPARAGUS VINAIGRETTE

International   *6 servings*

One of the culinary joys of spring is the abundance of fresh asparagus. In many countries, the asparagus season is honored with festivals, as in Germany with the Spargelfest—the white asparagus festival. White asparagus, favored in Europe, and green asparagus, popular in North America, are of the same family. Because white asparagus is grown underground without sunlight, the stalks do not receive any color from nature's photosynthesis process.

For a German-style Spargelfest, you would serve several courses, each featuring asparagus. One might be this asparagus vinaigrette.

3 pounds fresh asparagus

Simple Vinaigrette Dressing (makes approximately 1 cup)

   Juice of ½ lemon
2 tablespoons tarragon vinegar
¾ cup olive oil
2 tablespoons minced chives

Salt and pepper to taste

1 to 2 heads butter lettuce

Garnish

1 to 2 tablespoons sliced pimiento

Trim the bottom ½ to 1 inch off tough white asparagus stalks, and then roll-cut one asparagus at a time. To do this, place an asparagus spear on a cutting board and diagonally cut a 2-inch piece; then partially rotate the spear and cut again, to get as many angles as possible. Once all the asparagus has been cut, drop it in a large pot of boiling water; return water to a boil and cook 4 or 5 minutes. Immediately drain and rinse with running cold water and ice cubes to set the color and stop the cooking. Drain asparagus and pat dry with paper towels.

To make the vinaigrette: Whisk together the lemon juice and vinegar in a measuring cup or small bowl. Slowly whisk in the olive oil. Stir in the minced chives. Season to taste with salt and pepper (be especially generous with the fresh pepper).

Place asparagus in a shallow glass or porcelain bowl and gently toss with the vinaigrette. You can marinate the asparagus overnight in the refrigerator, occasionally spooning the dressing over top.

To serve, place lettuce leaves on individual salad plates and spoon asparagus with dressing into the center. Garnish generously with pimiento and spoon any extra dressing over all.

Additional Light Salads and Vegetable Dishes

Bill's Birthday Party Caponata

Caesar Salad

Chirashi-Zushi

Dashi-Wasabi Somen

Eggplant and Pepper Salad

Fettuccine with Marinated Broccoli, Tomato, Olives, and Peppers

French White Bean Salad

Fried Plantains

Greek Salad

Indonesian Gado Gado

Japanese Cucumber-Trout Appetizer

Mediterranean Ratatouille

Menrui with Dipping Sauce

Onigiri

Oriental Asparagus with Sesame Seed Sauce

Pancit Salad

Pasta with Garden Vegetables

Pennsylvania Dutch Beet, Apple, and Egg Salad

Pickled Mushrooms

Seafood Pancit Salad

Sherried Onions and Almonds

Sliced Tofu with Condiments

Spinach and Cheese Pie

Spinach Pasta Salad

Tequila-Marinated Avocado Appetizers

Hearty Salads and Main Dishes

AFRICAN FISH CONE
MY MOM'S FRIED CHICKEN
HERB-BAKED GUINEA HENS
MOTHER'S CHICKEN SALAD HAWAIIAN
SEA SLAW
PENNSYLVANIA DUTCH BEET, APPLE, AND EGG SALAD
PORK-STUFFED HALIBUT
COLD POACHED SALMON IN ASPIC GLAZE
NEW ORLEANS SHRIMP REMOULADE
IN CREAM PUFF BASKET
MOM'S APRICOT GLAZED BAKED HAM
ARMENIAN–RUSSIAN SALAD
CAMBODIAN CHICKEN AND TOFU SALAD
CARIBBEAN COLD POACHED FISH WITH
AVOCADO SAUCE
WON TON CHICKEN SALAD
MAIFUN WITH CHICKEN SALAD
SZECHWAN CHICKEN BREASTS
CHINESE CHICKEN AND VEGETABLE SALAD
SZECHWAN CHICKEN, VEGETABLE, AND NOODLE SALAD
SCOTCH EGGS
PANCIT SALAD
SEAFOOD PANCIT SALAD
SALADE NIÇOISE
FRENCH WHITE BEAN SALAD
MICHAEL JAMES'S WONDERFUL QUICHE

GREEK SALAD
INDONESIAN GADO GADO
VITELLO TONNATO—VEAL TONNATO
PASTA PRIMAVERA—PASTA WITH GARDEN VEGETABLES
FETTUCCINE WITH MARINATED BROCCOLI, TOMATO,
OLIVES, AND PEPPERS
GREEN FETTUCCINE WITH TUNA, OLIVES, AND CAPERS
DASHI-WASABI SOMEN
MENRUI WITH DIPPING SAUCE
JAPANESE PORK LOIN ROAST
CHIRASHI-ZUSHI—SCATTERED SUSHI SALAD
TAMAGO—THIN EGG SHEETS
MISO-GRILLED TROUT
BROCCOLI AND SHRIMP WITH TRANSPARENT NOODLES
TERIYAKI MARINATED STEAK SLICES
CAESAR SALAD
POACHED CHICKEN BREASTS WITH TKEMALI SAUCE
CHILLED POACHED TUNA WITH CUCUMBER SAUCE
THAI SHRIMP SALAD
VIETNAMESE CHICKEN SALAD
VIETNAMESE SHRIMP AND GREEN PAPAYA SALAD
COLD TROUT IN ASPIC
TURKEY SALAD WITH A HINT OF THE ORIENT

AFRICAN FISH CONE

African   *6 servings*

In this African version of a cold fish salad, the dill flavor in the salad and dressing complements the fish and vegetables. The variety of garnishes makes this dish very festive.

2 cups flaked poached whitefish

1 clove garlic, minced

2 tablespoons finely chopped dill pickle

1 hot yellow chile, seeded and finely chopped

¾ cup finely shredded cabbage

2 tablespoons mayonnaise

2 tablespoons fresh lemon juice
Salt and pepper to taste
Additional shredded cabbage for serving platter

African Dilled Dressing (makes approximately ½ cup)

¼ cup mayonnaise

3 tablespoons fresh lemon juice

2 tablespoons minced fresh parsley

1 tablespoon fresh dill or 1 teaspoon dried dillweed

½ to 1 teaspoon turmeric
Salt and pepper to taste

Garnish

2 tomatoes, diced

1 hard-cooked egg, chopped

2 tablespoons chopped roasted peanuts

2 tablespoons chopped green pepper

Combine fish, garlic, pickle, chile, ¾ cup shredded cabbage, mayonnaise, and lemon juice in a bowl. Season salad to taste with salt and pepper. Spread extra cabbage on a medium-size serving platter. With your hands, place salad on top of cabbage bed, molding salad into the shape of a cone. Refrigerate salad until serving time.

To make the dressing: In a small bowl, combine the dressing ingredients; refrigerate until serving time.

At serving time, pour dressing over the top of the fish cone. Serve any extra dressing in a separate bowl to spoon over individual servings. Garnish perimeter of salad with tomatoes, eggs, nuts, and green pepper.

Variation: Cooked chicken can be substituted for the white fish. Other garnishes might be used, including chopped green onions, chopped cucumber, chopped avocado, and chopped sweet red bell pepper.

MY MOM'S FRIED CHICKEN

American   *3 to 4 servings*

People often brag about their mom's fried chicken, but wait until you try this. The water seems to enhance the flavor without making the chicken greasy or oily.

6 cut-up chicken pieces
(breasts, thighs, legs)
2 eggs
Salt, pepper, and garlic
powder to taste

¾ cup unseasoned bread
crumbs
Cooking oil
½ cup water

Pat chicken clean with a damp paper towel.

Lightly beat eggs in a shallow dish and add salt, pepper, and garlic powder. Dip chicken in the seasoned eggs, turning pieces until well coated. Place bread crumbs in a second dish and coat chicken thoroughly. Sprinkle the coated pieces with a little more of the seasonings. Place chicken on a platter, cover lightly, and refrigerate ½ hour before cooking, which helps set the crust. Bring chicken to room temperature before final cooking.

Pour cooking oil to a ¼-inch depth in a large heavy skillet or electric frypan. In a single layer, brown chicken pieces on both sides until golden. Pour water into the pan; it will steam and sizzle immediately. Quickly cover skillet and reduce heat to a low simmer. Cook chicken for 20 to 25 minutes. Cook another 10 minutes uncovered to crisp the crust.

This chicken can be made in advance and frozen, as it freezes very well. Bring chicken to room temperature to take along for picnics. Accompanied by Grandma Fisher's Potato Salad and a cabbage slaw, it makes an all-American outdoor lunch.

HERB-BAKED GUINEA HENS

American   *3 to 6 servings*

These small game hens are ideal for picnic fare or brown-bagging.

3 1½-pound guinea hens or
Rock Cornish game hens,
split in half
1 lemon, cut in half
3 cloves garlic, lightly
smashed

Herb mixture: 1
tablespoon each dried
rosemary leaves, oregano,
marjoram, sage, thyme,
and sesame seeds (see
Note)
4 to 5 tablespoons olive oil

Rub each hen half inside and outside with lemon and garlic. Using your fingers, press herbs into the hens. Pour olive oil into a baking pan and roll the hens in it. Then press herbs into them again.

Place hens in a 375° oven and bake for about 45 minutes, or until tender. Spoon the pan juices on top of the hens several times.

Allow hens to cool and then refrigerate until serving time.

Note: You can select your own favorite herb-seasoning mixture— about ⅓ cup.

MOTHER'S CHICKEN SALAD HAWAIIAN

American   *8 servings*

The combination of chicken with pineapple and nuts has become identified with Hawaii. My mother created this luscious chicken salad that is served in a pineapple shell. Since most of the preparation can be done hours in advance, this is an excellent and most attractive main-course salad to serve when entertaining. By increasing the proportions, I once served this as an entree at a wedding shower for fifty.

8 chicken breasts, boiled
4 ripe pineapples (reserve juice)
1 medium red onion, finely diced
2 cups walnut halves
1 11-ounce can Mandarin oranges, drained

Hawaiian Salad Dressing
(makes approximately 1½ cups)
1 cup mayonnaise
½ cup sour cream
2 tablespoons reserved fresh pineapple juice
Salt, pepper, and garlic powder to taste
Curry powder to taste (optional)

Skin and bone chicken; cut into large chunks. Place in a large bowl and set aside.

Cut pineapples in half vertically. Using a grapefruit knife, hollow out the center pulp, leaving about ½ inch of pineapple so that the shell stays intact; take care not to pierce it. Pour any juices into a glass to save. Invert pineapple shells on a paper-towel-lined platter and drain in the refrigerator. The pineapple shells can be prepared several hours in advance. Cut pineapple into bite-size cubes, removing the tough center core. Again, reserve any juice.

Add 4 cups pineapple cubes (reserving remaining pineapple for another recipe), onion, and walnuts to chicken; toss carefully but thoroughly. Add half the can of oranges and again carefully toss.

To make the dressing: In a bowl, combine the mayonnaise and sour cream. Thin to a pouring consistency with pineapple juice. If necessary, add a little more juice. Season to taste with salt, pepper, garlic powder, and, if desired, curry powder.

To serve, pour dressing over chicken mixture and carefully toss. Fill pineapple shells with salad and garnish tops with remaining oranges.

Note: If you wish to make the chicken salad in advance, it is best not to add the pineapple until serving time, as the natural acids of the fresh fruit seem to break up the consistency of the chicken if refrigerated too long. In this case, toss the chicken with the onion, nuts, and oranges, and refrigerate. Mix the dressing ingredients; refrigerate. At serving time, toss with the pineapple and dressing, fill pineapple shells, and garnish with remaining Mandarin oranges.

SEA SLAW

American   *6 servings*

You may never have thought of adding cooked fish to your cole slaw, but after you taste this salad I'm sure you'll try it many times.

1½ pounds poached rockfish
    or other whitefish fillets
    (refer to Fish-Poaching
    Basics—see Index)
1   quart court bouillon (see
    Index) or 1 quart salted
    water
¼   cup plain yogurt or
    mayonnaise
2   tablespoons chopped onion
2   tablespoons sweet pickle relish

1   tablespoon fresh lemon
    juice
    Salt and pepper to taste
1   cup shredded green
    cabbage
1   cup shredded red cabbage

Garnish

Lemon wedges

After poaching, flake the fish, discarding any skin or bones. Combine yogurt or mayonnaise, onion, relish, lemon juice, salt, pepper, and fish. Refrigerate at least one hour to blend all flavors. Add cabbage and gently toss.

Spoon salad onto lettuce-lined individual plates and serve with lemon wedges.

PENNSYLVANIA DUTCH BEET, APPLE, AND EGG SALAD

American   *10 to 14 servings*

When I was a child, my family often took long Sunday rides in the country areas outside metropolitan Philadelphia. At the end of these rides there was always a restaurant—often a big farmhouse-style inn that specialized in multicourse dinners. I remember with much fondness the many unusual dishes, particularly the salads that were brought to the table on Lazy Susan trays. Every restaurant had at least one "house" beet salad, and the recipe I have created here, with its sweet-tart cooked dressing, is very close to these childhood taste memories.

2   pounds beets, washed and
    trimmed (don't cut off
    roots)
1½ pounds tart green apples,
    peeled, cored, and diced
    (about 4 cups)
4   hard-cooked eggs, chopped

Cooked White Salad Dressing
(makes approximately 1½ cups)
½   cup sugar
1   tablespoon flour
1   teaspoon dry mustard
2   eggs
½   cup hot water
½   cup white vinegar
    Salt (optional)

Boil beets in water to cover 30 to 50 minutes, or until tender; drain, cool, slip off skins, and dice. Beets can also be baked. Place in a large salad bowl along with apples and eggs; toss gently.

To make the dressing: In the top of a double boiler, thoroughly mix the sugar, flour, and mustard. Whisk in the eggs, one at a time. Slowly whisk in the hot water and vinegar. Place saucepan over a second pot of simmering water and cook about 15 minutes, whisking almost constantly, until thick. Cool and season with salt, if desired.

Toss with salad, cover, and refrigerate until needed.

Note: Since the beets take from about 30 to 50 minutes to cook, depending upon size, I make the dressing while they are cooking. This also allows time for the dressing to cool.

Variation: Boiled and diced potatoes can be added.

PORK-STUFFED HALIBUT

American   *8 servings*

Stuff and bake a whole halibut early in the day and serve either chilled or at room temperature for an unusual supper.

1 9- to 10-pound halibut, cleaned and boned
2 pounds ground pork sausage
3 onions—2 coarsely chopped; 1 thinly sliced
1 lemon, thinly sliced
2 strips bacon

Juice of 2 lemons
1½ cups dry red wine
1 16-ounce can peeled whole tomatoes, with the liquid
Pepper to taste

Garnish

Lemon wedges

Stuff the cavity of the fish with the sausage and the chopped onions. Lace up the cavity or securely skewer, place in a large roasting pan, and surround with sliced onion and lemon. Place the bacon strips over the fish. Add the lemon juice, wine, and tomatoes with their liquid, and season with pepper.

Bake at 350° for 45 to 55 minutes, depending upon the thickness of the fish. The fish should just barely flake; do not overcook. Allow to cool to room temperature and then chill for several hours. Serve with lemon wedges.

COLD POACHED SALMON IN ASPIC GLAZE

American   *6 servings*

This aspic glaze is quite simple to prepare, and the result is a delightful fish dish. Another time, you might try another fish, such as halibut, or poached chicken breasts.

1 3-pound salmon fillet,
poached and chilled (refer
to Fish-Poaching
Basics—see Index)

Aspic Glaze

⅔ cup sour cream
⅓ cup creamed white
horseradish
2 tablespoons lemon juice
2 envelopes plain gelatin

1½ cups court bouillon
(reserved from the
poaching liquid)

Garnish

Capers
Chives
Pimiento
Black olive slices
Cucumber slices
Hard-cooked egg slices

Triple-fold a length of heavy-duty aluminum foil to the width of your salmon fillet and extending a few inches beyond each end. Lightly oil the top surface of the foil, place the poached salmon on it, and then place the foil on a wire rack over a platter.

To make the aspic: Combine the sour cream, horseradish, and lemon juice. Soften 1 envelope of gelatin in ¼ cup court bouillon and beat the softened gelatin into the sour-cream mixture.

Spread the aspic over the cold salmon, using a spatula; any excess will fall through the rack onto the platter. Refrigerate until the aspic is set, about an hour.

To make the glaze: Soften the second envelope of gelatin in ¼ cup of the court bouillon. Heat the remaining court bouillon, add it to the softened gelatin, and stir until completely dissolved. Cool the gelatin until it is the consistency of raw egg white.

When the aspic is set, decorate as desired with garnishes, first dipping them in the gelatin glaze. Refrigerate until the decorations are set on the aspic, about 30 minutes.

Pour two layers of gelatin glaze over the aspic, chilling between each layer until the glaze is set.

When ready to serve, lift the glazed salmon, still in the foil, onto a serving platter. Insert a wide spatula under one end of the salmon and slide the foil out.

NEW ORLEANS SHRIMP REMOULADE IN CREAM PUFF BASKET

American   *4 to 8 servings*

My first taste of shrimp remoulade was many years ago at one of the French Quarter's leading restaurants. The piquant reddish sauce is an excellent dressing for shrimp or other shellfish. You can serve this shrimp simply on individual lettuce-lined plates or, more extravagantly—as I have suggested—in an edible cream puff basket.

I have created many varieties of edible pastry containers to hold salads and sauces—using all-purpose flour, whole wheat flour, or cornmeal as well as tortillas and bread loaves. The following basket is basically one giant cream puff that has been deflated and crisped. By lining the bottom with lettuce leaves, you can fill it with your choice of salad.

1½ pounds medium shrimp, steamed or boiled just until color turns pink, peeled, and deveined
½ cup minced green onions
¼ cup minced celery
¼ cup minced fresh parsley

1 teaspoon salt
½ to 1 teaspoon dry mustard
¼ to ½ teaspoon cayenne pepper
Dash hot pepper sauce
Dash Worcestershire sauce
⅔ cup olive oil

Remoulade Sauce (makes approximately 2 cups)

¼ cup fresh lemon juice or wine vinegar
2 tablespoons Dijon mustard
2 teaspoons prepared horseradish
1 tablespoon paprika

Cream Puff Basket (enough for 4 to 8 servings)

¾ cup water
6 tablespoons butter, cut up
¼ teaspoon salt
¾ cup all-purpose flour
3 eggs, at room temperature

Combine shrimp, green onions, celery, and parsley in a mixing bowl.

To make the sauce: In a food processor or blender, combine all ingredients, except olive oil, until well-blended. Slowly add the oil in an even stream, as when making mayonnaise. (See Note.) Toss shrimp and vegetables with dressing. Any extra dressing should be stored to spoon on top later. Cover and refrigerate several hours to let flavors mellow.

To make the basket: In a large saucepan, combine the water, butter, and salt. Bring to a boil, stirring with a wooden spoon to melt the butter. Remove from heat and add flour all at once, stirring until smooth. Add eggs, one at a time, continuing to beat until mixture is smooth.

Spoon batter into a buttered 9-inch springform pan, spreading evenly but thinly around the bottom and up the sides to create a basket or bowl shape. Since this is cream puff batter, the dough will puff up during the baking. Bake in a preheated 375° oven for 40 minutes.

Unlike individual cream puffs, from which the tops would be cut off and the centers scooped out, this basket remains intact. Therefore, after 40 minutes, prick the pastry all over with a wooden skewer to deflate, turn off oven, and bake the basket another 10 minutes. Remove from oven and cool before removing from pan. Cool thoroughly before filling with salad.

If you make the basket a day in advance, loosely cover with foil and store at room temperature. It can also be frozen; to recrisp, bake for 10 minutes at 375°.

To serve, line the bottom of basket with lettuce or spinach leaves and fill with salad. Cut into large wedges.

Note: If you want to use this dressing for other recipes, you may wish to add the celery, green onions, and parsley directly to the dressing.

Variation: Crabmeat, lobster chunks, or scallops are excellent substitutes for the shrimp. Try a single vegetable such as peeled and julienne-sliced celery root that has been tossed with lemon juice to hold the color with the remoulade sauce.

MOM'S APRICOT-GLAZED BAKED HAM

American   *15 to 18 servings*

You'll find this recipe for baked ham not only simple but one of the best you've ever served. Make sure you purchase a fully cooked ham and that the butcher removes the heavy outer skin and trims off the excess fat.

1 fully cooked butt end half or whole ham (these generally weigh 10 pounds or more)

Apricot Glaze (makes approximately 1⅓ cups)

⅔ to 1 cup apricot preserves
⅓ teaspoon dry mustard
1 tablespoon brown sugar

Wipe ham with damp paper towels. Place on a wire rack or trivet in a large roasting pan and bake at 325°, allowing 20 minutes per pound. Add glaze an hour before ham is done.

To make the glaze: Soften apricot preserves in a bowl with the back of a wooden spoon. Add the dry mustard and mix; add the brown sugar and mix again.

Remove ham from the oven, score the fat, and coat all over with glaze. Increase heat to 400° and return ham to oven. Bake for 5 minutes at this high temperature to set the glaze, and then reduce heat to 325° for remaining 55 minutes of baking time.

To serve, cool ham to room temperature, slice thinly, and arrange slices on a serving platter.

ARMENIAN–RUSSIAN SALAD

Armenian/Russian   *6 to 10 servings*

Armenian–Russian Salad, referred to as salat olivier in the Russian cuisine, is a very delicious chicken, potato, and vegetable salad with a generous amount of chopped crisp dill pickles. These pickles add an outstanding tang and texture to the creamy dressing.

1½ to 2 pounds chicken breasts, boiled until tender (reserve stock for another recipe)

1½ pounds red-skinned potatoes, boiled, cooled, peeled, and diced
2 to 3 carrots, scraped, cut

into small cubes, and
boiled until tender
2 hard-cooked eggs, chopped
1 cup frozen peas, defrosted
¾ cup kosher pickles (or more
to taste), cut up very fine

⅔ cup mayonnaise
⅔ cup sour cream
Salt to taste

Remove skin and bones from chicken breasts. Shred the meat with your fingers and place in a large bowl with the potatoes, carrots, eggs, peas, and pickles. Carefully mix everything together, adding the mayonnaise, sour cream, and salt to taste.

This salad can be made in advance, covered, and refrigerated for several hours. Remove from refrigerator about 30 minutes before serving time to soften the chill. Carefully mix again and serve in a large lettuce-lined salad bowl or on individual lettuce-lined plates.

CAMBODIAN CHICKEN AND TOFU SALAD

Cambodian

*4 main-dish servings;
6 to 8 side-dish servings*

This Cambodian main-dish salad was created by a cooking friend, Christina Hurn, who has spent much time researching many of the lesser-known Asian cuisines.

6 ounces medium-firm tofu
2 tablespoons peanut oil
2 chicken breasts, poached or boiled, cut crosswise into ¼-inch slices
1 sweet green pepper, seeded and cut into matchstick juliennes
1 cucumber (preferably European hothouse variety), peeled and cut crosswise into ¼-inch slices
½ cup fresh mint leaves
½ cup minced scallions, separated into rings

Cambodian Dressing (makes approximately 1¼ cups)

½ cup coconut milk (see Index)
2 tablespoons sugar
⅓ cup coarsely ground roasted peanuts or chunky peanut butter
¼ cup lemon juice
1 teaspoon grated lemon rind
3 tablespoons peanut oil

2 cups shredded iceberg lettuce

Garnish

⅓ to ½ cup cilantro leaves

Cut tofu into 1½- by ½-inch pieces. Heat oil in a small skillet and gently saute tofu chunks until they just begin to turn brown; remove from heat. Place chicken, pepper, half the cucumber slices, mint leaves, and scallions in a large bowl and gently toss. Add tofu and any oil from the skillet and toss again.

Combine dressing ingredients until well blended. Pour over salad and gently toss again, taking care not to break up tofu.

Line a platter or shallow serving bowl with the shredded lettuce. Place salad on top and arrange remaining cucumber slices around the outer edges. Garnish top with cilantro leaves; refrigerate. Serve well chilled.

CARIBBEAN COLD POACHED FISH WITH AVOCADO SAUCE

Caribbean Islands 6 to 12 servings

For an elegant buffet dish, a whole fish need only be poached in a seasoned court bouillon and then chilled. You can serve it au naturel with a variety of sauces, glaze it with an aspic decorated with edible garnishes, or spread a sauce over the top, as if to mask it, in the style of the Caribbean Islands recipe that follows.

1 5- to 6-pound scaled whole fish such as a bass, halibut, or red snapper, poached and chilled (refer to Fish-Poaching Basics—see Index)

Avocado Sauce (makes approximately 1 cup)

2 avocados, mashed to a puree

Juice of 1 lemon
1 tablespoon grated onion
3 tablespoons olive oil
Salt and pepper to taste

Garnish (optional)
Black olive slices
Capers
Chili slices
Lemon slices
Greens

Carefully remove main skin from main body of fish, keeping head and tail intact. Place chilled fish on a large serving platter. Just before serving, mix together the avocado sauce ingredients and spread evenly over top and sides of the center part (peeled section) of the fish (see Note). Decorate, if desired, with garnishes.

Note: Avocado sauce should not be mixed in advance or it will darken.

WON TON CHICKEN SALAD

Chinese 3 to 4 servings

Although won ton skins are generally stuffed, they can be sliced matchstick size and used in a salad. The chicken in this salad is especially delicious if roasted or baked with a teriyaki sauce.

1 2-pound chicken roasted with teriyaki sauce (or use leftover chicken)
2 teaspoons sesame seeds
8 scallions, thinly sliced into 1-inch lengths
1 tablespoon sesame oil
1 tablespoon dry mustard

Salt and pepper to taste
1 tablespoon hoisin sauce
1 8-ounce package of won ton skins, sliced into shreds
Cooking oil for deep-frying

If you have a teriyaki-roasted chicken, slice with the skin into 1-inch-long matchstick shreds. Reserve some of the teriyaki sauce for the salad. If you are using leftover chicken, remove the skin and shred in a similar manner. You should have about 1 to 1½ cups of shredded chicken. Put the chicken in a salad bowl.

Place sesame seeds in an unoiled heavy skillet and toast on very high heat, shaking constantly, for 1 to 2 minutes (see Note).

Add the sesame seeds, scallions, sesame oil, mustard, salt, pepper, and hoisin sauce to the chicken. If you are not using teriyaki-roasted chicken, add a teaspoon of commercial teriyaki sauce. Toss salad to mix well.

Deep-fry the shredded won ton skins, a few slices at a time, in hot cooking oil (375°). Drain on paper towels. Add warm won ton skins to the salad; toss again and serve immediately.

Note: Toasted sesame seeds are great for all salads and many other recipes. A Japanese sesame toaster will greatly aid in this process and eliminate the mess of sesame seeds popping all over your stove.

MAIFUN WITH CHICKEN SALAD

Chinese   *4 servings*

This Chinese chicken salad has always been one of my favorites to make and eat. The noodles puff up when deep-fried. The final salad has a combination of textures and tastes. It is similar to the traditional American mayonnaise-based chicken salad, but I find it lighter and spicier.

Cooking oil for deep-frying
1 to 2 ounces maifun (rice stick noodles)
1 head iceberg lettuce, shredded
½ pound cooked chicken, shredded by hand into matchstick pieces

Soy-Vinegar-Oil Dressing (makes approximately ½ cup)
2 teaspoons soy sauce
3 tablespoons rice vinegar
1 tablespoon sesame oil
¼ cup vegetable oil
2 tablespoons sugar
½ teaspoon dry mustard

Pour about 3 inches of cooking oil into a large pot or wok and heat to about 375°. Break maifun into small portions, about 3 inches long and drop a small handful into the hot oil; they will puff up within seconds. Turn the noodles over with two spoons to let them brown on both sides. Remove the noodles as soon as they stop "crackling" and place on paper towels to drain. Continue process with remaining noodles.

Place lettuce in a large salad bowl; top first with shredded chicken and then with noodles.

To make the dressing: Place all ingredients together in a glass jar, cover, and shake well. Or mix the dressing ingredients in a small bowl with a wire whisk.

To serve, pour dressing over salad and toss gently.

SZECHWAN CHICKEN BREASTS

Chinese

4 main-dish servings;
8 to 10 appetizer servings

This Szechwan chicken dish gets its marvelous pungent flavor from the chili oil and Szechwan peppercorns. It should be served well chilled, so make it several hours in advance.

- 2 chicken breasts, poached or steamed
- 1 small head of cabbage or iceberg lettuce, shredded

Szechwan Peppery Dressing
(makes approximately ⅓ cup)

- 1 clove garlic, finely minced
- 1 teaspoon finely minced fresh ginger
- *a pinch* 1 teaspoon ground Szechwan peppercorns

- ¼ teaspoon sugar
- 2 teaspoons sesame oil
- 1 tablespoon rice vinegar
- 1 tablespoon chili oil *½ teaspoon*
- 3 tablespoons soy sauce

Garnish

- 2 tablespoons chopped roasted peanuts
- Cilantro leaves

When chicken breasts have cooled enough to handle, remove skin and bones, and slice into thin bite-size pieces. Make a bed of the cabbage (or lettuce) on a serving platter and arrange chicken on top to resemble two whole chicken breasts.

To make the dressing: Thoroughly mix all dressing ingredients and refrigerate.

At serving time, pour dressing over chicken and garnish with peanuts and a few cilantro leaves.

CHINESE CHICKEN AND VEGETABLE SALAD

Chinese

4 servings

There are several unusual ideas in this Chinese chicken salad. The ingredients are not tossed together as in most chicken salads, but instead are attractively

*layered. The steamed chicken is not cut into chunks, but rather shredded by
hand to resemble the bean sprouts and cucumber juliennes. You can assemble
the ingredients several hours in advance and then pour the dressing on top at
the last minute. Serve this as one of many courses at a Chinese feast or as a
delightful alternative at lunchtime to the well-known mayonnaise-based
chicken salad.*

1 whole chicken breast, or 2
halves (approximately ¾
pound)
2 cups fresh bean sprouts
4 to 6 green onions,
including firm green tops
1 large cucumber

**Chinese Chicken Salad
Dressing (makes approximately
⅓ cup)**

3 tablespoons soy sauce

2 tablespoons rice vinegar
1 tablespoon dry mustard
½ teaspoon sugar
2 tablespoons sesame oil

Garnish

1 tablespoon chopped
roasted peanuts

Put chicken in a Chinese bamboo steamer (see Note), cover, and place in
a wok over about 2 inches of boiling water (the water must not enter the
steamer). Steam chicken for 12 to 15 minutes, or until tender; chill.

In a large saucepan, bring 2 quarts of water to a boil. Add bean
sprouts for a few seconds, stirring, and then drain. Rinse with cold water
and ice cubes to stop the cooking. Drain again, wrap in paper towels,
and refrigerate.

Slice green onions into matchstick juliennes 2 to 3 inches long, to
resemble the bean sprouts. Wrap in paper towels and refrigerate. Peel
cucumber and cut into 2- to 3-inch sections; then cut in half vertically
and remove seeds. Thinly slice cucumbers to resemble the bean sprouts
and green onions. Wrap in paper towels and refrigerate.

When the chicken has cooled, remove skin and bones. With your
fingers, pull apart into shreds the same size as the vegetables.

Put the bean sprouts on a large serving platter to make a bed. Next
add a layer of cucumber and green onion, and place a layer of chicken on
top. Cover and refrigerate until serving time.

To make the dressing: Combine the soy sauce, vinegar, mustard,
sugar, and sesame oil, stirring to dissolve sugar. Refrigerate until needed.

At serving time, pour dressing over salad and garnish with chopped
peanuts.

Note: If you do not own a steamer, you can improvise by using a fish
poacher, or you can easily construct your own device by placing a footed
wire rack or several metal rings (empty small metal cans, such as tuna or
pineapple, with tops and bottoms removed) in steaming water in a
Dutch oven. Put the chicken in a heat-proof cooking dish, or place on

the rings, and cover with the Dutch oven lid. To prevent condensation from dripping down on the chicken, wrap a tea towel under and around the lid.

Variation: Whole steamed or boiled shrimp or shredded crabmeat can be substituted for the chicken. Other vegetables can be added or substituted, such as green beans and carrots.

SZECHWAN CHICKEN, VEGETABLE, AND NOODLE SALAD

Chinese   *4 to 8 servings*

This salad is best made several hours in advance so that the chicken, vegetables, and noodles absorb the wonderfully piquant flavors of the sauce.

1 whole chicken breast or 2 halves (approximately 1 pound)

1 cucumber, peeled, halved, and seeded

Salt

2 to 3 carrots, scraped

4 scallions, including firm green tops

2 ounces saifun noodles (cellophane noodles), soaked in boiling water for 10 minutes, or until soft, and drained

Szechwan Salad Dressing (makes approximately ⅓ cup)

3 tablespoons soy sauce

4 teaspoons rice vinegar

4 teaspoons sesame oil

2 teaspoons hot chile oil

¼ teaspoon Szechwan peppercorn powder, or to taste (see Note)

Salt to taste (optional)

The chicken breasts should be steamed or poached. To steam using a Chinese bamboo steamer, place chicken inside steamer on the bamboo rack; cover. Place steamer in a wok over several inches of boiling water. Cover wok. Steam chicken for 15 to 18 minutes, or until barely cooked. Remove from steamer and allow to cool.

To prepare the vegetables: Thinly slice cucumbers, carrots, and scallions into 2-inch-long matchstick shreds, in a food processor if you have one. Place cucumber in a colander, sprinkle with salt, and allow to drain for 10 minutes. Rinse and drain cucumber; pat dry with paper towels. Cut noodles into 2-inch lengths. Combine vegetables and noodles in a large serving bowl.

When chicken is cool enough to handle, remove the skin and bones. With your fingers, carefully tear chicken into thin 2-inch shreds to match the vegetables. (One of the beauties of this recipe is the similarity in size and quantity of all ingredients.) Add chicken to the vegetables and thoroughly mix, tossing with your fingers.

To make the dressing: In a small bowl, mix the soy sauce, vinegar, sesame oil, hot chile oil, and peppercorn powder. Stir mixture, adding salt to taste, if desired.

Pour dressing over salad and toss well. Cover and refrigerate for several hours, tossing occasionally.

Note: If Szechwan peppercorn powder is not available, you can grind the peppercorns in a mortar and pestle, as you would black peppercorns, for a fresh and pungent flavor. If the peppercorns are not available, you can substitute cayenne pepper, although it does not have the same flavor.

Variation: Abalone, small shrimp, crab, or cooked pork can be substituted for the chicken.

SCOTCH EGGS

English   *6 servings*

Practically a complete meal in a single package, Scotch Eggs are a favorite among English outdoorsmen and picnickers. They make terrific appetizers, too.

1 pound well-seasoned ground pork sausage	1 raw egg
6 hard-cooked eggs, peeled and well chilled	½ cup bread crumbs
	Cooking oil for deep-frying

Divide sausage into 6 equal portions and flatten into patties large enough to encase the hard-cooked eggs. Place one egg in the center of each patty and mold the meat around the egg.

Lightly beat the raw egg in a medium-size plate. Roll each sausage-encased egg first in beaten egg and then in bread crumbs, firmly pressing the crumbs into the meat.

In a medium-to-large pot, heat oil to 375° and deep-fry the eggs for 4 to 6 minutes. Drain on paper towels and chill until serving time.

PANCIT SALAD

Filipino   *4 to 6 servings*

Pancit, a rice stick noodle, puffs beautifully when deep-fried. This dressing is delicate and excellent to use on other salads, too. The slight saltiness comes from the fish sauce, patis, which is used in almost all Filipino recipes. It is not as strong as fish sauces found in Vietnamese, Thai, or Indonesian cooking.

1 ounce pancit Cooking oil for deep-frying	1 medium cucumber, peeled, seeded, and diced
1½ cups coarsely chopped watercress	6 scallions, chopped
	1½ cups bean sprouts, chopped

Filipino Pancit Dressing (makes approximately ⅓ cup)

- 2 tablespoons soy sauce
- 1 tablespoon rice vinegar, or more to taste
- 1 tablespoon patis (fish sauce), or more to taste
- ¼ teaspoon minced fresh ginger
- 2 tablespoons sesame seeds or chopped roasted peanuts

Dash sesame oil

Freshly ground black pepper to taste

Break noodles into smaller pieces. Heat cooking oil in a deep pot or wok to 375°. Deep-fry a handful of noodles at a time. When puffed and golden, remove with strainer onto paper towels to drain off excess oil. Set aside for a few minutes until salad is completed.

In a large wooden salad bowl, mix together the pancit, watercress, cucumber, scallions, and bean sprouts.

To make the dressing: In a small bowl, combine the salad dressing ingredients.

Pour dressing over salad, toss carefully a few times, and serve.

SEAFOOD PANCIT SALAD

Filipino

2 to 3 main-course servings;
4 to 6 first-course servings

To complete your lunch or dinner, accompany this salad with pineapple spears or melon wedges and a basket of muffins or flatbreads—and don't forget a glass of crisp white wine.

- 1 ounce pancit
  Cooking oil for deep-frying
- 4 giant mushrooms (about ¼ pound), sliced very thin
- 6 large scallions, including firm green tops, sliced thin
- ½ cup chopped watercress
- ½ English (hothouse) cucumber, sliced very thin (see Note)
- 3 ounces cooked large shrimp, rinsed with salt, lemon juice, and water to freshen
- 1 ounce crabmeat, shredded by hand into matchsticklike pieces

Pancit Dressing (makes approximately ⅓ cup)

- 3 tablespoons soy sauce
- 1 tablespoon rice vinegar
- 1 to 3 teaspoons patis (fish sauce), optional
- ¼ teaspoon minced fresh ginger
- 2 tablespoons sesame seeds

Dash sesame oil

Freshly ground pepper to taste

Break noodles into smaller pieces. Heat cooking oil in a deep pot or wok to 375°. Deep-fry a handful of noodles at a time. When puffed and golden, remove with strainer onto paper towels to drain off excess oil. Set aside for a few minutes until salad is completed.

Place mushrooms, scallions, watercress, and cucumber in a salad bowl. Toss lightly, adding the shrimp and crabmeat.

To make the dressing: In a small bowl, combine all the salad dressing ingredients. Pour the dressing into the salad and toss.

Prior to serving, top with noodles and gently toss again.

Note: If substituting regular cucumber, peel skin, thinly slice, and allow to drain on paper towels to remove excess water.

SALADE NIÇOISE

French   *4 to 6 servings*

A rustic country salad featuring a variety of fresh seasonal vegetables and herbs. The tuna is the centerpiece, surrounded by the vegetables and condiments.

1 head Romaine lettuce
  Salt
3 medium red-skinned
  potatoes
½ pound green beans, ends
  trimmed
1 beefsteak tomato or 2 to 3
  medium tomatoes
1 clove garlic, cut in half
2 7-ounce tins tuna, drained
10 Kalmata olives (Greek
  olives)
10 large pimiento-stuffed
  olives
1 green pepper, seeded and
  cut into thin rings
½ cup chopped celery
3 hard-cooked eggs,
  quartered

1 2-ounce tin anchovies,
  drained and patted dry
2 scallions, chopped
2 tablespoons minced fresh
  thyme or other fresh herb,
  such as tarragon or basil
2 tablespoons minced fresh
  parsley

Niçoise Dressing (makes
approximately ¾ cup)

3 tablespoons red wine
  vinegar
1 clove garlic, finely minced
2 teaspoons Dijon mustard
5 tablespoons peanut oil or
  other salad oil
5 tablespoons olive oil
  Salt and pepper to taste

Wash the Romaine lettuce ahead of time. Cut off core end, separate the leaves, wash, and pat dry with paper towels. Wrap in dry paper towels and place in refrigerator vegetable compartment for several hours.

Boil potatoes in salted water until barely tender, about 20 minutes. Drain, peel, cut into thin slices, and set aside.

Cut string beans into 2-inch lengths. Boil in salted water until barely tender, about 5 minutes. Drain and rinse with cold water, adding ice cubes to help set the color; set aside.

Cut tomato into wedges. If you want to peel it first, place the tomato in boiling water for a few seconds to loosen the skin, rinse in cold water, and, with the tip of a paring knife, peel off skin.

To assemble the salad: Rub a large wooden salad bowl with cut garlic; discard garlic. Tear lettuce into nice-size pieces and put in bowl. Place large chunks of tuna in the center. In a circular fashion, surround tuna with tomato wedges, green beans, potatoes, olives, green pepper, celery, and egg. Place anchovies on top of the tuna. Scatter red onion rings over the salad and, finally, sprinkle with green onions, thyme, and parsley. Cover with plastic wrap and refrigerate until serving.

To make the dressing: Place vinegar, garlic, and mustard in a medium-size bowl and whisk to combine. Slowly whisk in the oils, until dressing is smooth and thick. Season to taste with salt and pepper.

At serving time, pour dressing over salad and toss.

FRENCH WHITE BEAN SALAD

French   *8 to 10 servings*

White beans tossed with an herby lemon and oil dressing make an excellent alternative to the more common red kidney bean salad.

2 cups white beans (haricots blancs), Great Northern, or navy, soaked overnight and drained
1 large onion, studded with 2 cloves
1 stalk celery
1 carrot
1 bay leaf

¼ cup minced fresh parsley
1 tablespoon minced fresh rosemary or tarragon leaves
1 clove garlic, pureed or mashed
Juice of 1 lemon
⅔ cup olive oil
Salt and pepper to taste

Herb and Lemon Dressing (makes approximately 1½ cups)
¼ cup capers, drained

Garnish (optional)
Additional minced parsley

Place the beans in a large pot, cover with fresh water, and bring to a boil. Add the onion, celery, carrot, and bay leaf. Cover and simmer about 1 to 1½ hours. Skim surface as "shum" (a film) rises. If necessary, add boiling water to keep beans fully covered with liquid. When beans are tender, drain and discard aromatic vegetables. Place beans in a bowl.

To make the dressing: Whisk together the capers, minced herbs, garlic, lemon juice, and olive oil. Season to taste with salt and pepper.

Pour dressing over beans while they are still warm so that they absorb the flavor. Gently toss, taking care not to break up the beans. Let salad rest at room temperature several hours, occasionally tossing gently. Serve in a lettuce-lined salad bowl.

This bean salad can be made a day in advance, covered, and refrigerated. Bring to room temperature before serving.

MICHAEL JAMES'S WONDERFUL QUICHE

French   *3 to 4 servings*

In Paris, quiche is such a popular choice for a quick park-bench lunch or picnic that it is available all over town from small take-out food stores and charcuteries (delicatessens). You can purchase small quiche either whole or by the slice. Cool or room-temperature quiche is excellent as a main dish for a summer picnic, a year-round luncheon dish, or an elegant party appetizer.

Many years ago, I first studied French cookery with Michael James, one of Simone Beck's very talented American protégés. The following recipe is a simplified version of the classic French quiche that we made for one afternoon's meal.

Quiche Dough

- 10 tablespoons butter, at room temperature, cut into small pieces
- 1¾ cup all-purpose flour
- 1 egg, lightly beaten
  Water to moisten
- ½ teaspoon salt

Leek or Spinach Filling (select one—see Note 1)

Leek Filling
- 6 leeks, including white and firm green parts
- ¼ cup butter
  Salt, pepper, and nutmeg to taste, freshly ground

Spinach Filling
- 2 pounds fresh spinach, cleaned
- 2 tablespoons butter
  Salt, pepper, and nutmeg to taste, freshly ground

Custard Filling (see Note 2)

- 4 eggs
- ½ pint heavy cream
- ¼ cup milk
  Salt to taste
- 3 ounces imported Swiss cheese, grated

Garnish

Additional grated Swiss cheese

To make the crust: In a large bowl, fork together the butter and flour; add the beaten egg and moisten with water as needed. Place dough on a floured board and knead for a few minutes. Shape into a round ball, wrap in plastic, and refrigerate. After the dough has slightly hardened in the refrigerator, roll out—on a lightly floured surface—to a circle slightly larger than a 9-inch quiche or pie pan. Place dough in the pan and trim it to fit. Prick all over the bottom with a fork and put in the freezer for 5 to 8 minutes to help prevent the dough from rising into bumps while baking. Then bake in a preheated 425° oven for 8 to 10 minutes. Cool on wire rack.

To make the leek or spinach filling: Clean leeks, taking care to remove all sand and dirt, and chop them. Saute in a skillet with butter and seasonings a few minutes, until barely tender. The spinach filling is handled in the same manner, using a little less butter and sauteing a little more quickly.

To make the custard filling: In a large measuring cup or glass bowl, whisk together the eggs, cream, milk, and salt. Stir in the grated cheese. (See Note 2.)

To assemble: For the leek quiche, add 1 to 2 tablespoons of custard sauce to the leek filling and spoon it into the prepared shell. Add another ¼ cup custard or more, if shell can hold it. Garnish with additional cheese. For the spinach quiche, place all the sauteed spinach on the bottom of the prepared shell; add ¼ cup or more, if possible, of the custard and garnish with grated cheese. Refrigerate any leftover custard for another recipe.

Bake quiche in a preheated 400° oven for 18 to 20 minutes. Remove from pans (I use quiche pans with the removable bottoms) and allow quiche to cool to room temperature. If you plan to take the quiche along on an outing, return cooled quiche to pans for support. Cut into slices at serving time.

Note 1: You can use one of these fillings or both, in which case prepare two recipes for dough. This recipe supplies enough custard filling for more than one quiche.

Note 2: This custard can be used for other fillings, such as sausage, bacon, mushroom, zucchini, broccoli, and carrot.

GREEK SALAD

Greek   *6 to 10 servings*

A traditional Greek salad is a combination of the freshest of greens and vegetables, including lettuce, onions, tomatoes, cucumbers, anchovies, and feta cheese as the essential ingredients. With its contrasting colors, it is aesthetically stimulating as well as delicious. Greek salad is often dressed with only olive oil and dried oregano, but I think that adding lemon juice brings out the fresh flavors.

1 large head Romaine lettuce	4 radishes, thinly sliced
1 clove garlic, cut in half	2 large scallions, thinly sliced
1 red onion, sliced into thin rings	12 Kalamata olives (Greek olives)
1 green pepper, seeded and sliced in thin rings	1 tablespoon capers
2 beefsteak tomatoes or 4 to 6 smaller tomatoes, cut into wedges	4 ounces feta cheese, cut into 1-inch cubes (see Note)
	2 tablespoons minced fresh parsley
1 cucumber, peeled and thinly sliced	1 2-ounce tin anchovies, drained and wiped dry

Greek Salad Dressing (makes approximately 1½ cups)

   Juice of 1 lemon
2 tablespoons vinegar
3 tablespoons minced fresh mint

1 tablespoon dried leaf oregano, crumbled through your fingers
1 cup olive oil
   Salt and pepper to taste

Wash the Romaine lettuce ahead of time. Cut off core end, separate the leaves, wash, and pat dry with paper towels. Wrap in dry paper towels and place in refrigerator vegetable compartment for several hours.

Rub large wooden salad bowl with cut garlic; discard garlic. Tear lettuce into large pieces and place in bowl. Arrange salad ingredients decoratively; for example, place the red onion rings over the lettuce, the green pepper rings along the outer circle, the tomatoes in another circle near the peppers, and the cucumbers in the center with the radishes in the center of the cucumbers and green onions on top. Place the olives near the tomatoes, capers on the cucumbers, and feta cheese on the tomatoes. Sprinkle parsley on the tomatoes and cheese, and anchovies over everything. Cover with plastic wrap and refrigerate until serving.

To make the dressing: Combine lemon juice, vinegar, mint, and oregano in a bowl. Using a wire whisk, slowly mix in the olive oil. Season to taste with salt and pepper.

At serving time be sure to display the handsome salad before adding the dressing and tossing.

Note: If you wish to use this dressing on another salad that does not include feta cheese, add several tablespoons of crumbled cheese.

INDONESIAN GADO GADO

Indonesian   *6 to 12 servings*

One of the most famous of all Indonesian salads to grace the rijsttafel or "rice table" banquet is this sweet-sour-spicy dish combining raw and cooked vegetables with garnishes of tofu and hard-cooked egg slices. This is a perfect dish for the adventurous vegetarian. I have included substitutions for several of the more difficult-to-obtain ingredients, but if you have access to an Indonesian market or a mail order supplier, you may prefer to use the traditional items. However, for most cooks these may be difficult to obtain. The resulting recipes are quite similar and most delicious.

1 pound (2 bunches) spinach, trimmed of tough stems
   Salt
½ pound green beans, ends trimmed, cut into 2-inch lengths

1 pound fresh bean sprouts
4 small light-skinned new potatoes

8 ounces tofu
¼ cup cooking oil
1 medium head iceberg

lettuce or cabbage, shredded

½ to 1 European hothouse cucumber, unpeeled and thinly sliced, or a waxed cucumber, peeled and then sliced

2 hard-cooked eggs, thinly sliced

Gado Gado Peanut Dressing
(makes approximately 2½ cups)

2 cloves garlic, finely minced

1 small to medium onion, minced

3 tablespoons cooking oil

½ teaspoon trassi (shrimp paste) or anchovy paste

½ cup crunchy peanut butter (see Note)

2 lemon rinds, grated

1 teaspoon grated kentjur root or fresh ginger

Salt to taste

1 tablespoon brown sugar

1 small hot red or green chile, seeded and finely chopped

1 cup hot water

¼ cup tamarind juice or lemon juice

1 cup coconut milk (see Index)

Quickly blanch spinach in boiling salted water, drain, and rinse with cold water and ice cubes, to set the color. Drain and squeeze dry with paper towels; set aside. Repeat process with green beans, cooking just until barely tender. Next, place bean sprouts in boiling salted water and as soon as the water returns to a boil, remove, drain, and pat dry. Cook potatoes in boiling salted water until barely tender, remove, and cool enough to handle. Peel and thinly slice them and set aside.

Drain tofu from container, rinse, and slice into 2-inch cubes. Place between layers of paper towels for about 20 minutes to drain off excess liquid. In a wok or medium skillet, heat oil and pan-fry tofu on all sides until golden. Remove and drain on paper towels.

To make the dressing: Cook garlic and onion in a medium-size saucepan with the oil until tender and transparent. Stir in shrimp or anchovy paste, peanut butter, grated rind, kentjur or ginger, salt, sugar, and chile. Stir well and add hot water and tamarind or lemon juice. Bring sauce to a boil, stirring. Reduce heat to a simmer and gradually stir in coconut milk. Continue to simmer for 15 minutes, or until sauce has thickened. Spoon dressing into serving bowl and set aside at room temperature.

To assemble the salad: Place shredded lettuce (or cabbage) as the first layer in a large salad bowl or on a serving platter. Cover with spinach and then green beans, and place bean sprouts and tofu in the center. Arrange the sliced potatoes, eggs, and cucumbers around the edge.

Serve salad accompanied by the dressing.

Note: Traditionally, fresh unsalted peanuts are ground to a butter. If you wish, you can make peanut butter in a food processor or blender, using about ⅔ cup roasted unsalted nuts. But this step is not really necessary, as excellent peanut butter is now widely available.

Variation: A simple version of this recipe called lalab can be made by tossing together raw vegetables such as cabbage, cucumber, and bean sprouts and serving them with a spicy sambal dressing (refer to Indian Tomato-Cucumber-Onion Salad—see Index). For a West Javanese variation of gado gado, vinegar would also be added to the dressing, making the final taste a little more tart.

VITELLO TONNATO—VEAL TONNATO

Italian   *6 to 8 servings*

The origin of the famous Italian Vitello Tonnato is an example of a creative cook's use of on-hand items for last-minute entertaining. It is reported that the cook for Marchese Casati of Milan topped leftover sliced veal roast with a sauce flavored with tuna and anchovies—an unusual yet amazingly successful combination of flavors. The original Caesar Salad, from Tijuana, Mexico, offers a similar glimpse into culinary history.

Traditionally, a veal roast is poached in a liquid with aromatic vegetables. After it has properly cooled and is sliced, it is topped with the tonnato sauce and then refrigerated for at least 24 hours or, even better, for several days before serving. Because veal is so expensive, however, sliced turkey breast or pork loin roast can be substituted.

I have made a small change in the traditional sauce by folding in half mayonnaise and half cream into the tuna-anchovy-oil puree, rather than all mayonnaise. I find the cream makes for a light, smooth sauce, and guests have told me it is the best tonnato sauce they've ever tasted. Tonnato sauce without veal, carefully tossed with pasta, becomes Pasta Tonnato.

1 2- to 3-pound veal roast (see Note)
4 quarts water
1 stalk celery, quartered
1 carrot, quartered
1 medium onion, quartered
1 sprig parsley
1 sprig fresh thyme or other favorite fresh herb
1 bay leaf
2 peppercorns

Tonnato Sauce (makes approximately 2½ cups)

1 2-ounce tin anchovies, drained, patted dry, all bones removed
1 6½-ounce can oil-packed tuna (preferably Italian), drained

2 tablespoons capers
1 tablespoon minced fresh parsley
2 tablespoons fresh lemon juice
½ teaspoon Dijon mustard
Salt and pepper to taste
½ cup mayonnaise (preferably homemade)
½ cup heavy cream

Garnish

Capers
Minced parsley
Lemon slices

In a large pot, make a court bouillon (see Index) with the water and vegetables, as you would for poaching fish. Bring to a boil and add meat, making certain the liquid covers the meat; if not, add more water. (Some cooks use part water and part dry white wine.) Allow liquid to return to a boil, cover, and reduce heat to a gentle simmer. Continue to cook at a simmer for about 1½ hours, or until meat is tender. Occasionally check the meat, making certain it is covered by liquid and turning it once or twice.

When meat is tender, allow it to cool completely at room temperature for several hours in its broth. Then remove the roast from the broth and strain the broth; you can refrigerate or freeze it for use in other recipes requiring a simple veal stock.

To make the sauce: Use a food processor or blender to puree anchovies, tuna, capers, parsley, lemon juice, and mustard. Slowly, drop by drop, add the olive oil. Patience must be taken, as with making mayonnaise, so that the mixture absorbs the oil. Season to taste with salt and pepper. In a small bowl, whisk together the mayonnaise and cream. Fold this mixture into the tuna-anchovy mixture and set aside or refrigerate until veal is ready; it can be prepared well in advance.

Remove the string and thinly slice the veal roast. Place it on a large platter and then completely cover it with the tonnato sauce. Cover and refrigerate for 24 hours or for several days so that the flavors have time to mature and mingle.

Bring to room temperature an hour before serving. Garnish top with capers, parsley, and lemon slices.

Note: If you have a butcher with whom you place special orders, call and request that he bone and tie a veal roast for this recipe. The approximate starting weight is 3 to 4 pounds. I like to use the sirloin tip cut which comes from the veal leg.

PASTA PRIMAVERA—PASTA WITH GARDEN VEGETABLES

Italian   *6 to 8 servings*

Pasta salads have become standard in the culinary world, as they place no limit on a cook's creativity. You can toss your favorite flat noodle or pasta shape with vegetables and/or meats, seafood, chicken, and then dress it with herbs and an oil or mayonnaise-based dressing. The red and green colors in this Italian pasta salad, featuring fresh spring garden vegetables (primavera), will be very handsome on your buffet table.

1½ pounds plum (Italian) tomatoes, peeled, seeded, and coarsely chopped	3 tablespoons capers, rinsed and drained
⅓ cup minced fresh basil	1 large sweet red pepper
⅓ cup minced fresh parsley	½ pound broccoli flowers

<table>
<tr><td>½ pound small young
zucchini</td><td>(your choice), cooked al
dente, drained, rinsed,</td></tr>
<tr><td>2 tablespoons red wine
vinegar</td><td>and drained again
Salt and pepper to taste</td></tr>
<tr><td>⅔ cup olive oil</td><td>Freshly grated Parmesan</td></tr>
<tr><td>12 ounces pasta noodles</td><td>cheese to taste (optional)</td></tr>
</table>

Place tomatoes, basil, parsley, and capers in a large salad bowl. Set aside at room temperature while preparing the remaining ingredients.

To roast pepper: Place it on a sheet of foil under the broiler and broil on all sides until entire outside is charred black. Wrap in a clean kitchen tea towel or plastic bag and place in refrigerator about 20 minutes so that the pepper sweats. To peel, rub off black with your fingers. Cut open, seed, and slice into 2-inch-long juliennes. Add to tomato mixture.

Place broccoli in boiling water and, after water returns to a boil, cook about 2 minutes until barely tender; rinse with cold water and ice cubes to set the color, and drain completely. Pat dry with paper towels and add to tomato mixture.

Boil zucchini for a few seconds, then drain and rinse with cold water and ice cubes. Drain completely and dry, then add to vegetable mixture.

Carefully toss vegetables with vinegar; slowly add the olive oil and toss. Add the cooked pasta, toss, and season to taste.

Pasta salad can be served immediately or it can be refrigerated for several hours to let flavors mellow. Serve at room temperature. Pass the Parmesan cheese to top individual servings.

FETTUCCINE WITH MARINATED BROCCOLI, TOMATO, OLIVES, AND PEPPERS

Italian   *4 to 6 servings*

These marinated vegetables are so delicious they can stand alone as an antipasto dish, but they are even more interesting when tossed with fettuccine for a pasta garden salad.

<table>
<tr><td>2 to 3 stalks broccoli</td><td>2 tablespoons vinegar
(preferably rice vinegar)</td></tr>
<tr><td>2 large green peppers,
roasted, peeled, and cut
into strips (see preceding
recipe for roasting
instructions)</td><td>2 tablespoons olive oil
2 tablespoons safflower oil
or other cooking oil
Salt and pepper to taste</td></tr>
<tr><td>1 beefsteak tomato, diced
16 pitted black olives</td><td>8 ounces fettuccine or other
pasta, cooked al dente,
drained, rinsed, and
drained again</td></tr>
</table>

Oil and Vinegar Dressing
(makes approximately ⅓ cup)

¼ cup parsley "flowers"
2 cloves garlic

Trim the very tough ends off broccoli and peel the thick green stems. Cut into bite-size pieces and boil a few minutes until barely tender; drain and rinse with cold water and ice cubes. Combine broccoli, peppers, tomato, and olives in a large salad bowl.

To make the dressing: In a food processor fitted with the metal chopping blade, process the parsley and garlic until well chopped. Add the vinegar and then very slowly add the oil. Season to taste with salt and pepper.

Pour about three-fourths of the dressing over the vegetables, toss gently, and allow to marinate at room temperature from 30 minutes to several hours. Then add pasta and toss again. The salad can sit at room temperature, if necessary, for a few hours. Serve additional dressing on the side.

Note: If desired, toasted pine nuts are an excellent addition to this salad. Add when tossing vegetables with pasta.

GREEN FETTUCCINE WITH TUNA, OLIVES, AND CAPERS

Italian   *4 to 6 servings*

Spinach pasta tossed with tuna, parsley, olives, and capers makes a beautiful dish. All the ingredients can be kept on hand in case company drops by around dinnertime.

½ cup olive oil (or more to taste)

½ cup chopped fresh parsley

2 large cloves garlic, minced

½ cup fresh grated Parmesan cheese

¼ teaspoon salt

⅛ teaspoon pepper

⅓ cup lemon juice

1 tablespoon of minced fresh basil leaves or 2 teaspoons dried, crumbled

1 2½-ounce can minced black olives, drained

2 tablespoons capers, drained

2 7-ounce cans tuna, drained (if packed in oil, add it to the olive oil)

¾ pound spinach fettuccine, cooked, drained, rinsed, and drained again

Garnish (optional)

Additional Parmesan cheese

Combine the olive oil, parsley, garlic, Parmesan cheese, salt, pepper, lemon juice, basil, olives, and capers in a large wooden salad bowl; let sit for 30 minutes at room temperature for flavors to mingle. Break tuna into large chunks and add; toss carefully. Add cooked fettuccine, toss again, and serve. If desired, garnish with additional Parmesan cheese.

This salad can be made in advance and refrigerated; it is best served at room temperature.

DASHI-WASABI SOMEN

Japanese   *4 servings*

This spicy version of cold somen (wheat noodles) features horseradish, seaweed, and green onion as condiments.

1 pound somen, boiled and
  rinsed in ice water
3 cups dashi
3 tablespoons reconstituted
  wasabi

½ sheet nori, quickly toasted
  over a flame and crushed
  into flakes
2 scallions, finely chopped

Place somen in a large serving bowl with 1 to 2 quarts of ice water. Place dashi in four small serving bowls and little piles of wasabi, nori, and scallions in four small dishes. Each person should season his own dashi to taste with the wasabi, nori, and scallions. Noodles are eaten communally, with each person taking a small portion with chopsticks and dipping it into the flavored dashi.

MENRUI WITH DIPPING SAUCE

Japanese   *4 to 6 servings*

Japanese cold-noodle dishes are often chilled further with ice cubes before serving. This sauce for dipping cold noodles is flavored with mirin, soy sauce, dashi, and bonito flakes. The strong-tasting garnishes are not added until the last minute so that they do not lose their texture in the sauce.

4 to 6 ounces somen, cooked
  and drained

**Mirin-Soy Sauce-Dashi Dipping
Sauce (makes approximately
1½ cups)**

  ¼ cup mirin
  ¼ cup soy sauce
  1 cup dashi
  2 tablespoons dried bonito
    flakes
    Salt

Garnish

3 tablespoons finely grated
  daikon
1 tablespoon grated fresh
  ginger
4 scallions, green top part
  only, very thinly sliced

Place mirin in a saucepan over medium heat and add the soy sauce, dashi, bonito flakes, and a pinch of salt. Bring to a boil, then strain through a sieve. Cool to room temperature.

Place cold noodles in a glass bowl, along with ice cubes. Each person is served an individual bowl of sauce and an individual plate of garnishes. Noodles are eaten communally with chopsticks; each person takes a small portion of noodles and dips it into the sauce.

JAPANESE PORK LOIN ROAST

Japanese 8 to 10 servings

My guests have been most impressed by this Japanese-style pork loin roast. If you prepare the recipe early in the day, slice the meat after it has cooled and serve it with a ponzu sauce. You can reserve the strained pan juices for use as a base for a sauce or as a "soup" for cooked noodles.

2 1½- to 2-pound boned
  pork loin roasts (have
  butcher bone and tie with
  string)
2 to 3 tablespoons cooking
  oil
16 slices ginger (1 large knob)
3 cups chicken stock
1 cup sake
½ cup soy sauce

3 to 4 large carrots, cut into
  thick julienne strips
4 large celery stalks, cut into
  julienne strips
24 scallions, including firm
  green tops

Ponzu Sauce (makes 1⅓ cups)

⅔ cup soy sauce
⅔ cup fresh lemon juice

Bring roasts to room temperature. Heat oil in a large Dutch oven and add half the ginger to flavor the oil. When the ginger is browned, remove and discard. Brown pork on all sides in the flavored oil. Discard excess oil. Add stock, sake, and soy sauce and stir. Add remaining ginger.

Add carrots and celery to the pot; cover, reduce heat, and simmer about 30 minutes. Add the scallions, baste the pork, cover again, and cook another 15 minutes, or until pork is tender (160°).

To make the sauce: combine soy sauce and lemon juice.

Allow pork to cool before slicing. Serve at room temperature with vegetables accompanied by ponzu sauce.

CHIRASHI-ZUSHI—SCATTERED SUSHI SALAD

Japanese 6 to 10 servings

Scattered sushi—chirashi-zushi—while in some ways the simplest form of sushi to assemble, may take the most time to prepare. It is a free-form scattering of fish and vegetables on top of sushi rice. The rice is first placed in a layer on the bottom of a large platter, bowl, or box. The other ingredients are attractively scattered over the top, and the garnishes are arranged in the center. Sometimes the sushi rice is first tossed with a few of the ingredients before it is placed in the container. Chirashi-zushi can also be assembled in individual serving dishes.

The number of ingredients is at the cook's discretion. You can make a simple chirashi-zushi with only a few ingredients, two or three items tossed with rice. Typical ingredient choices are separately cooked vegetables, eggs, and fish (though not usually raw, as in most sushi dishes). Traditionally, it has nine ingredients because this number is believed to bring good luck. Of course, the more ingredients you use, the more time you need for cutting and cooking. You can prepare everything in advance and assemble at the last minute.

I find chirashi-zushi excellent entertaining fare. Your guests serve them-selves from the large platter. Using a rice paddle, they scoop under the rice and place the desired amount in their bowl or dish, much as they might help themselves to pizza. Chirashi-zushi is eaten with chopsticks, not by hand as with most sushi dishes.

Shari Mixture (Sushi Rice Mixture)

2½ cups hot cooked rice
½ cup rice vinegar
2 tablespoons sugar (or more to taste)
2 teaspoons salt

Vegetable Mixture

2 ounces pea pods, blanched
2 carrots (about ¼ pound), scraped and slivered into pencil shavings
6 medium fresh mushrooms (about 3 ounces), washed and thinly sliced (reconstituted dried Oriental mushrooms can also be used)
2 whole takenoko, sliced (if canned, wash and parboil to refresh)
½ to 1 ounce kanpyo (half the cellophane package), reconstituted

3 ounces (½ cake) kamaboko, cut into bite-size pieces (optional)

Vegetable Seasonings

6 to 8 cups dashi or chicken stock
4 tablespoons sugar (or more to taste)
2 tablespoons soy sauce
1 teaspoon salt

Garnish (optional)

Crumbled nori, about 1 sheet
Beni shoga
Tamago sheets, thinly sliced (see next recipe)
Minced green onion
Japanese cooked fish fillets (refer to Miso-Grilled Trout—see Index)

Place hot rice in a wood tub or bowl and fan a few seconds to cool slightly. In a small mixing bowl, combine the vinegar, sugar, and salt, stirring until sugar has dissolved. Pour dressing over rice and mix thoroughly. As if cutting the rice, use a wooden paddle to turn the rice and blend it with the dressing. Continue to fan until cooled.

The vegetables should be cooked and seasoned separately. I find it best to use one large pot and start with the mildest-tasting vegetable. As one vegetable is cooked, remove it and repeat the process with each remaining vegetable.

Thinly slice pea pods into 2-inch-long matchstick juliennes. Place in a pot with 1 cup dashi (or chicken stock) and 2 tablespoons sugar. Simmer until tender and seasoned, about 2 to 3 minutes. Remove pea pods with a slotted spoon and place on a platter. Add carrots and simmer about 3 minutes, or until tender, adding dashi as needed. Remove carrots. Add mushrooms, another cup of dashi, 1 tablespoon sugar, 1 tablespoon soy sauce, and ½ teaspoon salt. Simmer 5 minutes. Remove. Add takenoko and another cup of dashi and remaining sugar, soy sauce, and salt. Simmer about 5 minutes and remove.

Meanwhile, in a second pot, boil reconstituted kanpyo in water for about 10 minutes, or until almost translucent. Remove, cut into 1- to 2-inch lengths, and place in pot with the remaining seasoned dashi. Add any remaining dashi and simmer about 5 minutes. Add sugar, if desired. Remove kanpyo and—unless you're preparing a vegetarian dish—add kamaboko to the pot; simmer a few minutes and remove.

There are two ways to assemble the chirashi-zushi—tossed together or scattered. *To toss:* In a large bowl, combine the sushi rice with all the vegetables and toss. You can also prepare individual bowls. Garnish with crumbled nori, pickled ginger, tamago shreds, green onions, and tiny shreds of fish. *To scatter:* Lightly pack the sushi rice at the bottom of a large serving platter or individual bowls and then sprinkle everything on top. Place nori, ginger, tamago, green onion, and fish shreds in the center.

If you make this in advance for a party, do not add the nori until the last minute because it loses its crispness quickly. You may want to try a make-your-own chirashi-zushi party. Set out bowls of various toppings and garnishes and suggest that your guests top their own sushi rice. Serve at room temperature with additional soy sauce.

Variations: Other ingredients can be added or substituted, such as shiitake, bits of raw fish or seafood, slivered string beans, peas, gobo, cucumber, tofu, vinegared celery, or lotus root.

TAMAGO—THIN EGG SHEETS

Japanese   *4 to 6 sheets*

Tamago, a sweetened "omelet," is a favorite among adults and children alike in Japan, and is eaten as part of a meal or as a snack. Although tamago is generally made in thick cylindrical shapes, it can also be made in thin sheets to be used as a "wrapper" for other foods, or it can be sliced into thin juliennes to be used as a garnish for other recipes.

4 eggs	**½ teaspoon salt**
1 tablespoon sugar (or more to taste)	**Cooking oil**

Beat eggs with sugar and salt and pour through a fine-holed strainer to eliminate any sticky membrane.

Heat skillet (a rectangular or square tamago pan is traditionally used) and oil well. Pour a small amount of egg mixture (about ⅙ to ¼ of total) into the skillet and tilt the pan to spread it around. (If you are familiar with making crepes, this step will remind you of that recipe.) When the bottom of the egg mixture has set, in a few seconds to a minute, remove from heat and carefully lift up egg sheet with your fingers and chopsticks, taking care not to tear the sheet. Turn the mixture over, return to heat, and cook lightly for a few seconds, until the second side is golden.

Carefully remove the egg sheet and place it on paper towels to drain off excess oil. Oil the pan again and repeat the process until all the egg mixture is cooked.

MISO-GRILLED TROUT

Japanese   *6 servings*

The Japanese serve room-temperature miso-grilled fish at breakfast, as part of a bento lunch (picnic style), and as a fish course with dinner.

6 **small trout, cleaned and boned**	3 **tablespoons rice vinegar**
Salt	1 **tablespoon soy sauce**
½ **cup miso**	1 **tablespoon sugar**
1½ **tablespoons fresh lemon juice**	**Garnish**
	6 **thin slices lemon**

Pickled Ginger

1 **whole medium-size ginger root**

Skewer each trout lengthwise with dampened bamboo skewers. Generously sprinkle fish with salt. In a small bowl, combine the miso with lemon juice, mixing until smooth.

Place trout on a well-oiled grill over a charcoal fire or under the broiler, and barbecue or broil for about 4 minutes. Brush fish thickly with prepared miso, turn fish, and continue grilling for another 4 to 6 minutes, or until golden. Cool fish at room temperature and brush with remaining miso sauce.

To prepare the pickled ginger: Pare ginger and cut into very thin slices. Combine vinegar, soy sauce, sugar, and ginger and set aside for several hours.

When the trout has totally cooled, serve it with garnishes of pickled ginger and lemon slices.

Variation: Other small fish or fillets can be prepared in this same manner.

BROCCOLI AND SHRIMP WITH TRANSPARENT NOODLES

Japanese   *4 servings*

You can serve this delightful Japanese salad as part of a multicourse dinner. It is ideal to add to your New Year's Day Osechi Table, as the shrimp symbolically represent long life and the noodles represent good fortune in the year to come.

1 pound broccoli
½ pound (about 18) small to medium shrimp, shelled, deveined, and cleaned (see Note)

1 ounce saifun, soaked in boiling water about 10 minutes, or until soft, and drained
1 tablespoon very thin julienne slices of fresh ginger

Japanese Vinegared (Su) Dressing (makes approximately ⅓ cup)

¼ cup rice vinegar
1 tablespoon sugar
1 teaspoon salt
2 tablespoons cooking oil
¼ teaspoon sesame oil

Cut off and discard the very tough bottom stems of broccoli. Cut flower parts into medium-size portions. Peel middle tender stalk and cut into sections the same size as the flowers. Place broccoli stems in a pot of rapidly boiling salted water. After 1 minute, add the flower parts and continue to boil another minute or two until broccoli are barely tender. Drain and immediately rinse with cold water and ice cubes to set the color. Drain and pat dry with paper towels. Place in a serving bowl.

Place shrimp in rapidly boiling salted water for a few seconds until the color turns pink, and immediately drain and rinse. Do not overcook shrimp or they will toughen. Place in serving bowl with the broccoli.

Cut drained noodles the same length as the broccoli and shrimp; add to serving bowl.

Place ginger shreds in a small bowl of cold water for 1 minute; drain and add to broccoli mixture.

To make the dressing: Pour vinegar in a small bowl. Add sugar and stir until fully dissolved. Add salt and stir until dissolved. Slowly stir in cooking oil and sesame oil.

Toss salad ingredients. Add dressing and toss again. Cover and refrigerate until serving time.

Note: To clean shrimp easily, swish peeled and deveined shrimp in a bowl of su water (1 tablespoon vinegar to 1 quart of cold water), then rinse again in plain water and pat dry.

Variation: Toasted sesame seeds can be added. Other seasonal vegetables, such as string beans, cauliflower, and peapods, can be substituted for the broccoli, and other shellfish, such as crab, can be substituted for the shrimp.

TERIYAKI MARINATED STEAK SLICES

Japanese/American   *6 servings*

This teriyaki-marinated steak is ideal for a dinner party, elegant picnic fare, or a busy day, as the steak is marinated the day before, broiled early the following day, and then refrigerated until serving time. Do not slice the steak until serving time to assure the beautiful rare quality of the meat. A simple ponzu sauce, for dipping, completes the dish.

1 2-pound London broil or top sirloin steak (approximately 2 inches thick)

2 teaspoons finely chopped fresh ginger
1 clove garlic, minced
Salt

Teriyaki Marinade

½ cup soy sauce
2 tablespoons mirin or sweet sherry
1 tablespoon sugar

Ponzu Sauce (makes ½ cup)

¼ cup soy sauce
¼ cup fresh lemon juice

Place meat in a glass, porcelain, or plastic container. In a small bowl, combine the marinade ingredients and pour on top of meat. Cover and refrigerate at least 8 hours, or even for 1 or 2 days, occasionally turning meat.

To cook meat, remove from marinade and, for rare meat, broil approximately 8 minutes per side, occasionally basting with marinade. You will have to adjust the cooking time depending upon the thickness of meat and desired degree of doneness. This dish is best served rare. After cooking, cover and refrigerate for several hours.

Meanwhile, prepare the ponzu sauce by mixing the soy sauce and lemon juice and placing it in a small serving bowl.

At serving time, thinly slice steak; London broil is best sliced at an angle. Place steak slices on a serving platter and serve with ponzu sauce as a dipping sauce.

CAESAR SALAD

Mexican   *3 to 6 servings*

Caesar Salad was first created at the famous Caesar Hotel in Tijuana, Mexico. The first Caesar Salad was a last-minute composition of on-hand ingredients tossed together by a creative cook for a visiting dignitary. In the kitchen, the inspired restaurateur-chef found romaine lettuce, bread, eggs, oil, Worcestershire sauce, and Parmesan cheese. Caesar Cardini has since become world-famous for his salad.

Authentic Caesar Salad did not contain anchovies—this is an American addition—and the Romaine lettuce (primarily the hearts) was served in large pieces to be eaten by hand, not by fork. The croutons were originally made of Mexican white-bread cubes baked in the oven with a brushing of olive oil in which garlic cloves were steeped for several days. This same olive oil was used for the dressing. I have eaten this salad several times at the Caesar Hotel, and have always found the lettuce served at room temperature. I do not know if this is another "secret" of the originator or if the hotel waiters are so busy preparing the salad tableside that they have wooden bowls of greens always waiting.

Every home cook and restaurant chef has a particular way of preparing Caesar Salad. The following is close to the classic, with the much-loved addition of anchovies and a hint of the Mexican-favored herb, dried leaf oregano.

2 large cloves garlic
¾ cup olive oil
1 large head Romaine lettuce
2 cups French bread (about
  1 medium baguette), crusts
  removed, cut into ½- to
  1-inch squares
1 2-ounce tin anchovies,
  drained and patted dry
1 egg at room temperature
1 to 2 teaspoons

Worcestershire sauce
¼ teaspoon dried leaf
  oregano
Juice of ½ lemon
Salt and pepper to taste
2 tablespoons freshly grated
  Parmesan cheese

Garnish (optional)

Additional Parmesan
cheese

Early in the day, or one to two days in advance, crush 1 clove garlic and add to olive oil. Cover and steep garlic in oil to flavor.

Several hours before serving, the lettuce must be properly washed, dried, and chilled. Cut off core end, separate the leaves, wash, and pat dry with paper towels. Wrap in dry paper towels and place in refrigerator vegetable compartment for several hours.

To make the croutons: Place French-bread cubes on a cookie sheet. Remove ¼ cup garlic-seasoned oil and, using a basting brush, "paint" croutons on all sides with this oil. Bake croutons in a 350° oven about 15 minutes. When the tops of the cubes are golden, turn them, and make sure they do not burn. Drain on paper towels. The croutons can be made early in the day.

At serving time, cut up 6 anchovies; reserve remaining anchovies to garnish salad. Cut remaining garlic in half and rub all over inside of large wooden salad bowl; discard garlic.

Place egg in boiling water to cover and immediately turn off heat. Steep egg for 1 minute and remove. The egg should be warmed (coddled) only, not cooked.

Tear lettuce into bite-size pieces (or, if desired, larger hand-held lengths) and place in salad bowl.

In medium-size bowl, whisk the remaining olive oil and Worcestershire sauce. Crumble oregano through your fingers into oil and whisk again. Pour olive oil mixture over lettuce and toss. Add cut-up anchovies and toss. Add lemon juice, salt, and pepper, and toss. Crack egg over the center of the salad and toss again. Add Parmesan cheese and croutons, tossing once more. Place remaining anchovies over top of salad and serve immediately.

If desired, you can sprinkle the salad with additional cheese and freshly cracked black pepper.

POACHED CHICKEN BREASTS WITH TKEMALI SAUCE

Russian   *3 to 6 servings*

This Russian plum sauce is often served with vegetables. I have found it a beautiful sauce to spoon over poached chicken breasts, which are then allowed to "rest" for several hours so that the flavors mingle. The sauce is also excellent as an accompaniment to simple roasted meats, game, and sliced pâté.

6 chicken breast halves or 3 whole breasts

Chicken Poaching Liquid
Water to cover
1 onion, studded with 2 whole cloves
1 stalk celery, cut in half
1 sprig parsley
1 sprig cilantro
3 whole peppercorns

Tkemali Sauce (makes approximately 1½ cups)
6 deep-red-fleshed plums (such as elephant heart or Damson), peeled and pitted

3 tablespoons sugar
1 tablespoon red wine vinegar
1 tablespoon minced fresh cilantro
1 tablespoon minced fresh basil
2 to 3 cloves garlic, minced
¼ teaspoon cayenne pepper (or more to taste)
Salt and pepper to taste

Garnish
3 tablespoons minced fresh cilantro

Place chicken in a large soup pot with water to cover. Add onion, celery, parsley, and peppercorns. Bring to a boil, reduce heat to a gentle simmer, cover, and cook 18 to 20 minutes. Remove from heat, uncover, and allow chicken to sit in its broth for about 15 minutes. Remove chicken and allow to cool enough to handle. Remove skin and bones. Strain the broth and save it for another recipe. Place chicken on a serving platter.

To prepare the sauce: Place plum flesh in a medium-size saucepan over low heat. Stir for a few seconds, then slowly stir in the sugar. Cook about 10 minutes, or until slightly thickened; set aside. Puree cilantro, basil, and garlic in a food processor or blender. Add the cooked plums and process until smooth. Season with cayenne pepper, salt, and pepper.

Spoon sauce over chicken breasts and leave at room temperature for several hours so that the chicken will absorb much of the sauce. Spoon any sauce that has dripped to the sides of the chicken to the top. This recipe can also be made in advance and refrigerated; bring to room temperature before serving.

Prior to serving, garnish generously with cilantro.

CHILLED POACHED TUNA WITH CUCUMBER SAUCE

Scandinavian   *6 to 8 servings*

If fresh albacore is available, try poaching it for this delicate tuna dish.

1 albacore fillet (about 2½ pounds) or other firm whitefish

Cucumber Sauce (makes approximately 4 cups)

3 cucumbers

Salt
1 cup sour cream
1 cup mayonnaise
1 tablespoon minced fresh dill or 1 teaspoon dried dillweed

Poach the albacore according to Fish-Poaching Basics (see Index) and then refrigerate.

To make the sauce: Peel the cucumbers, cut them in half lengthwise, and remove the seeds. Finely chop cucumbers and sprinkle with salt. Chill for an hour. Drain and mix cucumbers with the sour cream, mayonnaise, and fresh dill.

Serve sauce with chilled albacore fillet.

THAI SHRIMP SALAD

Thai   *4 to 8 servings*

In this very attractive and delicious salad from Thailand, the fresh shrimp are quickly poached and then marinated in a spicy, tart, and slightly sweet aromatic dressing. The Thai fish sauce nam plai is the "secret," and key ingredient in this recipe. Nam plai is as important to Thai cuisine as soy sauce is to Japanese and Chinese. Do not turn up your nose to the idea of a fish sauce flavoring; it is very mild when properly added to your recipes.

2 pounds fresh shrimp
Simple court bouillon (see Index)
1 large red onion, chopped
2 shallots, chopped
2 cloves garlic, minced
1 tablespoon minced fresh ginger

1 bunch fresh cilantro leaves, minced
5 tiny green Thai or serrano chiles
Juice of 3 limes
2 to 3 tablespoons nam pla
1 tablespoon sugar
Salt to taste

Wash shrimp, but do not peel.

Make a simple court bouillon with ingredients on hand. Pour 1 to 2 quarts of water into a large pot and add pieces of leftover uncooked vegetables, herbs, wine, and seasonings. (I once heard a chef say, "One should never shop for a court bouillon.") Bring liquid to a boil; then reduce to a simmer for at least 15 minutes.

To cook the shrimp, return court bouillon to a boil and add shrimp, stirring thoroughly. When liquid returns to a boil, remove shrimp—do not overcook. Immediately drain and rinse shrimp in cold water. (The court bouillon can be saved for another recipe.) When shrimp have cooled enough to handle, peel and clean dark veins, using the tip of a sharp knife. Leave shrimp whole.

Place shrimp in a large salad bowl and add the onion, shallots, garlic, ginger, and cilantro. Using a sharp knife, slit chiles in half and discard the seeds. Finely chop and add to shrimp mixture (see Note).

In a small bowl, mix the lime juice, fish sauce, and sugar, stirring until sugar is dissolved. Pour over salad and toss well. Season to taste with salt. Allow salad to chill several hours (even overnight) for flavors to all mingle.

Note: These chiles are very spicy. Be careful not to burn any open cuts. Do not rub your eyes, and wash your hands as soon as you have finished handling the chiles.

Variation: Substitute small Japanese squid for shrimp. (Refer to Giant Squid Vinaigrette—see Index.)

VIETNAMESE CHICKEN SALAD

Vietnamese   *6 to 8 servings*

Vietnamese cooking has successfully incorporated the influences of both Chinese and French cuisines. The resulting dishes are both artistic and light. Very little oil is used. Outstanding ingredients in many recipes are vinegar and nuoc nam, a fish sauce used in place of salt.

4 **whole chicken breasts or 1 small cut-up chicken, steamed and cooled**
1 **head iceberg lettuce**
1 **cup chopped bok choy**

Vietnamese Dressing (makes approximately ¾ cup)

½ **cup white vinegar**

¼ **cup nuoc nam**
2 **teaspoons sugar**

Garnish

2 **tablespoons roasted unsalted peanuts, coarsely chopped**

Chop chicken into small chunks, discarding the bones but including the skin if you like the taste (and calories). Slice lettuce into thin shreds.

Toss chicken, lettuce, and bok choy together in a salad bowl. Combine the dressing ingredients in a small bowl; stir until sugar is dissolved.

Pour dressing over salad and toss. Garnish with nuts, toss, and serve.

Variation: If you wish to make this salad more complex, add about 2 tablespoons each minced cilantro leaves, lemon grass, mint, and shredded coconut.

VIETNAMESE SHRIMP AND GREEN PAPAYA SALAD

Vietnamese   *4 to 8 servings*

Fruits are often combined with seafood in Vietnamese recipes. In this one, a special green papaya is traditionally called for. I have substituted unripe (still green) fresh papaya, which is more readily available. Because the unripe fruit is somewhat starchy, it should be soaked and massaged to tenderize it. Serve this salad as an unusual main dish or party appetizer.

1 pound medium unshelled
  shrimp
  Vinegar
1 large green papaya, peeled,
  seeded, and shredded
1 teaspoon salt
¾ cup chopped bok choy or
  celery

Vietnamese Dressing (makes approximately ¼ cup)

2 tablespoons white vinegar

1 tablespoon nuoc nam
1 teaspoon sugar

Garnish

2 tablespoons roasted
  unsalted peanuts, coarsely
  chopped

Quickly steam shrimp in a steamer over simmering water until it turns pink. Do not overcook shrimp or they will toughen. Rinse with cold water to help stop the cooking. When cool enough to handle, peel the shrimp and, with the tip of a paring knife, clean dark veins. To clean shrimp, make a vinegar-water mixture of 1 quart water to 1 tablespoon vinegar and swish 1 shrimp at a time in solution to help remove all veins. Chop cleaned shrimp and place in an attractive salad bowl.

Place shredded papaya in a small bowl with salted water to cover. Let sit for five minutes, "massage" with your fingers, and then drain well. Add papaya and bok choy to shrimp.

Prepare dressing ingredients, stirring well to dissolve sugar. Pour over shrimp and toss well. Cover and refrigerate.

At serving time, toss shrimp mixture and garnish with peanuts.

COLD TROUT IN ASPIC

International   *3 servings*

One of the most beautiful buffet presentations is cold trout in aspic. Decorated with truffles, pimiento, scallion stems, and eggs in a gelatin, it can display a spring-flower personality.

3 small trout, cleaned
3 cups clam juice

2 tablespoons white wine
  vinegar

Aspic

  1 envelope unflavored gelatin
  ½ cup water
  1½ cups bouillon (reserved
     from cooking trout)

Garnish

  Scallion stems
  Hard-cooked egg whites,
  sliced
  Truffles
  Pimiento

Add trout to a pot in which the clam juice and vinegar have been brought to a boil. Cover and simmer for 6 minutes, or until the fish barely flakes when tested with a fork. Remove the trout and reserve the cooking bouillon.

To make the aspic: Soften the gelatin in ½ cup cold water and thoroughly mix in 1½ cups of the reserved hot fish bouillon. Let the gelatin cool until it reaches the consistency of raw egg white.

Place the trout on a wire rack and set the rack over a dish. Make two diagonal cuts a few inches apart on one side of each fish. Pry under the cuts to loosen the skin and then peel off the skin with your fingers, leaving the heads and tails intact. Spoon a layer of aspic over each fish and refrigerate until the aspic is set.

Create a flower design by trimming green parts of scallions to make the stems. Cut the egg white slices to look like petals. Use truffles and pimiento strips as the flower buds. Dip these decorations in aspic and arrange on each fish. Chill. Cover with layers of aspic, chilling after each layer is applied.

To serve, place the trout on a platter and serve with seasoned mayonnaise of your choice (refer to Homemade Mayonnaise—see Index).

TURKEY SALAD WITH A HINT
OF THE ORIENT

International   *4 to 5 servings*

There is always an abundance of leftover turkey in most American households, particularly after holidays. This turkey salad is a favorite for all ages. You might even find yourself roasting a small turkey breast just so you'll have an opportunity to prepare this salad with the leftovers. The dressing is just as good with other vegetable, meat, and seafood salads.

  1 pound leftover roasted
     turkey or chicken, cut into
     1- to 2-inch chunks
     (approximately 3 cups)
  ⅓ cup chopped water
     chestnuts (see Note)

  ⅓ cup finely chopped celery
  2 tablespoons finely minced
     onion
  1 small tart green apple,
     cored, seeded, and coarsely
     chopped

Juice of ½ lemon

Hint of the Orient Dressing
(makes approximately ¾ cup)

½ cup mayonnaise
3 tablespoons olive oil or
other salad oil

1 tablespoon rice vinegar
1 teaspoon sesame oil
¾ teaspoon dry mustard
Salt and white pepper to
taste

Place turkey in a large salad bowl. Add water chestnuts, celery, and onion to the turkey. Place cut apple in a small bowl with the lemon juice to hold the color. Add apples and juice to turkey mixture; toss well.

To make the dressing: Whisk together the ingredients in a small bowl. (The sesame oil gives a lovely hint of the Orient to this dressing.) Toss dressing with salad and refrigerate until serving time:

Note: When using canned water chestnuts (and many other canned goods), refresh in the following way: place in a small strainer, pour boiling water over, drain, rinse with cold water, drain again, and dry.

Variation: Substitute a combination of cooked shellfish for the turkey for another wonderful salad.

Additional Hearty Salads and Main Dishes

Acapulco Shrimp Ceviche

Armenian Potato Salad with Red Onions and Green Pepper

Ceviche con Alcáparras

Ceviche/Scallop Ceviche

Ecuador Pickled Fish

Escabeche of Poached Whitefish

Gravlax with Mustard-Dill Sauce

Greek Baked and Marinated Spring Garden Vegetables

Guatemalan Potato and Vegetable Salad

Indonesian Mixed Salad

Marinated Artichoke Heart and Rice Salad

Potato and Roasted Green Pepper Salad with Mustard Vinaigrette

Potato Salad with Tangy Blue Cheese Dressing

Russian Bean Salad with Satsivi (Walnut) Sauce

Salmon Mousse in the Shape of Salmon

Sushi and Sashimi

Tabbouleh

Desserts

CHOCOLATE MOUSSE–ANGEL FOOD CAKE DESSERT

DOUBLE RICH CHOCOLATE BROWNIE CAKE

WHITE CHOCOLATE CAKE

ANABEL'S ALL-AMERICAN PIES (LEMON PIE, BANANA CREAM PIE, PUMPKIN CHIFFON PIE, AND FRESH STRAWBERRY PIE)

PECAN FESTIVAL CREAMY PECAN PIE

LEMON CUSTARD ICE CREAM PIE

ANNIE'S VERY RICH GINGER CHEESECAKE WITH STRAWBERRY GLAZE

OLD-FASHIONED FRUIT CAKE

BAKED RICE PUDDING

HAUPIA—HAWAIIAN COCONUT CUSTARD

CHOCOLATE-DIPPED STRAWBERRIES

CHEESECAKE SAUCE FOR FRESH FRUITS

FROZEN STRAWBERRY SOUFFLE

FRENCH VANILLA-PEACH ICE CREAM

ROSEMARY'S LEMON ICE CREAM

STRAWBERRIES-IN-A-BASKET PAVLOVA

TROPICAL LIME-RUM PIE

ENGLISH TRIFLE

STRAWBERRY FOOL

RASPBERRY FLUFF

PUMPKIN-RUM FLAN

FREE-FORM APPLE TART

ALMOND TORTE WITH PEACHES AND CREAM

COEUR À LA CRÈME

FIGS WITH BLUEBERRIES

SWEET POTATO AND ALMOND HALVA

CHRISTINA'S INDONESIAN AVOCADO DESSERT

COCONUT CREAM PUDDING

SICILIAN CASSATA

BOCCONE DOLCE—MERINGUE, WHIPPED CREAM,
CHOCOLATE, AND FRESH FRUIT DESSERT

FROZEN MANGO MOUSSE

CINNAMON CUSTARD

CHEESE PASHKA

CARAMEL EGG CUSTARD

CHOCOLATE MOUSSE IN MOUSSE SHELL

CHOCOLATE BAVARIAN CREAM

OVEN-POACHED PEARS IN A WHISKEY ORANGE SAUCE

STEWED RHUBARB

OASIS FRUITS

GINGER-MELON ICE

WATERMELON ICE

NUT TORTES WITH ZABAGLIONE CUSTARD AND BERRIES

CHOCOLATE MOUSSE–ANGEL FOOD CAKE DESSERT

American   *12 to 14 servings*

The airiness of angel food cake molded in layers combined with the creamy richness of chocolate mousse results in this heavenly dessert. Although it takes many steps, it's well worth the time.

Angel Food Cake (see Note 1)

1½ cups egg whites (12 to 14) at room temperature
½ teaspoon salt
1 teaspoon cream of tartar
1 cup cake flour
1½ cups sugar
1 teaspoon vanilla extract

Creamy Chocolate Mousse Filling (see Note 2)

12 ounces semisweet chocolate
1 tablespoon instant coffee, diluted in 3 tablespoons hot water
1½ teaspoons vanilla extract or liquor such as rum or Kahlua

6 eggs at room temperature, separated
Pinch salt
2½ cups heavy cream

Chantilly Cream Icing (makes approximately 2½ cups)

1½ cups heavy cream
2 tablespoons confectioner's sugar
½ teaspoon vanilla extract or the same liquor used in mousse filling

Garnish (optional)

Glacé cherries or toasted sliced almonds

To make the angel food cake: In the large bowl of an electric mixer, beat the egg whites until foamy. Mix in the salt and then the cream of tartar and continue to beat until soft round peaks form but egg whites are still moist.

Sift together the flour and sugar. Sprinkle a few tablespoons of these dry ingredients over the egg whites and gently fold in. Continue folding in dry ingredients, a little at a time, taking care not to deflate the egg whites. Fold in vanilla extract.

Turn batter into a 10-inch removable-bottom tube pan and bake in the center of a preheated 350° oven 45 to 50 minutes, or until the top of the cake springs back when gently touched. Remove from oven, invert pan, and cool cake in pan.

To make the mousse filling: Melt the chocolate with the coffee in the top of a double boiler over barely simmering water. Remove from heat, add vanilla, and cool for a few minutes. Beat egg yolks and stir into chocolate. In a large bowl, beat egg whites until foamy. Add a pinch of salt and continue beating until egg whites are stiff but not dry. Lighten chocolate mixture with a little of the egg whites, then fold chocolate mixture into egg whites. Whip cream until soft peaks form and then fold into chocolate mixture.

To assemble the dessert: Tear the cake into bite-size pieces and place half of them in the bottom of a well-buttered 10-inch springform pan (without the center tube). Spoon half the mousse on top. Add remaining cake pieces and then smooth mousse all over top. The pan will be filled to the very top. Refrigerate until firm, about 6 hours. If you are in a hurry, you can place it in the freezer until firm, about 2 hours. When cake is firm, unmold onto a platter.

To make the icing: Whip the cream, adding sugar and vanilla after it has begun to thicken, until soft peaks form.

Ice the cake with the chantilly cream and garnish, if desired, with glacé cherries or toasted almond slices. Refrigerate until serving time.

Note 1: Angel food cake can be used for many other recipes. It makes excellent use of leftover egg whites, and it can be made in advance and frozen for later use. In a pinch you can substitute a commercial angel food cake.

Note 2: The mousse filling can also make 8 to 10 servings, by itself, as a dessert. Spoon into individual goblets or a large mold and refrigerate several hours.

Variation: A simple variation of this dessert can be made by cutting a 1-inch-thick slice from the top of the Angel Food Cake and removing the center of the cake, leaving about an inch of the bottom and sides. Mix 6 tablespoons each cocoa and sugar with a pinch of salt and 3 cups heavy cream; chill this mixture for 1 hour and then whip until stiff; add ½ cup sliced toasted almonds. Fill cake with ⅓ of the whipped mixture. Return cake top and frost the top and sides with remaining whipped mixture. Chill at least 2 to 3 hours before serving.

DOUBLE RICH CHOCOLATE BROWNIE CAKE

American   *8 to 12 servings*

What chocoholic wouldn't walk a mile for fabulous brownies or a double-rich chocolate cake! This dessert serves the two as one. Start with thin slices, as it's very rich, and then offer seconds.

Brownie Cake

½ cup cocoa
1 cup water
½ cup butter, cut up
½ cup cooking oil

2 cups cake flour
2 cups sugar
1 teaspoon baking soda
   Dash salt

2 eggs at room temperature
½ cup buttermilk
1 teaspoon almond extract
⅓ cup finely chopped
   almonds, walnuts, or
   Macadamia nuts

Chocolate Fudge Glaze

¼ cup butter
½ cup cocoa

| 6 table spoons milk | 1 teaspoon almond extract |
| 2 cups confectioner's sugar, sifted | Hot water, if necessary |

In the top of a double boiler over simmering water, stir together the cocoa and water. Add butter and oil. Cook, stirring, until everything is thoroughly blended.

Sift the flour, sugar, baking soda, and salt into a large bowl. Slowly pour in the chocolate mixture, blending well. Beat in 1 egg at a time, then the buttermilk and the almond extract. Stir in the chopped nuts.

Pour batter into two well-buttered and wax-paper-lined 9-inch cake pans, smoothing with a spatula. Bake in a preheated 350° oven for about 30 minutes, until a toothpick inserted in the center is barely dry. Do not overbake or the cake may be dry.

Remove pans from oven and allow to cool on racks for 10 minutes. Turn out of pans onto racks and remove wax paper. Allow to cool.

When cakes have cooled, place the layer with the flattest top on a rack over a sheet of wax paper. (You may have to slice a little off the top of this layer to flatten it.)

To make the glaze: Melt the butter in a saucepan over low heat. Add cocoa and milk, stirring constantly until mixture thickens. Do not boil. Place sugar in a large bowl and blend chocolate mixture into the sugar. Stir in almond extract. If necessary, thin with a little hot water (1 to 3 teaspoons). Spread about ⅓ of the warm glaze over top of cake. Place second layer on top and spread remaining glaze over top and sides. Set cake aside at room temperature for about an hour, then refrigerate overnight.

WHITE CHOCOLATE CAKE

American   *Approximately 20 servings*

The ultimate in dessert decadence lies in the realm of chocolate sweets. In search of a grand finale more extravagant than the finest of dark chocolate pastries, I began experimenting with white chocolate. Although the white variety isn't classified as a true chocolate because it doesn't contain chocolate "liquor" (the essence that is extracted from cocoa beans), its taste is similar to a sweet, mild milk chocolate. White chocolate is a candy composed of a white-colored cocoa butter as well as milk, vanilla, and sugar.

As I was very fond of cookbook author and caterer Martha Stewart's recipe for Double Diabolo, I began experimenting with white chocolate, ground almonds, golden raisins, rum, butter, cake flour, sugar, cream, and eggs, and whipped together this simple yet elegant candylike cake. In the spring and summer months, I decorate it with petals and blossoms from my garden. For the Christmas table, I use sprigs of holly with vivid red "beads."

White Chocolate Cake

- 6 ounces blanched almonds
- 10 tablespoons cake flour
- ¼ teaspoon salt

- 6 eggs at room temperature, separated
- ⅔ cup sugar

- 14 ounces white chocolate
- 2 tablespoons golden rum (Puerto Rican light-colored variety)
- 2 tablespoons water
- ¼ pound butter
- ½ cup golden raisins, soaked several hours in ½ cup golden rum

White Chocolate Glaze

- 8 ounces white chocolate
- ½ cup heavy cream
- 2 teaspoons golden rum

Grind almonds in a food processor or blender and place in a small bowl. Sift cake flour and salt into this bowl; mix.

In a large bowl, beat the egg yolks with the sugar until well blended, light, and creamy.

Place the white chocolate, rum, and water in the top of a double boiler over simmering water. Stir to melt the chocolate, then add the butter, a teaspoon at a time, continuing to stir until smooth. Remove from heat and add a spoonful of egg mixture to lighten. Gradually stir the melted chocolate into the egg mixture, continuing to beat constantly to retain the smooth quality of the batter. Stir in the ground almonds and flour, then the raisins and rum.

In another bowl, beat the egg whites until they hold firm peaks. Fold into the batter.

Prepare a 12-inch cake pan by cutting a wax-paper circle to fit the bottom. Butter the pan and wax-paper liner. Pour in batter and bake in a preheated 350° oven for about 30 minutes. When cake is tested with a toothpick, it should just be clean; do not overbake.

Remove from oven and allow to cool in pan 10 minutes. Carefully turn cake out of pan, using the palms of your hands, onto wire cooling racks. (Since the cake is so large, extra patience must be taken not to break it.) Carefully remove wax-paper liner.

Allow the cake to cool thoroughly before glazing. This cake can be made several days in advance, wrapped, and refrigerated, or placed in the freezer for longer storage.

To make the glaze: Melt the white chocolate with the cream in the top of a double boiler over simmering water, stirring with a wooden spoon. Remove from heat and add rum. Allow to cool slightly, stirring occasionally to retain smooth texture.

Place the cake on a wire rack over wax paper. Pour glaze over cooled cake, spreading evenly over top and sides with a spatula. Chill the cake to harden glaze.

At serving time, decorate the cake with cut garden flowers or Christmas holly.

ANABEL'S ALL-AMERICAN PIES (LEMON PIE, BANANA CREAM PIE, PUMPKIN CHIFFON PIE, AND FRESH STRAWBERRY PIE)

American   *Approximately 8 servings each pie*

My mother-in-law, Anabel Hoy, was truly the greatest home pie baker I have ever known. There was always a pie in the oven and another cooling on the kitchen counter. If she asked which pie you would like and you were undecided between two, she'd bake them both, and maybe another. Pies were served for desserts at lunch, tea, dinner, and supper. Sometimes we'd even sneak them at breakfast. Her repertoire ran to the dozens. These are a few of my favorites.

All-Purpose Pie Shell (single 9-inch pie)

⅓ cup cooking oil

3 tablespoons water
1 cup flour
1 teaspoon salt

Pour oil and add water into a medium-size bowl, stirring well. In a larger bowl, place flour and sprinkle salt on top; stir. Add oil/water to flour and mix well. The consistency should be similar to soft clay. Cut two pieces of wax paper slightly larger than desired pie shell. Place dough between the sheets and roll out to desired size. Place rolled-out dough on top of 9-inch pie plate and carefully press into the plate to shape. With the tines of a fork, prick little holes all over. Trim edges with a knife and patch any tears with this extra rolled-out dough. (You may need a little water to help repair the crust.)

Bake in a preheated 400° oven 10 to 12 minutes. Cool and fill with desired filling.

Lemon Pie Filling

2 tablespoons cornstarch
½ to ¾ cup sugar, depending on how tart you like the pie
Juice of 1 lemon and grated lemon rind (optional)

3 egg yolks, beaten
1¼ cups warm water
1 tablespoon butter at room temperature

Meringue

3 to 5 egg whites
½ cup sugar

Mix cornstarch and sugar in the top of a double boiler over simmering water. Add juice, lemon rind (if desired), and egg yolks. Pour in water, stirring constantly, until mixture thickens. (If you have a problem getting the mixture to thicken, you can add another tablespoon of cornstarch that has been diluted with 1 tablespoon water.) When mixture has thickened, allow it to cool; then add butter, which makes the custard richer.

Pour lemon custard into fully cooled pie shell.

To make the meringue: Beat the egg whites (from the eggs whose yolks were used in the custard plus another 2 or 3 whites, depending on how much meringue you want), until frothy. Gradually beat in the sugar, a tablespoon at a time, until meringue is thick, full bodied, and has greatly increased in volume. It should not be dry.

Spoon egg whites over pie and place in a 350° oven to brown. Watch carefully so that the meringue doesn't burn. Allow pie to cool before eating.

Banana Cream Pie Filling

3 tablespoons cornstarch
2 tablespoons flour
½ cup sugar
⅓ teaspoon salt

2½ cups milk, heated
3 egg yolks, beaten
1 tablespoon butter
1 teaspoon vanilla extract
2 bananas, sliced

Mix cornstarch, flour, sugar, and salt together in a medium saucepan. Add milk, stirring constantly. Place saucepan over low to medium heat and cook, stirring constantly, until thickened. Add egg yolks and continue to cook another minute. Stir in the butter and vanilla extract. Allow custard to cool.

Line cooled pie shell with the sliced bananas. Pour creamed custard over bananas and top with whipped cream or meringue, if desired.

Variation: For a Chocolate Banana Cream Pie Filling, add 2 squares of semisweet chocolate to the milk when heating, stirring until melted.

Pumpkin Chiffon Pie Filling

3 eggs, separated
1 cup sugar
1¼ cups pumpkin puree
½ cup milk
½ teaspoon salt

½ teaspoon ground ginger
½ teaspoon nutmeg
½ teaspoon cinnamon
1 envelope unflavored gelatin
¼ cup water

In the top of a double boiler, beat egg yolks and ½ cup sugar until a rich, thick yellow. Add the pumpkin, milk, salt, ginger, nutmeg, and cinnamon. Place over the bottom of the double boiler, filled with simmering water, stirring until thick.

Soak the gelatin in ¼ cup water for 5 minutes to soften and add to the pumpkin mixture, stirring and cooking until gelatin is dissolved. Allow pumpkin mixture to cool.

Beat egg whites with the remaining sugar until stiff, not dry, and fold into pumpkin mixture. Pour filling into the cooled pie shell and chill for several hours.

Glazed Fresh Strawberry Pie Filling

2 pints strawberries
¾ cup sugar

½ cup water
3 tablespoons cornstarch
1 cup heavy cream, whipped
    with 1 tablespoon sugar

When cleaning the strawberries, set aside 1 cup of the softer (or bruised) berries and mash them with the sugar and ¼ cup water. Then, in a saucepan, gently heat them until very soft. Dilute the cornstarch with the remaining water and stir into the mashed berries. Continue to cook over low heat until the mixture is thick and clear; cool.

Spread half the whipped cream in the pie shell. Top with remaining berries, stem end down. Spoon glaze over the berries and top with remaining whipped cream. Refrigerate until serving.

PECAN FESTIVAL CREAMY PECAN PIE

American   *8 to 10 servings*

According to my southern friends, a summer cookout is not complete without a pecan pie. You'll love the triple nuttiness of this recipe: pecans in the crust, in the creamy cheese middle, and on the top. Years ago, I adapted this wonderful pie from a prize-winning Georgia recipe.

Pecan Crumb Crust

1½ cup graham cracker crumbs
½ cup butter, softened
⅓ cup finely chopped pecans

Pecan-Cheese Filling

2 8-ounce packages cream cheese, softened
1 cup sugar

¾ cup coarsely chopped pecans

Pecan Topping

1 cup sour cream
2 tablespoons sugar
2 teaspoons vanilla extract

Garnish

Pecan halves

Combine the crust ingredients well and press into the bottom and sides of a 9-inch pie plate. Chill at least 20 minutes.

To make the filling: Beat the cream cheese until fluffy; beat in the sugar until smooth and then add the chopped pecans. Spoon mixture into the prepared crust and bake in a preheated 325° oven for 20 minutes.

To make the topping: Mix the sour cream, sugar, and vanilla, and spoon over filling.

Return pie to oven and raise temperature to 350°; bake another 10 minutes.

Garnish with pecan halves and chill until serving time.

LEMON CUSTARD ICE CREAM PIE

American   *8 servings*

If lemon pie is already a favorite in your household, wait until your family tastes this outstanding lemon custard ice cream pie.

Cookie Crust

6 tablespoons butter at room temperature
1 cup flour
¼ cup confectioner's sugar

Lemon Custard Filling

2 eggs, beaten
¾ cup sugar
2 tablespoons flour
Juice of 1 lemon
1 teaspoon grated lemon rind

4 cups lemon ice cream, softened (refer to Rosemary's Lemon Ice Cream—see Index)

Topping

1 cup heavy cream
2 tablespoons sugar
1 teaspoon vanilla extract

Garnish

1 lemon, very thinly sliced
Chocolate curls or shavings (optional)

Combine the crust ingredients and press into the bottom and sides of a well-buttered 9-inch pie plate. Bake in a preheated 350° oven for 15 minutes and remove from oven.

To make the filling: Mix together the eggs, sugar, flour, lemon juice, and rind. Pour lemon mixture into the hot crust and return to the oven for another 20 minutes. Allow to cool and then top with softened ice cream. Place pie in the freezer.

To make the topping: Whip cream with the sugar and vanilla until stiff peaks form.

Decorate the frozen pie with the whipped cream and garnish with lemon slices and chocolate. Return to the freezer for several hours.

Prior to serving, allow pie to sit at room temperature a few minutes to soften somewhat.

ANNIE'S VERY RICH GINGER CHEESECAKE WITH STRAWBERRY GLAZE

American   *6 to 10 servings*

My dear friend Annie first created a dense, rich cheesecake and then experimented by adding chopped candied ginger. This outstanding dessert has won her the applause of friends as well as ribbons from country fairs.

Ginger Cheesecake

5 8-ounce packages cream cheese at room temperature
1¾ cups sugar
3 tablespoons flour
2 teaspoons grated lemon rind

1½ teaspoons grated orange rind
¼ teaspoon vanilla extract
5 eggs, plus 2 extra egg yolks
¼ cup heavy cream
⅔ cup chopped candied ginger

Strawberry Glaze

1 pint strawberries
¾ cup water
½ cup sugar
1 tablespoon cornstarch

1 teaspoon plain gelatin
3 tablespoons Grand Marnier or other orange liqueur

Using an electric mixer, blend cheese, sugar, flour, grated lemon and orange rinds, and vanilla at high speed. Beat in eggs, one at a time, until smooth. Beat in cream. Fold in candied ginger.

Pour batter into a 9-inch springform cake pan and bake in the center of a preheated 450° oven for 10 minutes. Lower heat to 250° and bake another 1 to 1½ hours. After an hour, begin checking cake by inserting a knife in the center; it is done when the knife comes out clean. Place on a wire rack to cool. Prior to glazing, remove the side of the springform pan.

To make the glaze: Set aside the nicest half of the strawberries to remain whole. Clean and hull all the strawberries and place the remaining half in a saucepan and crush with a potato masher. Add water and sugar and simmer 5 minutes. Strain to remove pulp and let the juice cool. In a bowl, blend cornstarch and gelatin with ¼ cup of the cooled berry juice, stirring to remove any lumps, and then add this mixture to the remaining berry juice in the saucepan. Cook over medium heat, stirring constantly, until it becomes thick and clear. Stir in liqueur.

Arrange whole strawberries on top of the cooled cake. Carefully glaze each strawberry, allowing glaze to drip down the sides. Chill for several hours before serving.

Variations: This basic cheesecake responds beautifully to other toppings or glazes. You can vary it with your favorites.

OLD-FASHIONED FRUIT CAKE

American   *2 loaves*

This classic old-fashioned fruit and nut cake, created by a lovely elderly family friend, Jessie Hoy, has been a treasured Christmas recipe for many years.

3 cups pitted dates, quartered
3 cups raisins, rinsed with warm water and drained
2 cups walnut or pecans, chopped
1 pound candied fruit mix
¼ cup molasses
¼ cup sherry or fruit juice
1 cup butter at room temperature

1½ cups packed brown sugar
4 eggs at room temperature

2 cups flour
1 teaspoon cinnamon
½ teaspoon ground cloves
½ teaspoon mace
½ teaspoon salt
¼ teaspoon baking soda

Place dates, raisins, nuts, fruit mix, molasses, and sherry in a mixing bowl. In another large bowl, cream butter and sugar. Beat in one egg at a time. Pour this mixture over fruit and nut mixture.

Sift dry ingredients together and add gradually to the fruit mixture. Spoon batter into two 9-inch loaf pans that have been lined with wax paper and well greased. Place a shallow pan filled with water in the bottom of the oven and preheat to 275°. This will help keep cake moist while baking and ensure a proper crust and coloring. Bake the cakes for 2½ hours.

Remove cakes from pans and cool on racks. Do not remove wax paper until cake is used. Wrap in plastic or foil and refrigerate until needed. The cakes will keep several weeks in the refrigerator.

If desired, the cakes can be wrapped in cheesecloth that has been soaked in additional sherry, and then wrapped in foil and refrigerated for several weeks. Additional sherry can be added occasionally.

BAKED RICE PUDDING

American   *6 servings*

There are certain foods that I refer to as comforting foods. They recall childhood memories of my grandmother wrapped in her apron, standing in a kitchen crowded with ingredients, ready to make one of my favorite desserts—in this case, a creamy rice pudding.

½ cup raisins
¼ cup fresh orange juice, strained
1 tablespoon lemon juice
1 tablespoon grated orange rind
1 teaspoon grated lemon rind
2 eggs at room temperature
½ cup sugar
½ teaspoon vanilla extract

½ teaspoon salt
½ teaspoon powdered cinnamon
2 cups milk or half-and-half
1½ cups cooked white rice
Sprinkling of freshly grated nutmeg (optional)

Garnish (optional)

Grated nutmeg
Whipped cream

Soak raisins in a bowl with the orange and lemon juices and grated rinds for 1 hour. In a large bowl, beat eggs and sugar until thick, creamy, and white-colored. Add vanilla, salt, and cinnamon. Stir in the milk or half-and-half, cooked rice, and raisin mixture. Pour into a buttered 5-cup baking dish. Sprinkle with freshly grated nutmeg, if desired.

Set baking dish in a larger pan of hot water and bake in a preheated 350° oven 1 hour 15 minutes. Allow to cool to room temperature, then chill.

Prior to serving, garnish with whipped cream, if desired. Some people prefer to pour milk or half-and-half on this pudding.

Note: Rice pudding is a nutritious alternative to cereal for a child's breakfast.

HAUPIA—HAWAIIAN COCONUT CUSTARD

American   *8 servings*

A classic Hawaiian luau dessert is haupia, a fresh coconut custard. Traditionally molded in a square pan and sliced in squares, haupia has a creamy, light texture.

1 **quart fresh coconut milk (see Index)**	½ **cup milk**
1 **cup sugar**	**Garnish (optional)**
Pinch salt	**Toasted fresh coconut**
½ **teaspoon almond extract**	**Whipped cream**
¼ **cup cornstarch**	

In a medium-size saucepan over low heat, heat coconut milk until bubbles begin to form. Slowly add the sugar, salt, and almond extract, stirring to dissolve the sugar. In a small bowl, add milk to cornstarch and stir to dissolve. Slowly add dissolved cornstarch to coconut mixture, taking care that lumps do not form. Continue to cook over low heat, stirring constantly, until mixture thickens, about 8 to 10 minutes, or until mixture coats the back of a wooden spoon.

Pour coconut mixture into a well-oiled 8-inch square pan, a 1½-quart mold, or individual serving dishes or goblets. Cool the custard somewhat, cover, and refrigerate for several hours.

At serving time, garnish with toasted coconut and/or whipped cream, if desired.

CHOCOLATE-DIPPED STRAWBERRIES

American   *4 to 6 servings*

Très chic to serve as a finale to a romantic supper, chocolate-covered strawberries are also an excellent accompaniment to Coeur à la Crème. They can be prepared several hours in advance, thus allowing the hostess to enjoy the last sips of wine with her guests before bringing out the dessert.

1 **pint strawberries, with stems on (preferably a very long-stemmed variety), washed and patted dry**	4 **ounces semisweet chocolate**
	1 **tablespoon cooking oil**

Spread strawberries on a working surface with a wax-paper-covered tray nearby. You will also need 1 or 2 bamboo skewers or other picks. In the top of a double boiler over hot water, melt the chocolate with the cooking oil, stirring to mix thoroughly. (The cooking oil will add a beautiful shine to the completed sweet.) Place melted chocolate near working surface, but keep the chocolate warm. One at a time, insert the skewer in the stem end of a strawberry and dip into the chocolate. Lift out and shake any excess chocolate back into the pot. Place the strawberry on the wax paper and continue with remaining berries. The strawberries should set for about 10 minutes before being served.

Chocolate-dipped strawberries can be refrigerated for up to 24 hours, during which time the chocolate will harden.

Variation: If desired, the strawberries can be injected with your favorite liqueur prior to dipping in chocolate. Other fresh fruits or sliced fruits can be dipped in chocolate, following this recipe.

CHEESECAKE SAUCE FOR FRESH FRUITS

American   *Approximately 2 cups*

A simple alternative to the classic cheesecake is this sauce to top fresh berries or a medley of cut-up seasonal fruits. Accompanied by party cookies, this is an excellent buffet dessert.

8 ounces cream cheese
½ cup sour cream
½ cup confectioner's sugar
4 egg yolks
4 tablespoons Triple Sec or other orange liqueur
1 teaspoon vanilla extract

Combine all ingredients in a food processor fitted with the metal chopping blade and process until creamy. Spoon into a serving bowl, cover, and refrigerate for several hours or several days. Spoon over fresh fruit.

Variation: This sauce can be served over a mixture of halved grapes and kiwi and banana slices. It's also outstanding with strawberries or raspberries.

FROZEN STRAWBERRY SOUFFLE

American   *6 to 8 servings*

Frozen fruit souffles make marvelous sweet endings to luncheons or dinners.

2 pints strawberries, washed and hulled
2 egg whites
1 cup sugar
1 tablespoon fresh lemon juice
1 teaspoon almond extract
1 teaspoon minced lemon rind

Cut up enough strawberries into small pieces to equal 2 cups, reserving a few large berries for garnish.

In a large bowl, beat egg whites at high speed until they start to hold a peak. Beat in sugar gradually, until egg whites are stiff. Continue at high speed, gradually adding the lemon juice and almond extract. Reduce the speed and carefully add the cut-up strawberries and lemon rind.

Lightly oil a 5-cup mold and pour in strawberry mixture. Cover and freeze several hours until firm. This dessert can be made a day or two in advance.

To serve, turn out of mold onto dessert platter and garnish top with reserved whole strawberries. Don't worry if the strawberry mixture separates into layers, as the resulting tastes are delicious—one very creamy and the other sherbety.

Variation: Other fruits, particularly berries, can be substituted for the strawberries.

FRENCH VANILLA-PEACH ICE CREAM

American   *6 to 10 servings*

Homemade ice creams are wonderful year-round, but especially for a 4th of July crowd.

3 **extra-large peaches (about
2 cups when cut up)**
Juice of ½ lemon
¼ **cup sugar (optional)**

Basic French Vanilla Mixture

¾ **cup sugar (see Note)**

2 **tablespoons flour**
⅛ **teaspoon salt**
1 **pint half-and-half**
2 **eggs, beaten until fluffy**
1½ **teaspoons vanilla extract**
1 **pint heavy cream**

Early in the day, or the day before, cut peaches into small pieces and place in a glass or plastic container. Squeeze lemon juice on top to hold color and mix thoroughly with the sugar, if desired. Cover and refrigerate.

To make the French vanilla mixture: Combine sugar, flour, and salt in the top of a double boiler over simmering water. Slowly add the half-and-half, stirring constantly. Cook mixture over low heat for about 15 minutes, until the sugar is fully dissolved and the cream lightly coats a wooden spoon.

Mix a little warm cream mixture into the beaten eggs to lighten them. Beat or whisk lightened eggs into cream mixture to prevent the uncooked eggs from hardening. Cook for another minute, stirring constantly. When fully cooled, stir in vanilla extract and heavy cream. Cover and refrigerate for 2 to 3 hours.

To complete the recipe, you can use either an ice cream maker or ice trays. *To use an ice cream maker:* Puree or mash half the peaches with all the juice and combine thoroughly with the cream mixture. Pour mixture into an ice cream maker and follow manufacturer's instructions for processing. Swirl the remaining peaches through the ice cream. Cover and freeze for several hours.

To use ice cube trays: Process the frozen mixture at least two times to ensure the best texture. When making homemade ice cream, the more often you take it out of the freezer and beat it, the creamier it will be.

Note: If the fruit has not been sweetened, increase the sugar to 2 cups.

Variation: Amaretto liqueur (2 to 4 tablespoons) can be added when presweetening the peaches, and other fruits can be substituted for peaches.

ROSEMARY'S LEMON ICE CREAM

American   *6 to 8 servings*

Many years ago, my dear friend and cooking buddy Annie Marino shared her mother's lemon ice cream recipe with me. I have made this recipe countless times. It's an excellent creamy homemade ice cream that can easily be made in the freezer. It will cool a spicy dinner for a tired soul.

 2 eggs
½ cup sugar
½ cup light corn syrup
¼ cup fresh lemon juice

1 teaspoon grated lemon rind
2 cups half-and-half

In a large bowl, beat the eggs until lemon-colored. Gradually add sugar, beating until mixture has a thick, custardlike consistency. Add remaining ingredients. Spoon into ice cube trays (without dividers) or any shallow container and place in freezer. When fairly stiff but not completely frozen, beat with an electric beater until light and fluffy. Return to freezer. Repeat process one more time. Freeze until needed.

Note: If desired, the ice cream can be frozen in a decorative mold and then brought to the table, unmolded, on a platter garnished with fresh mint leaves.

STRAWBERRIES-IN-A-BASKET PAVLOVA

Australian   *6 to 8 servings*

Here's a mouth-watering Pavlova, named after the famous ballerina: an elegant basket made of baked meringue, then a thin layer of whipped cream, and finally the crown filled with giant strawberries. You may also wish to fill the basket with kiwi slices in the traditional Australian manner.

4 egg whites at room
  temperature
  Dash salt
1 cup sugar
1 scant tablespoon
  cornstarch
1 teaspoon white wine
  vinegar

1 teaspoon vanilla extract
1 cup heavy cream, whipped
  and sweetened to taste
  with sugar
2 pints strawberries (or
  more), washed and hulled

In a large mixer bowl, beat egg whites at high speed, adding the salt. When the eggs become frothy, slowly add the sugar, one tablespoon at a time, continuing to beat at high speed. In a small bowl, mix 1 tablespoon of the sugar with the cornstarch; add this mixture after all the other sugar has been added. Next, beat in the vinegar, and then the vanilla extract. The final mixture should have a stiff and shiny appearance.

I like to shape this meringue mixture into a "basket" so that the final product will hold the strawberries. I have also been Pavlova shaped into a mound resembling half a football, with the whipped-cream icing the top and the fruit around the edges. With a spatula, spread the meringue into an 8- or 9-inch pie plate, "pulling up" around the edges to form a basket shape. Place in a preheated 250° oven for 1½ hours, or until lightly browned and dried. Cool completely on a wire rack.

At serving time, place whipped cream in the bottom and fill to the top with strawberries.

Variation: Softened vanilla ice cream can be substituted for the whipped cream.

TROPICAL LIME-RUM PIE

Caribbean Islands   *8 to 10 servings*

If you haven't visited the Caribbean Islands or another tropical hideaway, this lime and rum pie will make you feel like you're there. The simple coconut and almond crust is also excellent for other no-bake pies, such as a chocolate cream.

Coconut Almond Pie Shell

1 cup flaked sweetened
  coconut, finely chopped
  (see Note)
1½ cups blanched almonds,
  ground (see Note)
2 tablespoons sugar
¼ cup butter, melted

Lime Filling

Juice of 2 large limes (½
  cup)
2 lime rinds, grated

1 envelope unflavored gelatin
5 eggs, separated
1 cup sugar
2 tablespoons golden rum
  (or more to taste)
1 tablespoon brandy
  Few drops green food
  coloring (optional)
1 cup heavy cream, whipped

Garnish

½ cup toasted almond slices

In a small bowl, combine the coconut and almonds with the sugar and butter until well blended. With your fingers, press evenly into a 9-inch pie plate and bake in a preheated 350° oven for 10 minutes. Allow to cool thoroughly before filling.

To make the filling: Place lime juice in a small bowl and sprinkle gelatin on top; let sit 5 minutes to soften. Place egg yolks and ½ cup sugar in the top of a double boiler and beat with a wire whisk or electric beater until thick and light-colored, about 2 minutes. Place pot over second pot of simmering water, spoon in softened gelatin, and beat for about 6 minutes, or until the mixture becomes a thick custard. When you lift the beater, the custard will form mounds. Remove from heat and cool. Stir in reserved lime rind, rum, brandy, and green food coloring, if desired.

Beat egg whites until soft peaks form. Gradually beat in the remaining ½ cup sugar. Continue to beat until thick and white, as when making a meringue. Fold a spoonful of egg whites into the lime custard to lighten. Then gradually fold the custard into the egg whites. Gently fold whipped cream into the custard—do not overmix. Spoon into prepared pie crust and refrigerate several hours until firm. This pie can be made a day in advance.

To serve, garnish generously with toasted nuts.

Note: The coconut can be chopped and the almonds ground in a food processor.

ENGLISH TRIFLE

English   *6 to 8 servings*

This classic party trifle was created by my close friend Bobbi Felsot. Don't be fooled by its simplicity; it's as elegant as can be.

1 9-inch pound-cake loaf, purchased or homemade (refer to Sicilian Cassata—see Index)
¼ cup seedless raspberry jam
1 cup slivered blanched almonds
1 cup dry sherry
¼ cup brandy
3 or 4 firm bananas, sliced
2 pints fresh strawberries, washed and hulled, or 2 10-ounce packages frozen strawberries, defrosted and drained
1 pint fresh blueberries, washed, or 1 10-ounce package frozen blueberries, defrosted and drained
3 cups custard (refer to Nut Tortes with Zabaglione Custard and Berries—see Index) or 1 large package instant French vanilla pudding, prepared according to package instructions
½ pint heavy cream, whipped

Garnish

Additional fresh berries and nuts

Cut pound cake into 1-inch slices. Spread three slices with jam and place cake, jam side up, on the bottom of a traditional trifle dish or glass bowl. Cut remaining cake into 1-inch cubes; scatter over slices in the dish. Sprinkle almonds on top. Pour sherry and brandy on top and let cake macerate in the liquor at room temperature for 30 minutes or more.

Place a layer of bananas over the cake. Scatter a layer of strawberries on top, and then a layer of blueberries. Gently smooth the custard over the fruit. Refrigerate 2 to 3 hours.

To serve, top with whipped cream and garnish with extra berries and nuts.

STRAWBERRY FOOL

English   *6 servings*

Fruit fools can be made with practically any pureed fruit and whipped cream—there's no trick to this dessert. "Fool" refers to the French word fouler, *meaning "to crush."*

2 pints strawberries, washed and hulled	**1 cup heavy cream**
½ cup sugar	**2 tablespoons brandy or other favorite liqueur**
2 drops fresh lemon juice	

Put strawberries through a sieve to crush, or mash them in a food processor or blender and then strain through a sieve to remove seeds. In a bowl, mix the strawberries with the sugar and lemon juice. In another bowl, beat cream until peaks start to form. Add brandy and continue to beat to form peaks. Fold the flavored brandy into the strawberry mixture. Spoon into individual dessert dishes or champagne glasses.

Serve immediately or refrigerate until serving time. If chilled, bring to room temperature for about 15 to 30 minutes to remove the chill. This is a soft, custardy-looking dessert.

Variation: Other fruits that you might try are blueberries, raspberries, nectarines, and cooked rhubarb.

RASPBERRY FLUFF

English   *8 servings*

A fresh-fruit fluff, similar to a fool, is a lovely dessert to end an elegant dinner.

4 to 5 cups fresh raspberries	**1 cup heavy cream, lightly whipped**
⅔ cup sugar	
½ cup kirsch (cherry brandy or liqueur) or other fruit liqueur	**1 cup sour cream or crème fraîche (see Index)**

Puree raspberries, using a food processor or blender. Strain fruit through a sieve, colander, or cheesecloth to remove all seeds. Although this process takes some time, it is well worth the effort for the final result.

Place raspberries in a large bowl and add the sugar and kirsch. Gently fold in the whipped cream and sour cream.

Spoon into dessert glasses (tall stemmed wine glasses are ideal), cover, and refrigerate. The consistency is best when made at least 4 hours in advance.

Variation: Frozen raspberries or other berries can be substituted. If they are presweetened, reduce sugar to taste.

PUMPKIN-RUM FLAN

Filipino/Spanish/Mexican   *8 servings*

Flans are found in many Latin American cuisines and in Filipino cookery, which has felt a Spanish influence. In the Philippines, this dish might be enjoyed as a snack or at merienda, which can be compared to the Spanish afternoon snack or English high tea.

¾ cup sugar

1 cup heavy cream
1 cup half-and-half
1 cup pureed cooked
   pumpkin
¼ cup golden rum
6 eggs
½ cup sugar

1 teaspoon pumpkin pie spice or a combination of ground cinnamon, ginger, and nutmeg
½ teaspoon salt
1 tablespoon vanilla extract

Garnish (optional)

Whipped cream

Melt the ¾ cup sugar in a heavy (preferably nonstick) skillet over low to medium heat, stirring with a wooden spoon to break up any lumps. Cook until it becomes a golden syrup. Immediately pour the syrup into a 5-cup ring mold or other baking dish, tilting the mold to coat as much of the inside as possible. (It is important to hold the mold with asbestos mitts, as it gets very hot.) Set mold aside to cool. (See Note.)

To make the custard: Heat cream, half-and-half, and pumpkin in a saucepan, stirring well, until bubbles appear. Remove from heat and stir in rum. In a large bowl, beat the eggs with the sugar, spices, salt, and vanilla and slowly add to the pumpkin mixture. Pour into prepared mold.

Set mold in a larger, shallow baking dish and add boiling water to a 1-inch depth. Carefully place in a preheated 325° oven and bake for about 50 minutes, or until a knife inserted near the center comes out clean. Cool at room temperature, then refrigerate overnight.

Unmold onto a platter at serving time, using a sharp knife to carefully loosen the edges.

If desired, garnish slices with a dollop of whipped cream.

Note: If any caramel hardens in the skillet or on the spoon, add warm water and heat to melt the caramel, and then wash immediately.

FREE-FORM APPLE TART

French   *10 servings*

These free-form apple tarts are typical French bistro fare. They're easy to make with step-by-step instructions.

Tart Dough

- 4 cups all-purpose flour
- 2 teaspoons salt
- 2 tablespoons confectioner's sugar
- ¾ pound butter, cut up and softened
- 2 eggs at room temperature

Apple Filling

- 6 medium-size apples (I use Pippins)
- Lemon juice—water bath: 6 tablespoons lemon juice and 1 quart water
- ½ to 1 cup apricot jam, melted
- Sprinkling of sugar (optional)

To make the tart dough: I use a mixer, but if you do not have one, work by hand. In the bowl of a mixer, combine the flour, salt, and sugar and then add the butter. When the mixture is crumbly, add the eggs and mix thoroughly. Turn out of the bowl and shape into a large ball. Wrap the dough ball in wax paper and refrigerate for several hours, or for a day.

To shape the crust: Place dough ball on a lightly floured surface (a board, marble slab, or formica kitchen counter) and roll out. I have found that the first few minutes of rolling out is very difficult since the dough is so hard that it takes a lot of patience and strength. Roll dough to about ¼ to ½ inch thick, in the desired shape. For a free-form tart, transfer the rolled-out dough to a large, lightly buttered baking sheet. (I line my sheet with parchment paper and then butter it.) At this point, it is not necessary for the shape to be perfect.

To make a large rectangle, the edges should be considerably thicker than the center. With the aid of a little water (have a dish of icy water handy), pull up the edges and shape into a proper rectangular "pan," with the edges coming up about 1 to 2 inches. Patch any holes, tears, or odd edges, using the ice water. Prick the bottom all over with a fork and place the dough in the freezer for 10 minutes to firm up.

Peel, core, and halve the apples and immediately place them in water bath to hold the color. Removing one half at a time, thinly slice the apples and return the slices to the water bath.

Using a pastry brush, coat the pastry with apricot jam. Decoratively overlap the apple slices on the jam. If you wish, sprinkle apples with sugar.

At this point, you can either bake the tart as is or spread jam over the top before baking. If the jam is brushed on at this point, the apples cook in a fair amount of liquid and the result is very moist and juicy. However, it is more traditional to bake the tart without the top coating and then to brush the jam on during the very last minutes.

Bake tart in a preheated 350° oven for 45 to 60 minutes. If you added the jam prior to baking, check the tart during the baking and spoon some of the liquid over the apples.

Remove tart when the crust becomes golden and the apples are tender. If you haven't already added the top layer of jam, do so now. Cover the edges of the crust with a little foil so that the crust won't become black, and place the tart under the broiler to "crisp up" the apples and add a rich color.

Remove tart from the baking sheet and allow to cool several hours at room temperature before serving.

ALMOND TORTE WITH PEACHES AND CREAM

French   *8 to 12 servings*

Fresh peach shortcake is one of my husband's favorite desserts. I created this French version after being inspired by Roger Vergé's almond butter cake recipe, which I have made a multitude of times. Rather than layering biscuits, pound cake, or shortcake as is traditionally done for American shortcake, I have layered a flourless cake of ground almonds, eggs, and butter with the fruit and whipped cream.

Almond Butter Cake

½ pound whole blanched almonds
1 cup sugar
4 eggs at room temperature
Pinch salt
1¾ sticks (7 ounces) butter

Peach Filling

3 tablespoons Damson plum preserves or other favorite preserves, softened at room temperature

4 large peaches or 5 to 6 medium peaches
2 tablespoons lemon juice
1 cup heavy cream
1 to 2 tablespoons Amaretto liqueur or other favorite liqueur

Garnish

2 tablespoons sliced almonds

Using a blender or a food processor with metal blade, process almonds until minced, about 40 seconds; add sugar and process a few more seconds. Add one egg at a time and process until smooth. Add salt and butter, about 1 tablespoon at a time, and process about 1 minute, until mixture is smooth. (You can also prepare batter with an electric mixer. In this case, the nuts should first be fully ground and the butter softened to room temperature.)

Butter bottoms and sides of three 8-inch round cake pans and cut circles of wax paper to fit bottoms and place inside. Butter the wax paper. Divide the batter equally among the pans.

Bake in a preheated 375° oven for 18 to 25 minutes, until well browned like a cookie. Remove pans to racks and cool for about 10 minutes; the cakes will begin to shrink from sides of pans and sink in the center. Carefully turn out, upside down, on the palm of your hand; remove wax paper and place the cakes right side up on racks. Allow cakes to cool totally before completing recipe. The cakes can be made a day in advance and refrigerated or considerably longer in advance and frozen.

To make the filling: Peel peaches by placing them in boiling water for a few seconds and then in cold water; remove the skin with a sharp knife. Cut peaches into thin slices and place in a bowl with the lemon juice to hold the color. In a large chilled bowl (preferably copper or stainless steel), beat cream until soft peaks appear. Slowly add the liqueur, continuing to beat until the peaks are soft and fluffy. Do not overbeat, or you will have butter.

To assemble the torte: Spread preserves evenly over the top of each layer. Using ⅓ of the peaches for each layer, place the slices in a circular pattern on top of the preserves. Spread ⅓ of the whipped cream on top of one of the layers and place the second layer on top; repeat the process. Add the third layer and spread the remaining cream on top, garnish with almonds, and refrigerate until serving time.

The assembled torte will keep several hours in the refrigerator. Even though the whipped cream may begin to "fall," the cake is still gorgeous and, during this time, the flavors will begin to mingle.

Variation: Other fruits, such as berries or kiwi, can be substituted for the peaches. Liqueur and preserves should be adjusted to taste when substituting fruits.

COEUR À LA CRÈME

French   *6 to 8 servings*

A Coeur à la Crème mixture is classically spooned into a proper heart-shaped porcelain mold or wicker basket and then refrigerated for several hours to drain off the whey. The resulting dessert is similar to a crustless cheesecake, although it is much lighter and fluffier. It is traditionally accompanied by a strawberry sauce or sugared fresh strawberries.

Many years ago, I adapted the following recipe from one I had read in Dione Lucas's book on French cooking. I have made it dozens of times, especially for anniversaries, birthdays, and Valentine's Day. There are many recipes for Coeur à la Crème. Some list cottage cheese in the ingredients instead of confectioner's sugar; the resulting dish is more cheeselike. There is also a version prepared as an appetizer instead of dessert.

Cold water, baking soda, and 1 tablespoon lemon juice (to prepare the cheesecloth)
8 ounces cream cheese, softened
⅔ cup confectioner's sugar
1¼ cups heavy cream
1 teaspoon vanilla extract

Strawberry Sauce
1 pint fresh strawberries, hulled, or 1 20-ounce bag frozen unsweetened strawberries, defrosted and drained
⅓ cup crème de cassis
¾ cup seedless red raspberry preserves

Cut a square of cheesecloth large enough to hang 3 inches over the sides of the mold. (If you are making individual molds instead of one large mold, you will need several squares of cheesecloth.) Soak the cheesecloth in ice water to which a pinch of baking soda and 1 tablespoon lemon juice have been added. Set aside.

In a bowl, beat the cream cheese until fluffy. Add sugar and beat again until well blended. In another bowl, begin whipping the cream. When it reaches soft peaks, add vanilla and continue to whip until a bit firmer. Carefully fold the cheese-sugar mixture into the whipped cream.

Remove the cheesecloth from the water, wring it dry, and line the mold. Spoon creamed mixture into the mold, carefully packing down, and fold excess cheesecloth over top. Place the mold on a dish so that the whey drips into the dish, and refrigerate for several hours. I find it easiest to prepare this recipe a day in advance.

To make the sauce: Place strawberries in a serving bowl and pour liqueur on them. In a small saucepan, melt the preserves over low heat; if there are seeds, strain the preserves through a sieve. Pour melted preserves over the strawberries and refrigerate for at least one hour.

To serve dessert, unmold onto serving platter and accompany with strawberry sauce. Cut a small wedge of this cream for each person, and top with sauce.

Variation: For the hors d'oeuvre variety of Coeur à la Crème, blend together 2 cups each softened cream cheese, sour cream, and heavy cream, and a pinch of salt. (If you like it sweeter, gradually beat in 2 tablespoons confectioner's sugar.) Proceed as in preceding recipe, but garnish with a dollop of caviar or salmon roe rather than the strawberry sauce.

FIGS WITH BLUEBERRIES

French   *6 servings*

Based upon a classic French recipe of figs with raspberries, I find this dessert a refreshing end to a spicy meal. Think about serving it for a luncheon dessert. You can make this several hours in advance and then serve it in individual crystal goblets or in one large beautiful dish. The crème fraîche is served on the side to be generously spooned on top.

6 fresh firm, ripe figs
1 pint blueberries
2 tablespoons Damson plum preserves or plum jelly

1 tablespoon crème de cassis or kirsch
1 cup crème fraîche (see Index)

Using a sharp paring knife, carefully pull back and cut off the skin of figs, trying not to lose too much flesh. Place figs, standing up, in individual dishes or one large serving dish and surround them with blueberries.

In a small saucepan, melt the preserves or jelly; do not bring to a boil. Add liqueur and heat thoroughly. With a spoon, carefully drizzle preserves over each fig. Cover and refrigerate.

At serving time, bring to room temperature. Generously spoon crème fraîche over individual servings.

SWEET POTATO AND ALMOND HALVA

Indian   *12 servings*

In India, street vendors sell a variety of candies and confections (halvais) made by professional sweetmakers. This sweet potato and almond halva resembles a sweet porridge and is a little softer than fudge. Halvas are also made from other grated vegetables, such as carrots, beets, or pumpkin.

1½ pounds sweet potatoes, peeled and coarsely grated
2 cups milk
½ cup sugar
2 tablespoons clarified butter or ghee (see Index)
¼ teaspoon ground saffron
¼ teaspoon ground cardamom

1 cup blanched almonds, ground

Garnish

Shelled pistachio nuts and/or toasted almond slices

Place grated potatoes in a heavy pot with the milk. Bring to a boil; then reduce heat and cook, stirring frequently, for 20 to 25 minutes, or until milk is fully absorbed. Stir in sugar, clarified butter, saffron, and cardamom. Simmer another 10 minutes.

Spread halva into a 9-inch pie plate, garnish generously with nuts, and allow to cool. Serve at room temperature. Cut into pieces as you would fudge.

CHRISTINA'S INDONESIAN AVOCADO DESSERT

Indonesian   *6 to 8 servings*

An Indonesian avocado dessert that is velvety and luscious to eat.

2 medium avocados, very ripe	1 teaspoon finely grated lime rind
1 cup heavy cream, whipped to the soft-peak stage	
½ to 1 cup sugar to taste	Garnish (optional)
Dash salt	Slivers of fresh pineapple
2 tablespoons lime juice	with skin on

In a food processor or blender, process the avocados until very smooth. Add cream, sugar, salt, lime juice, and rind and process for a few seconds until well blended.

To serve, spoon into individual parfait glasses or goblets and garnish with pineapple, if desired.

This dessert can be made a few hours in advance, covered, and refrigerated, but it will not keep more than 8 hours, as it will begin to separate.

COCONUT CREAM PUDDING

Indonesian/Brazilian   *8 servings*

Fresh coconut cream as the basis of sweets can be found in every tropical country where coconuts proliferate. This smooth pudding recipe, similar in technique to a French souffle or mousse, travels from as far away as Brazil, where it is an egg sweet called quindin (sometimes made without the egg whites), and Indonesia, where it is called serigaja. Coconut milk–based custards are also found in Filipino cooking.

¼ cup butter at room temperature	8 eggs at room temperature, separated
1 cup sugar	1¼ cups coconut cream (see Index)
¼ teaspoon cinnamon	

In a bowl, cream the butter with the sugar and cinnamon until light. Mix in 1 egg yolk at a time. Gradually add the coconut cream. (If the cream and creamed butter mixture should separate, process in a food processor or blender until well blended.)

Beat egg whites until fluffy and almost stiff, but not dry. Fold into coconut cream mixture.

Pour liquid into a well-buttered 4-cup souffle or custard dish, or into 8 well-buttered individual dishes. Place dish(es) in a larger baking dish and add enough hot water to come up about halfway.

Bake in a preheated 350° oven for 40 to 45 minutes, or until set and the pudding begins to pull away from the sides of the dish(es). Cool at room temperature and refrigerate until serving.

SICILIAN CASSATA

Italian   *8 to 12 servings*

This classic Italian dessert is a magnificent addition to any buffet. Although there are three major steps in this recipe, much can be made in advance. A

9-inch pound cake from a bakery can be substituted for the homemade, but you can make the cake base weeks in advance and store it in your freezer. The unusual chocolate glaze, which hardens when refrigerated and creates a brick-like cake, is the crowning glory of this recipe.

Pound Cake

½ **pound butter at room temperature**
1 **cup sugar**
5 **eggs**
2¼ **cups sifted cake flour**
¼ **teaspoon salt**
1 **teaspoon vanilla extract**
½ **teaspoon lemon extract**

4 **to 6 teaspoons Galliano liqueur or other favorite liqueur, such as Grand Marnier or Amaretto**

Cheese and Fruit Filling

½ **pound ricotta cheese**
½ **cup confectioner's sugar, sifted**
1 **teaspoon almond extract**
¼ **cup chopped candied fruits**
1 **small lemon rind, grated**
2 **to 4 tablespoons semisweet chocolate pieces**

Chocolate Glaze

6 **ounces semisweet chocolate pieces**
½ **cup heavy cream**
2 **teaspoons Galliano liqueur**

To make the pound cake: Beat butter with an electric mixer until soft. Add sugar in small amounts, beating until mixture is well blended. Beat in one egg at a time and gradually add flour and salt, beating until everything is fully mixed. Beat in vanilla and lemon extracts.

Spoon batter into a well-buttered 9-by-5-inch loaf pan and bake in a preheated 325° oven for about 1¼ hours, or until a toothpick comes out clean. Allow the cake to cool a few minutes in the pan and then turn out on a rack to cool fully. When cooled, the cake can be wrapped and refrigerated until needed or used immediately.

Trim the top of the pound cake, removing any high bump, so that cake resembles a brick, and slice horizontally into thirds. Place on a sheet of aluminum foil. Sprinkle the underside of the top layer and the tops of the other two layers with the Galliano; set aside.

To make the filling: Process cheese in food processor or push through a sieve until smooth. Add sugar and continue to process until well blended. Add almond extract; process again. Add candied fruits, lemon zest, and chocolate; quickly pulse to blend.

Spread half the cheese mixture on the bottom layer of cake. Add the middle slice of cake, spread with the remaining cheese mixture, and top with the last layer of cake. Wrap very tightly with foil and chill several hours or overnight.

To make the glaze: Melt chocolate with the cream in the top of a double boiler over barely simmering water. Cool slightly and stir in the Galliano.

A few hours before serving, place cassata loaf on a wire rack over wax paper. Spread glaze on the top and sides, using a pastry brush to help paint the sides. Refrigerate until serving. To serve, slice vertically.

The whole unsliced cassata will keep in the refrigerator for several days.

Variations: Toasted slivered almonds can be substituted for the chocolate pieces in the filling. Whipped cream can be substituted for the chocolate glaze; if desired, dust with unsweetened cocoa.

BOCCONE DOLCE—MERINGUE, WHIPPED CREAM, CHOCOLATE, AND FRESH FRUIT DESSERT

Italian   *8 to 10 servings*

The pièce de résistance of my classic Mother's Day Brunch is this sweet, mouth-watering dessert composed of a multilayered cake of meringues, chocolate, whipped cream, and fresh fruits. Although you need plenty of time to put this together, it should be done a day in advance, thus adding no last-minute demands to your other cooking chores.

Meringues
  6 egg whites at room
     temperature
     Pinch of salt
  ¼ teaspoon cream of tartar
  1½ cups sugar

Chocolate Layer
  6 ounces semisweet chocolate
  3 tablespoons water

Whipped Cream Layer and Icing
  2 pints heavy cream
  2 to 3 tablespoons crème de cassis or other favorite liqueur
  1 to 1½ pounds fresh seedless grapes, cut in half horizontally

Garnish
  4 large kiwi, peeled and thinly sliced

To make the meringues: In a large bowl, beat the egg whites with the salt until they are foamy. Add the cream of tartar and continue to beat until soft peaks form. Gradually beat in the sugar until the meringue batter is shiny and stiff.

There is an easy way to shape meringues. Place three 8-inch cake pans on a sheet of parchment paper and draw circles around them. Cut out the circles and place them on the inverted (upside down) pans. Then bake the meringues on the parchment circles, using the inverted cake pans as support forms.

Divide the batter into three parts and, with a spatula, spread it evenly on the three parchment circles. Place pans in a preheated 250° oven and bake for one hour. Turn off the heat and let the meringues dry for another hour. Remove the meringues from the oven, carefully pull off the parchment paper, and place on wire racks to cool completely.

Melt the chocolate and water together in the top of a double boiler over gently simmering water, stirring until smooth. Spread chocolate over the top of two of the meringues. Again, place on wire racks to cool. The chocolate will harden somewhat.

Whip the cream. As soft to medium peaks form, add the liqueur and continue to whip a few more seconds.

Assemble your meringue cake directly on the serving platter. (Because the whipped cream is not very stable and some of the liquid will drip, use a platter with raised edges to catch the excess. Otherwise, your refrigerator may get very messy.) Place one chocolate-covered meringue, chocolate side up, in the center of the platter. Using a spatula, spread about ½ to 1 inch of whipped cream on top. Cover with half the sliced grapes. Top with the second chocolate-covered meringue, chocolate side up. Again, cover it with whipped cream and then sliced grapes. Now, top with the plain meringue. Completely frost the top and sides with the whipped cream and garnish the top with the sliced kiwi.

Refrigerate the dessert for 24 hours, occasionally checking the whipped cream. If it is dripping or separating, wipe the platter clean with paper towels. During this period, the cake's flavors will mellow, the meringue will soften slightly, and the chocolate will harden.

Variation: You may substitute 2 pints fresh strawberries, hulled and sliced lengthwise, for the grapes. In this case, you may wish to garnish the top with 8 large whole strawberries instead of the sliced kiwi.

FROZEN MANGO MOUSSE

Latin American   *6 servings*

The color of this simple, refreshing dessert is a vibrant orange. Ideal to serve both with a luncheon or dinner, and excellent after a piquant entree, it can be made several days in advance.

3 ripe mangoes	1 envelope plain gelatin
Juice of 1 lemon	½ cup fresh orange juice
Lemon rind, grated	⅓ cup sugar
2 tablespoons rum or orange	1 egg white
liqueur	

With a sharp paring knife, slice through mangoes lengthwise around the central flat pit. Then, slice each half into quarters, peel off the skin, and cut the remaining mango flesh away from the pits. Puree the flesh in a food processor or blender. Blend in the lemon juice, rind, and rum; set aside.

In a small saucepan, soften the gelatin and the orange juice for about 5 minutes. Stir in sugar, place saucepan over low heat, and cook slowly until the gelatin and sugar are thoroughly dissolved. Stir gelatin mixture into mango mixture, and then spoon into a large, shallow metal pan and freeze until it begins to thicken, about 45 minutes to 1 hour.

In a small bowl, beat the egg white until light and fluffy. Beat into mango mixture and return to freezer overnight. (Mango mousse will keep several days in the freezer.)

Remove from freezer and leave at room temperature about 15 minutes before serving to soften somewhat. Slice into rectangles and serve on dessert plates or scoop into balls and serve in sherbet glasses.

Mango mousse can also be frozen in a souffle dish with a foil collar.

Variation: Papaya can be substituted for mango.

CINNAMON CUSTARD

Mexican   *6 to 8 servings*

Not too sweet, this cinnamony custard is a soothing, creamy finale to a spicy dinner.

4 cups milk	**Pinch salt**
4 eggs at room temperature	**1½ teaspoons vanilla extract**
¼ cup sugar	**Additional ground**
1 teaspoon ground cinnamon	**cinnamon for topping**

Pour milk into the top of a double boiler and heat over simmering water to scald. When a light layer of skin begins to form, remove from heat and cool slightly.

In a large bowl, lightly beat eggs. Beat sugar into eggs, then add the cinnamon, salt, and vanilla and pour into a 1½ quart baking dish. Sprinkle the top with cinnamon.

Place the baking dish in the center of a larger baking dish and put enough hot water in the second dish to come up at least 2 inches. Bake in a preheated 350° oven for about 35 minutes, or until a knife inserted in center comes out clean.

Place the baking dish on a rack and allow to cool to room temperature. Refrigerate several hours before serving.

CHEESE PASHKA

Russian   *12 to 18 servings*

Ukrainian cheese pashka (pashka translates to "Easter") is a traditional Easter sweet, resembling in texture and taste a crustless cheesecake studded with candied fruits and nuts. Classically, it is prepared in a pyramid-shaped wooden mold and then refrigerated for at least 24 hours to allow the whey to drain and the cheese and egg mixture to become firm. When unmolded, it is decorated with more slices of fruits and nuts and accompanied by a sweet yeast bread.

I find this dessert to be an excellent addition to my Christmas-sweets buffet table, especially since the candied fruits are easily available and most popular at that time of year.

This version is cooked for a creamy, rich, and custardy taste and texture.

6 ounc :s butter, softened
1½ cups confectioner's sugar,
 sifted
4 egg yolks, beaten until
 light-colored
2 pounds large-curd cottage
 cheese
1 cup heavy cream
1½ teaspoons vanilla extract
¼ teaspoon salt
½ cup candied citron or

mixed candied fruits, finely
 chopped
¼ cup golden raisins or
 currants
¼ cup dark raisins
½ cup slivered almonds,
 toasted and chopped
1 small lemon rind, grated

Garnish

Candied maraschino
 cherries, cut in half

Cheese pashka can be made in a traditional pyramid-shaped pashka mold, a clean clay or plastic flower pot (minimum size, 7 inches) with a hole in the bottom, a chinoise, or a Coeur à la Crème mold. Line the mold with four thicknesses of dampened cheesecloth, allowing enough cloth to be folded over the top of the filled mold.

Using an electric mixer with a stainless steel bowl, beat butter and sugar until well mixed and light-colored. Slowly beat in egg yolks. Process cheese in a food processor or press through a sieve until smooth and add to egg mixture, again beating until well blended. Stir in cream, vanilla, salt, candied citron, raisins, nuts, and lemon rind.

Place mixing bowl over a second large pot of gently simmering water to simulate a double boiler. (The quantity of pashka mixture is too great for a normal-size double boiler.) Stir constantly until the mixture thickens and bubbles begin to appear along the outer rim, about 30 minutes. Do not let it come to a boil. Allow the mixture to cool, stirring occasionally to assure a smooth, creamy texture. It will thicken considerably as it cools.

Pour pashka mixture into lined mold (I use a chinoise). The mold should be set on a plate to catch the whey drippings. Place another plate on top, weight down with a heavy object, and refrigerate for a minimum of 24 hours or, better, 2 to 3 days.

Prior to serving, carefully unmold and unwrap the cheesecloth. Decorate the sides, bottom rim, and top with candied maraschino cherry halves. Refrigerate until serving. Accompany with slices of a sweet yeast bread or pound cake (refer to Sicilian Cassata—see Index).

Variation: My dear friend Debbie Pipino has a simple family version of Russian pashka that calls for 3 egg yolks, ½ cup sugar, ½ cup milk, ⅓ pound butter, 2 pounds dry cottage cheese, 2 teaspoons vanilla extract, ¼ cup candied cherries, and 4 ounces blanched almonds. Beat eggs and sugar until light. Warm the milk and add butter, stirring until it melts. Slowly add the egg mixture to the warm milk. Let cool. Put cheese through a meat grinder or food processor and add to the egg mixture. Stir in fruit and nuts. Pour mixture into a cheesecloth-lined mold and proceed according to preceding recipe. Refrigerate 24 hours.

CARAMEL EGG CUSTARD

International   *6 to 8 servings*

Melted sugar becomes a syrupy glaze for this all-time-favorite French-American baked egg custard, which is called flan in Latin American cookery. You can make this in individual custard dishes for family dining or in one larger 5-cup ring or decorative mold for entertaining.

1 cup sugar	¼ teaspoon salt
5 eggs at room temperature	3½ cups milk, heated to a low simmer
2 to 3 teaspoons finely grated vanilla bean or 2 teaspoons vanilla extract	
	Garnish (optional)
2 to 3 teaspoons finely grated lemon or orange rind	Fresh berries

Over very low heat in a small, heavy skillet, melt ½ cup sugar, stirring occasionally with a wooden spoon. Do not allow sugar to burn. The result should be a rich golden brown caramel. Immediately pour into a 5-cup ring or decorative mold, tilting the mold to coat as much of the dish as possible before the caramel hardens. Set mold aside to cool.

In a large bowl, beat eggs. Slowly whisk in the remaining ½ cup sugar, vanilla, lemon or orange rind, and salt. When the sugar has fully dissolved, slowly whisk in the warm milk. Pour egg mixture into the caramel-coated mold.

Place the mold in a larger baking dish and put on the lower shelf of a preheated 325° oven. Immediately pour 1 to 2 inches of hot, almost boiling, water into the larger dish. As the custard cooks, the water should remain at a low simmer. Bake custard about 50 to 60 minutes, or until a knife inserted near the center comes out clean. Remove mold from water and place on a rack to cool to room temperature. Refrigerate for several hours before serving.

At serving time, unmold. Carefully loosen the sides of the mold with the tip of a knife or spatula. Place a serving dish on top of the mold and carefully turn over. Tap the mold so that the caramel runs down the sides.

If desired, you can fill the center of a ring-shaped custard or decorate the sides with fresh berries.

CHOCOLATE MOUSSE IN MOUSSE SHELL

International   *6 to 8 servings*

What could possibly be better than a luscious chocolate mousse? A mousse pie shell filled with mousse. This French-American recipe, created by my dear family friend Dori Phillips, is a most ingenious concept of baking half the mousse to create a pie shell and then filling it with the remaining rich chocolatey custard.

3 teaspoons instant espresso
coffee
8 ounces semisweet chocolate
¼ cup boiling water
8 eggs, separated
⅔ cup sugar
1 teaspoon vanilla extract
Pinch salt

Pinch cream of tartar
½ cup chopped walnuts
Butter
Fine bread crumbs

Garnish

Whipped cream
Shaved chocolate
(optional)

In the top of a double boiler over barely simmering water and very low heat, melt the chocolate with the coffee and boiling water. When the chocolate is almost melted, remove from heat and whisk the mixture until very smooth.

In a large bowl, beat egg yolks until thick. Gradually beat in ½ cup sugar until mixture is thick and lemon-colored. Gradually beat the chocolate and then the vanilla into the yolk mixture. Beat the egg whites until foamy, and add salt and cream of tartar. Continue beating until soft peaks form, then gradually add the remaining sugar and continue beating until stiff peaks form. Fold a dollop of whites into the chocolate mixture to lighten the batter. Carefully fold in remaining whites, combining thoroughly. Fold in the nuts.

Generously butter a 9-inch pie plate and dust with dry bread crumbs. Fill the plate with half the chocolate mixture—it should be even with the edge of the plate. Refrigerate remaining mousse.

Place pie plate on the middle rack in a preheated 350° oven and bake 25 minutes. Turn off oven and let the mousse remain for 5 more minutes. Remove to a wire rack and cool for about 2 hours. As the baked mousse cools, it will sink in the center, thus creating a pie shell.

Fill this shell with the remaining mousse and refrigerate at least 2 to 3 hours. At serving time, garnish with whipped cream and, if desired, shaved chocolate.

Variation: The mousse mixture, unbaked, can be served alone as a French mousse or as rich chocolate pots de crème, if you have individual demitasse cups. Pour into a large mold or individual pots de crème cups and refrigerate until firm and cold, even overnight.

CHOCOLATE BAVARIAN CREAM

International   *6 servings*

A light, delicate European dessert, often served with slices of fresh fruit such as strawberries or peaches, Bavarian creams are a summertime favorite. Made with gelatin and cream, this chocolatey one will be a favorite of yours year-round.

2 eggs at room temperature,
separated

1¼ cups milk
½ teaspoon vanilla extract

½ cup sugar
2 tablespoons cocoa
(preferably semisweet)
⅛ teaspoon salt

1 tablespoon unflavored
gelatin
1 cup heavy cream

With a wire whisk or an egg beater, beat egg yolks, milk, and vanilla together in the top of a double boiler. Whisk in ¼ cup sugar, cocoa, and salt. Sprinkle gelatin on the surface and allow to sit for 5 minutes to soften gelatin. Mix well. Place pot over second pot of gently boiling water and heat, stirring constantly, 3 to 5 minutes, or until mixture is thoroughly combined. Remove from heat and chill about an hour, or until slightly thickened.

In a large bowl, beat egg whites until peaks hold. Fold chilled gelatin mixture into the egg whites. Whip cream until soft peaks form. Slowly beat in remaining sugar. Fold a little whipped cream into the chocolate mixture to lighten it and then carefully fold chocolate mixture into the remaining whipped cream.

Turn chocolate mixture into a lightly oiled 4-cup mold or six individual molds. Chill several hours until firm.

Unmold and serve with fresh fruits and/or sugar-dusted cookies or a simple fruit sauce made of pureed fresh strawberries.

Variation: For a slightly tangy flavor, replace half the cream with plain yogurt.

OVEN-POACHED PEARS IN A WHISKEY ORANGE SAUCE

International   *4 servings*

When traveling in Europe I first enjoyed poached pears fragrant with orange and liqueur. In trying to re-create this delicacy, I devised this simple dessert.

4 pears, washed
1 cup whiskey, bourbon, or
Strega
½ cup sugar
1 6-ounce container frozen
orange juice concentrate,
defrosted

2 tablespoons Triple Sec or
other orange-flavored
liqueur
1 whole cinnamon stick

Garnish

Whipped cream

Place the whole, unpeeled pears stem up in a deep baking dish. Mix together the whiskey, sugar, orange juice, and liqueur, stirring to dissolve the sugar, and pour over the pears. Add cinnamon stick.

Cover and bake in a preheated 375° oven for 30 minutes; uncover and bake another 30 minutes, or until tender, basting occasionally. Chill.

At serving time, place pears in individual goblets or glass dishes, spoon sauce on top, and garnish with whipped cream.

Note: Some people prefer their poached pears peeled and cored. If so, peel prior to cooking and cut in half. Remove core and brush inside and outside with fresh lemon juice to help hold the color.

Variation: Fresh peaches that have been peeled, halved, pitted, and brushed with lemon juice can be substituted for the pears.

STEWED RHUBARB

International   *6 to 8 servings*

The first stalks of rhubarb at the produce stands are a sign that spring has arrived. Although most people associate rhubarb with pies, it is excellent when simply baked or simmered and then chilled. (I find the oven technique to be far gentler on the rhubarb.) The cooked fruit can be pureed and folded into whipped cream and served as a mousse or fruit fool; thickened with cornstarch and served as a Scandinavian pudding (rabarbragrøt); thickened with potato starch and served as a Russian pudding (kisel); or served with whipped cream or crème fraîche on the side.

A little caution should be taken with rhubarb: be sure not to eat the leaves, as they contain high levels of poisonous oxalic acid.

2 pounds rhubarb, washed and cut into 1- to 2-inch pieces	**¾ cup orange juice or water**
	1 tablespoon lemon juice
1 cup sugar (or more to taste)	

Place rhubarb in a large baking dish. Sprinkle with sugar and pour orange and lemon juices on top. Cover and bake in a 350° oven for 30 minutes. Chill until serving time.

Variation: To prepare the Scandinavian or Russian puddings, dilute 2 tablespoons of cornstarch or potato starch in ¼ cup cold water and add to stewed rhubarb. Bring to a boil, stirring constantly, then reduce to a simmer and cook about 3 minutes, until thickened; chill several hours.

OASIS FRUITS

International   *6 servings*

This combination of oranges, almonds, dates, and golden raisins hints at the influences of Israeli and Moroccan cuisines. It is sweet yet refreshing, like an oasis in the desert. Serve as a side dish with heavily spiced or simple roasted foods, or as an unusual dessert.

4 large oranges (about 2½ pounds), peeled and thinly sliced	**½ cup pitted dried dates, chopped**
	2 tablespoons golden raisins

⅓ cup almond slices   ⅓ cup brandy
⅔ cup fresh orange juice

Combine the fruits and nuts in a bowl. Mix the orange juice and brandy and pour on top of the fruits; toss gently. Cover and refrigerate several hours before serving, occasionally spooning juice on top.

To serve, place the fruit in a large dish, such as a footed trifle bowl, or offer individual portions, along with the brandied juice, in small goblets or bowls.

GINGER-MELON ICE

International   *6 servings*

This is one of my top choices to follow an Oriental luncheon or dinner.

1 large cantaloupe   2 tablespoons candied
⅓ cup sugar   ginger, finely minced
⅔ cup water
2 tablespoons fresh lemon
  juice

Remove rind and seeds from cantaloupe, cut into large chunks, and puree in a food processor or blender. You need about 2½ cups of fruit.

To make a simple syrup, mix the sugar and water in a saucepan, bring to a boil over medium heat, stirring to dissolve the sugar, and simmer another 5 minutes. Allow to cool.

Combine the cantaloupe and lemon juice and stir in the cooled simple syrup. Pour the mixture into an ice cream maker and follow manufacturer's instructions, or pour into ice cube trays, cover, and freeze.

If using an ice cream maker, add candied ginger before placing the mixture in the freezer. Cover and freeze several hours. If using ice cube trays, break up the firmed-up ice after a few hours, add the candied ginger, stir well, cover, and return to freezer.

WATERMELON ICE

International   *8 servings*

This simple sorbet or gratinée to enjoy on a hot summer afternoon or evening can be made in an ice cream maker or in ice cube trays. Other melons can be prepared in this same manner.

1½ cups water   4 cups pureed watermelon
 ¾ cup sugar   (simplest done in a food
                                       processor)
                                    1 lime, juice and grated rind

Make a simple syrup by bringing the water and sugar to a boil in a heavy saucepan over moderate heat; stir until sugar is dissolved. Reduce heat to a simmer for 5 minutes. The grated lime rind can be added while making the syrup. Allow to cool.

Mix the cooled syrup, pureed watermelon, and lime juice together and pour into an ice cream maker; follow manufacturer's instructions. Eat immediately or freeze for later use. Watermelon ice can also be made in ice cube trays. To ensure a smooth texture, after the mixture has become firm, process with an electric mixer or food processor and then return to ice cube trays. Freeze again until firm, about 3 to 4 hours.

This ice should be served a little soft, so remove from freezer 5 to 10 minutes before serving.

It is best to eat fresh fruit ices within a few days.

NUT TORTES WITH ZABAGLIONE CUSTARD AND BERRIES

International   *4 to 8 servings*

One of my favorite desserts is fresh raspberries with warm zabaglione, an Italian Marsala-flavored custard sauce. (Sabayon sauce, or wine custard, is zabaglione by another name.) When planning the menu for one dinner party, I decided to make the custard in advance and refrigerate it to use as a topping for assorted berries and kiwi slices. Another time, I decided to expand upon this Italian classic for an elegant evening picnic at the Hollywood Bowl. I created a chewy flourless nut-cookie base for the zabaglione, which was topped generously with raspberries.

Zabaglione Custard
- 3 egg yolks at room temperature
- ⅓ cup sugar
- ½ cup Marsala wine
- 1 cup heavy cream, whipped (optional)

Individual Nut Tortes
- 3 cups finely chopped walnuts or blanched almonds or a combination of the two

- ¼ cup sugar
- ¼ cup butter at room temperature
- ½ teaspoon vanilla extract
- 1 egg, lightly beaten

- ½ pint raspberries

To make the zabaglione: Place the egg yolks in a stainless steel or copper bowl and beat with a wire whisk or electric mixer until smooth and yellow (as when making mayonnaise). Slowly beat in the sugar until the mixture becomes a pale white and the texture resembles ribbons. This takes about 8 to 10 minutes. Do not rush the cooking process, or the egg yolks will stick to the pan and the sauce will not properly increase in volume.

Place the bowl over a larger pot of barely simmering water. Continue to beat very, very slowly, whisking in the Marsala, for about 20 minutes. Remove from the heat and whisk for another minute. You now have a beautiful warm zabaglione. The custard should be pale yellow and almost triple its original volume.

To cool immediately, place entire bowl of zabaglione in a larger bowl of cold water with ice cubes; continue to whisk custard until it is cold. Unfortunately, the volume deflates, but the taste is marvelous. One cup of whipped cream can be folded into chilled zabaglione for a lighter sauce. If not using immediately, place zabaglione in a plastic, glass, or porcelain container, cover, and refrigerate.

To prepare the nut tortes: In a food processor or blender, thoroughly mix the chopped nuts, sugar, butter, vanilla, and egg. Butter four 4½-inch tart pans (I prefer the small, fluted pans with easy-to-remove bottoms). Divide the nut mixture evenly among the pans and press into bottoms and sides. Each pan contains a generous portion, as the resulting torte base is actually a chewy flourless cookie; if you want a thinner base, the mixture is sufficient for six individual pans. Chill the torte bases in the freezer for 20 minutes to allow the butter to harden somewhat. Bake in a preheated 375° oven for about 18 minutes, or until nicely browned. Allow tortes to cool in pans before removing. (See Note.) The nut torte can also be baked in one large pan.

At serving time, fill the center of each torte base with zabaglione and top with raspberries.

Note: When I took these tortes to the picnic, I removed them from the pans, allowed them to cool fully, washed the pans, and then returned the tortes to the pans as containers in the picnic basket.

Variation: Other wines or liquors are often substituted for the Marsala, such as dry white wine, port, sauterne, sherry, or champagne. Other fruits may be substituted for raspberries—another favorite berry or sliced kiwi, peaches, or nectarines.

Additional Desserts

Blueberry Soup

Candied Sweet Potatoes

Crème Fraîche

Kaernemaelkskodskaal

Shrikhanp (variation of laban)

Special Ingredients and Techniques

SPECIAL INGREDIENTS

Throughout this book I have made great use of fresh produce and ethnic ingredients. In many cases, I have given explanations or suggested substitutions for the more unusual items, which may not be readily available. With the growing interest in ethnic cuisines and the constant immigration to the United States of peoples from other countries, most major markets carry an extensive selection of international items, and small ethnic markets are increasing in abundance. Check your telephone directory for their locations.

Azuki beans: Dried small red beans. Must be soaked several hours or overnight before use. In Japanese cooking they are most often prepared with sugar and/or honey to be eaten as a sweet. Other small red beans can be substituted. Available in most supermarkets and Oriental and health-food stores.

Bagoong alamang: Shrimp paste used in Filipino cooking, similar to Thai kapee, with an anchovylike flavor and aroma. Another Oriental fish paste or anchovy paste may be substituted. Available in Oriental markets.

Bonito flakes: *See* Katsuo bushi.

Bulgur: Cracked wheat. Found in three grades or thicknesses—fine, medium, and heavy. Must be soaked and drained before using. A popular ingredient for many Middle Eastern recipes. Available in Middle Eastern specialty and health-food markets.

Burdock root (gobo): Skinny, firm, woody-looking roots, usually a little thicker than a finger and about 1½ feet long. Store in the vegetable section of the refrigerator. Must be scrubbed well to remove the outer layer and then soaked in a vinegar-water solution to help retain the white color and crunchy texture. Used in many Japanese recipes. Available in Oriental specialty markets and many gourmet produce sections.

Cilantro: Also referred to as Chinese parsley; equivalent to *yuen sai* (Chinese) or *coentro* (Portuguese). Fresh coriander. A fragrant, flat-leafed herb that is an important ingredient in many international recipes, especially Latin American, Oriental, Russian, and African. Parsley can be substituted but the taste and aroma of the final dish will not be the same. It is also easy to grow. To store for several days, place stems in a glass of water (like fresh flowers), encase the leaves in a small produce plastic bag, and keep in the refrigerator. Generally available in the produce section of most supermarkets.

Coconut cream/milk: The final liquid made from soaking shredded, fresh coconut in warm water, massaging the pulp, and then pressing out the juice. The thickness depends upon the ratio of water to shredded coconut. The liquid will keep in a covered container in the refrigerator for several days; the heavier cream will rise to the top. Unsweetened canned coconut milk is available in gourmet markets and Oriental and Latin American specialty stores.

Daikon: Japanese white radish, generally about 3 feet long and weighing 1 to 2 pounds. The entire vegetable is edible. It is served raw and grated (squeeze out excess liquid), pickled, and cooked. Available in the produce section of most markets.

Feta cheese: Most feta cheeses belong to the goat cheese family. Imported feta comes from Greece, Bulgaria, Yugoslavia, Rumania, Sardinia, Hungary, Israel, Denmark, and Holland. It is also produced domestically in California, New York, and Wisconsin. It is a semisoft white cheese made from goat's, cow's, or ewe's milk. The top-quality fetas are generally packed in a brine solution and are available in Middle Eastern specialty markets and many cheese shops. The brine keeps the cheese fresh for a long period of time. Non-brine-packed fetas are available in most supermarkets.

Gari: Ginger seasoned in vinegar, often tinted a bright pink. Used in Japanese cuisine. Paper-thin slices of gari are eaten with sushi to refresh the palate. Available refrigerated in many supermarkets and Oriental specialty stores.

Ginger (ginger root): One of the most outstanding of seasonings used in Oriental recipes. Peel off the brown outer skin of only as much as you need, then wrap the remaining root in plastic and store in the refrigerator. Ginger can also be frozen, although the texture will become somewhat spongy. In appearance, fresh ginger resembles the knuckles and hands of a cartoon witch. Since fresh ginger is generally available in the produce section of most supermarkets, please do not substitute the powdered variety. Beni shoga—red pickled ginger—is available both bottled and cellophane-wrapped in most supermarkets and Oriental specialty stores.

Gefilte fish: Poached fish dumplings or balls, generally made with finely chopped white fish and onion and then bound with egg and matzo meal. Already-prepared gefilte fish, packed in a flavorsome stick, is available in the Jewish-food section of most supermarkets and in Jewish delicatessens. For a recipe for homemade gefilte fish, see Index.

Goma: *See* Sesame seeds.

Hoisin sauce: A dark, thick, sweet, and salty sauce used frequently in Oriental cooking. Made from fermented soybeans and rice, and seasoned with several ingredients, including vinegar, chili, garlic, sugar, and onion. Opened jars may be kept in the refrigerator. Available in the Oriental section of most supermarkets.

Hot chili oil: A piquant, highly fragrant red-colored oil often used in Oriental cooking. Made of sesame oil and vegetable oil in which spicy red peppers have been steeped. I prefer the varieties available in Oriental markets to those found in the Oriental section of most supermarkets, as the oil is more flavorsome, full-bodied, and pungent.

Jícama: A brown root vegetable that looks like a potato. When peeled, it is white, and its crunchy texture resembles that of a raw potato, radish, or water chestnut. Don't be fooled by its starchy appearance, as the flavor has an unusual sweet quality, and it is an excellent low-calorie substitute for potato chips to dunk in a dip. Popular in Mexican cooking. Available in most supermarkets or Latin American markets.

Kamaboko: Japanese fish-paste cakes. Kamaboko is the generic name of a variety of pureed, mixed (often bound with a starch), and then steamed or, sometimes, grilled fish products. Slice into decorative shapes. Available refrigerated in Oriental markets and most supermarkets.

Kanpyo (kampyo): Dried gourd (squash) shavings, the skin of a Japanese fruit. Long and ribbonlike, kanpyo is dried and packaged in cellophane. Before use, reconstitute by rinsing in water, rubbing with salt, and then soaking in water for several hours to overnight (the salt rub will hasten softening) or by parboiling. Available in Oriental specialty markets.

Kapee (kapi): Shrimp paste used in Thai cooking, similar to bagoong alamang, with an anchovylike flavor and aroma. Another fish paste or anchovy paste may be substituted. Available in Oriental specialty markets.

Katsuo bushi: Dried bonito flakes. Most often, katsuo bushi resembles sawdust, although it is also sold in larger shavings and strips. It looks woody and smells fishy. Used primarily for making dashi (the basic stock of Japanese cooking), occasionally as a garnish for sunomono (Japanese salads), and sometimes in sushi rolls. Packaged in paper or cellophane bags or boxes. Check the date for freshness, and use within six to twelve months. Store at room temperature in an airtight container. Available in the Oriental section of most supermarkets and Oriental specialty markets.

Kentjur root: A root related to fresh ginger, used in Indonesian cooking. Fresh ginger can be substituted. Available in Oriental specialty markets.

Kochu: Ground Korean red pepper powder, more pungent than cayenne (red) pepper. If substituting cayenne, increase to taste. Available in Oriental specialty markets.

Kombu (konbu): Dried cultivated kelp or sea tangle. This dark sea vegetation is primarily used for making dashi (Japanese stock). Store sheets at room temperature in an airtight container. Available in the Oriental section of most supermarkets, Oriental specialty markets, and health-food stores.

Lox (smoked salmon): Thinly sliced salt-cured filleted salmon. Available in many fish markets, the refrigerated delicatessen section of supermarkets, and Jewish delicatessens.

Maifun: Opaque white Oriental rice stick noodles, similar to spaghetti. They are brittle, dry, and hard, but become smooth and shiny when cooked. Available in the Oriental section of most markets.

Mirin: A sweet syrupy rice wine related to sake whose alcoholic content is approximately 13 to 14 percent. Used for cooking, not drinking. A popular Japanese ingredient. Available in the Oriental section of most markets and Oriental specialty markets. Light or sweet sherry may be substituted.

Miso: Fermented soybean paste made from sieved soybeans mixed with a grain (rice malt or barley), salt, water, and Aspergillus oryzae, a mold starter that encourages fermentation. There are numerous flavors, colors, and textures. To introduce your family to miso, it is best to start with a sweet, light-colored variety. Used in many Oriental cuisines, most extensively in Japanese. Available in most supermarkets, health-food stores, and Oriental specialty markets.

Nam plai: An amber-colored, salty Thai fish sauce that is basic to most Thai recipes. Other Oriental fish sauces, such as the Filipino patis, can be substituted. Worcestershire sauce or soy sauce can also be substituted, but the final taste will not be the same. Available bottled in the Oriental section of most supermarkets or Oriental specialty markets.

Nopales: Flat, broad prickly-pear-cactus leaves or paddles that somewhat resemble string beans when cooked. The pricklers must be carefully removed and the skin peeled. When cooking, baking soda is added to the water to prevent the vegetable from becoming slimy. Available at many produce stands and in Latin American specialty markets.

Nori: Although it is referred to as seaweed, nori is actually laver, a type of sea vegetation, used in Japanese cooking, especially sushi. Different qualities and types are available, but it is usually in thin, crisp, dark greenish-black sheets 6 to 10 inches square. Available in the Oriental section of most supermarkets, Oriental specialty markets, and health-food stores.

Nuoc nam: A clear, amber-colored liquid made from the fermentation of layers of fresh anchovies and salt. Although it may seem piquant and salty at first, the final taste when combined with other ingredients is excellent. Used instead of salt for Vietnamese cooking. Other Oriental fish sauces can be substituted. Available bottled in the Oriental section of most supermarkets.

Pancit: Opaque white, spaghettilike rice stick noodles. Brittle, dry and hard, they become smooth and shiny when cooked; when deep-fried, they expand and puff up. Used in many Oriental recipes, especially Filipino. Other rice stick noodles can be substituted, such as maifun. Available in the Oriental section of supermarkets and Oriental specialty markets.

Patis: An amber-colored, salty liquid fish sauce important in Filipino recipes. Other Oriental sauces, such as Thai nam pla, can be substituted. Available bottled in the Oriental section of most supermarkets and Oriental specialty markets.

Petis: An Indonesian fish sauce with a strong, salty flavor. Other fish sauces, such as patis or nuoc nam, or anchovy paste can be substituted. Available bottled from Oriental specialty markets.

Pine nuts: A small, white, soft-textured nut also called pignolia and piñon seeds, popular in Italian and Latin American cooking. Their flavor increases when toasted or roasted. Available in most supermarkets and health-food stores.

Plantain: A member of the banana family, the plantain resembles the banana but is about twice the size and is too starchy to eat raw. Cooked, it takes on a mellow flavor. It is ready for cooking when the outer skin is black. Popular in Indonesian and Latin American cooking. Available at many gourmet produce stands, in supermarkets that cater to a Latin American clientele, and Latin American specialty markets.

Rice vinegar (su): A white-colored vinegar used extensively in Oriental cooking. It has a delicate, crisp, clean taste and is somewhat sweet without the addition of sugar. I use rice vinegar almost exclusively. Use the unseasoned rice vinegar variety for recipes in this book. Available in most supermarkets and Oriental specialty markets.

Saifun: Very small, thin yam noodles. Should be steeped in boiling water rather than boiled, after which it is transparent. Available in the Oriental section of most supermarkets and Oriental specialty markets.

Sake: Rice wine. Popular for drinking and for cooking, especially Chinese and Japanese cuisines. Clear, colorless, and containing 12 to 18 percent alcohol, sake is often compared to beer because of the ingredients and fermentation process. It is as good as the quality of its water and rice. Store in a cool, dark place. Once it is opened, it should be used as soon as possible. Dry sherry can be substituted in cooking.

Serrano chiles: Small (1 to 2 inches long), spicy, bright green chiles used frequently in Latin American cooking. They are also an excellent substitute for the spicy smaller Thai chiles. Take care not to rub your eyes when seeding and chopping (some cooks wear rubber gloves when handling chiles). Available in most supermarkets and Latin American specialty markets.

Sesame oil (sesame seed oil): A highly fragrant golden- to dark-brown-colored oil made from toasted sesame seeds. Used extensively in Chinese and Japanese recipes, not as the main oil for cooking but as an accent oil or garnish. Store in a dark, cool place, preferably not in the refrigerator (or bring to room temperature before using). Available in the Oriental section of most supermarkets, Oriental specialty markets, and health-food stores.

Sesame seeds (goma): A popular Oriental garnish. White and black varieties are available. The white seeds are generally toasted in a small, dry skillet to bring out their full flavor, or are crushed to make a sauce with other ingredients for many Japanese dishes. The black seeds need not be toasted. Presalted black sesame seeds are also used for seasoning and as a garnish in many Japanese dishes, especially steamed white rice. Seeds stored in an airtight container will keep for several years. Available in the Oriental section of most supermarkets, Oriental specialty markets, and health-food stores.

Shallots: A member of the onion family, somewhat similar in appearance and taste to garlic. When substituting onions or leeks for shallots, I like to add fresh garlic to the recipe. Available at most produce stands and in many supermarkets.

Shiitake: Dried Oriental mushrooms, the most commonly used of the Oriental mushrooms. To reconstitute, soak in warm water for a minimum 3 to 5 hours, better yet 24 hours, according to Japanese technique; some Chinese cooks feel 30 minutes is sufficient soaking time. Remove and discard the tough center core after soaking. The longer soaking time results in a more tender texture, enabling the use of the entire mushroom, including the center core. Fresh American mushrooms may be substituted, but shiitake are easy to obtain and especially tasty. Available in cellophane packages in the Oriental section of most supermarkets, Oriental specialty markets, and health-food stores.

Soba: Japanese buckwheat noodles. Thin whole wheat or other noodles can be substituted. Available dried and fresh in the refrigerator or freezer section of supermarkets and Oriental specialty markets.

Somen: Japanese thin white noodles, similar to vermicelli. Thin spaghetti or vermicelli can be substituted. Available in the Oriental section of most supermarkets and Oriental specialty markets.

Star anise flowers: Hard eight-pointed pods encasing tiny brown seeds, used in many Oriental recipes. Related to magnolia flowers, anise flowers come from a small Chinese evergreen tree. The entire pod with seeds is used. Since it is dried, it will keep for a long time in a tightly covered container. A small amount of the spice will remind you of licorice. A few drops of anisette or licorice extract can be substituted for star anise. Available in jars or boxes in the Oriental section of most supermarkets and Oriental specialty markets.

Szechwan peppercorn powder: Very pungent powdered red pepper. Kochu, Korean powdered red pepper, is an excellent substitute, as is Indian ground pepper, but red pepper or cayenne pepper is not as pungent, so the quantity should be increased to taste. Available in both powdered form and peppercorns (which must be ground) in Oriental specialty stores.

Tahini: Sesame seed paste made from ground sesame seeds, somewhat similar in consistency to peanut butter. Available in jars and tins in many supermarkets, Middle Eastern markets, and health-food stores.

Takenoko: Japanese bamboo shoots, cut from the bamboo plant as it throws out new seasonal stalks. If using canned bamboo shoots, try to find whole sheets so that you can slice the cylinders yourself. To refresh canned shoots, parboil in fresh water for a few seconds, rinse, and drain. Available canned in the Oriental section of most supermarkets.

Tamarind juice: A tart juice made by steeping the dark dried pulp of the tamarind fruit in hot water. Used in many Latin American and Indonesian recipes. Fresh lemon or lime juice may be substituted. Available in Oriental and Latin American specialty markets.

Thai green chiles: One of the spiciest and smallest of fresh green chiles. Take care when chopping and seeding not to rub your eyes (some cooks like to wear rubber gloves when handling chiles). Serrano chiles, another small green chile used frequently in Latin American cooking, may be substituted. Available at gourmet produce stands and in Oriental specialty markets.

Tofu (soybean cake; bean curd): There are nine main classes of tofu. The two varieties used in this book are fresh tofu and deep-fried tofu pouches or puffs, referred to as *age*. The custardlike cakes of fresh tofu are generally packed with water in plastic containers. To store opened tofu for several days, it is best (though not mandatory) to change the water daily and keep the tightly covered container in the refrigerator. You can drain the fresh cakes, cut them into small squares, and add them to your recipes, or you can take more time to properly remove the excess liquid by placing slices between layers of paper towels for 30 minutes. Deep-fried age must be parboiled to rid them of excess oil. Available in the Oriental section of most supermarkets and Oriental specialty markets.

Trassi: A reddish-colored fermented shrimp paste used in Indonesian recipes. Anchovy paste can be substituted. Available in Oriental specialty markets.

Turmeric: The underground stem of a small plant, related to ginger (a rhizome) used in Indian cooking. Before turmeric is packaged, it is boiled, dried, and ground to a fine yellow powder. Many cooks use it as a substitute for the more expensive saffron, which it resembles. Ground turmeric is available bottled in the spice section of most supermarkets.

Umeboshi: Pickled Japanese plums, a popular ingredient in rice balls and many sushi recipes. Available canned or bottled in the refrigerated section of Oriental specialty markets.

Wakame: Dried sea vegetation popular in Japanese cooking. It is used once-reconstituted, primarily in salads and soups. Soaking time varies, depending upon the quality, generally 15 minutes to an hour; then it should be drained and squeezed dry, and the tough parts cut off. Available in Oriental specialty markets and health-food stores.

Wasabi: A member of the horseradish family, powdered wasabi is the mustard of Japanese cookery. It is essential for sushi and sashimi. To reconstitute this condiment, place a small amount of powder in a small mixing bowl, add a few drops of water, and mix thoroughly until you have a thick, pungent paste. Cover and let rest for 15 minutes to allow the flavors to mellow. Leftover paste can be stored, tightly covered, in the refrigerator. Tins of powder are available in the Oriental section of most supermarkets, Oriental specialty markets, and many fresh fish markets.

Won ton skins: Dumpling or skin noodle wrappers. They are generally filled and fried or steamed, but they can be sliced and used as a noodle. Available in the refrigerator or freezer section of most supermarkets and Oriental specialty markets.

SPECIAL TECHNIQUES

Most of the cooking techniques used in this book are basic knowledge for home cooks, cooking hobbyists, and professional cooks. I have tried to explain all the necessary steps for final completion of the dishes in the recipes themselves, but there are a few exceptions; they are presented here for reference.

CLARIFIED BUTTER/GHEE

Approximately ⅓ cup clarified butter;
¼ cup ghee

Clarified butter is melted butter in which the pure butter and milky solids have been separated. Ghee, used extensively in Indian cooking, is a long-simmered clarified butter, traditionally made from buffalo milk.

To make clarified butter, slowly melt ¼ pound butter in a heavy saucepan over low heat. Let rest. Skim off the foam. Pour butter through a very fine-meshed strainer or dampened cheesecloth into a cup. Repeat straining step a second time. Discard milky solids.

For ghee, the melted butter should be cooked in a heavy saucepan at a very low temperature for another 30 to 45 minutes. Do not let butter burn. Strain as with clarified butter. Ghee has a somewhat nutty flavor.

Store clarified butter or ghee, covered, in the refrigerator.

COCONUT MILK AND CREAM

Select a coconut with no bruises. The "eyes" should be firm, not weepy. When you shake it, you should hear plenty of juice.

To open, puncture one or two eyes with a sharp knife or an ice pick. Drain out liquid—this is a juice, not coconut milk. Save to drink, if desired, or discard.

Firmly but lightly tap the entire exterior of the coconut with a hammer. Then repeat the process, a little harder; the coconut should split in half. Pull apart. Again, tap each half until it breaks apart. You should now have four pieces.

Place the tip of a sharp knife between the flesh and the shell to loosen the flesh and separate the flesh from the shell. Break the flesh into a few smaller pieces and cut off the brown outer skin. Wash the coconut pieces. They are now ready to eat.

Another technique for cracking open a coconut is to puncture the eyes and drain out the liquid. Place the coconut in a baking dish in a 400° oven for 15 minutes, or until the shell starts to crack. Remove from the oven and cool enough to handle. Hit the coconut with a hammer to fully crack open the shell or first wrap the coconut

in a kitchen tea towel and then whack it with the hammer. Remove the flesh as described in preceding paragraph.

To grate, place a few pieces at a time in a blender or a food processor fitted with a fine grating blade, and finely grate. Or you can use a standard box-style grater if working by hand. The grated coconut is ready to be used for coconut milk. One medium-size coconut yields about 4 cups of grated meat.

To make coconut milk: Measure the coconut and place it in a large bowl. Pour hot, not boiling, water on it and soak it for 15 minutes. The proportion of water to coconut depends upon the desired strength of coconut milk or cream in the recipe(s) you will be making. Generally, for coconut milk, equal amounts of coconut and hot water are used. *For a thinner milk,* you may want 2 cups of hot water for each cup coconut. *For coconut cream,* use considerably less water—1 cup of hot water for each 2 cups of coconut.

An excellent tip I learned from my housekeeper, a native of Honduras, is to massage the soaking coconut, as if washing laundry. By rubbing the coconut with your fingers and palms, you will extract all the coconut milk. After the coconut is fully rubbed "dry" of its milk, squeeze all juice out of the grated coconut meat and discard the meat. You can also strain the coconut through a sieve, pressing it with a wooden spoon, or place the grated coconut in cheesecloth to squeeze out the milk. However, the hand-massaging method seems the most effective.

Place the coconut milk in a container, cover, and refrigerate until needed. The richest part will rise to the top, and this can be used in recipes calling for coconut *cream.* Before using coconut *milk,* stir to mix well. Coconut milk will stay fresh in the refrigerator for several days, or in the freezer for several months.

One medium coconut contains approximately 4 cups of grated coconut, thus yielding from 2 to 8 cups of coconut cream or milk, depending upon desired strength.

FISH-POACHING BASICS— SIMPLE COURT BOUILLON

There is a mystique about poaching fish. Why, I do not know. Some people think it is a tricky, time-consuming project, but I find it to be one of the easiest methods of cooking fish.

Poaching simply means cooking in a seasoned liquid at a low simmer, never a boil. The poaching liquid can be a basic salted-water bath (a friend of mine actually uses ocean water) or a slightly more complex court bouillon.

For seasonings, you might select from: spices and herbs (parsley, basil, thyme, bay leaf, garlic) and vegetables (onion, carrots, celery). Add a little vinegar, lemon, or wine and you've got the ingredients for a marvelous court bouillon. However, I do recommend being somewhat cautious in your selection, because the bouillon should not overpower the delicate flavor of the fish.

Almost any liquid can be used for poaching. I've used chicken broth, milk, fruit juices, and wine. Whatever you choose, do not discard the used liquid but recycle it for sauces, soup, aspic, or more fish poaching.

The necessary equipment is minimal. If you poach fish often, you may wish to invest in a proper fish poacher, available at most department stores and gourmet shops. Basically, it is a rectangular lidded pan (designed to accommodate a long whole fish) with a rack inside upon which to place the fish, thus protecting it from the direct heat source during cooking. The rack also makes it easy to lift the whole cooked fish from the pan.

For years I have managed without a poacher by using my everyday pots and casseroles with the aid of cheesecloth. Double-wrap the fish in the cloth, allowing approximately 4 inches of cloth at either end to hang outside the pot and be used as handles. After poaching, the fish remains in the cheesecloth wrapper for a few minutes until it is cool enough to handle, and then unwrapped. Remove the cloth before refrigerating the fish or the natural gelatin of the fish will cause the fabric to stick to it.

Whatever equipment you use, you can poach either on the stove or in your oven. Fill the pan with enough preheated prepared liquid to cover the fish (recipe follows) and carefully place the cheesecloth-wrapped fish in the pan or the unwrapped fish on the poacher's rack. (For added pro-

tection, you may want to use cheesecloth even when cooking with a fish poacher.)

It is important not to overcook the fish or it will toughen and dry out. Poaching is a fairly quick process. Allow approximately 10 minutes per inch of circumference (not length), measured at the fish's thickest part, a timing method developed by the Fisheries Council of Canada and popularized in the United States by cooking expert James Beard. Shellfish and squid need considerably less time. Generally, when the fish has changed color it is done.

A whole cold poached fish garnished with vegetables and sauces makes a handsome buffet dish. Individual fillets and steaks are a superb entree. These can be made even more elegant if decorated with vegetables cut to resemble flowers and then "painted" with a clear aspic (refer to Cold Trout in Aspic—see Index).

Place a medley of sauces in separate bowls and have guests select as many as they like. Some of my favorites include cucumber, sour cream, mustard, yogurt, herb, chili salsa, and aioli.

Simple Court Bouillon

2 quarts water
1 quart dry white or red wine or dry vermouth
¼ cup fresh lemon juice or vinegar
1 onion, sliced into rings
1 to 2 carrots, sliced into rounds
2 tablespoons fresh celery leaves or 1 stalk, sliced
1 to 2 bay leaves
2 sprigs parsley or other fresh herbs
4 peppercorns
1 to 2 cloves garlic, cut in half
Salt (optional)
Fish heads and/or tails (optional)

Put all ingredients in a deep saucepan, turkey roaster, or Dutch oven. (For large fish, you may have to increase the above portions, particularly the water and wine.) Bring to a boil, reduce heat, and let simmer for at least 20 minutes. This allows the liquid to pick up the flavors of the vegetables. Court bouillon can be used now or refrigerated or frozen for later use.

At cooking time, return court bouillon to a boil, carefully drop cheesecloth-wrapped fish into the liquid, placing the ends of the cheesecloth over the sides of the pot. At a gentle simmer, not a boil, poach for 10 minutes per inch of circumference; do not overcook.

Slightly cool the fish before unwrapping and chill thoroughly before serving.

CLEANING SMALL SQUID

To clean small squid, place them on newspaper near running water. Lay out squid horizontally with the tentacle end to the right and the pointed tip to the left. Using both hands, hold the pointed base end in your left hand and the tentacle end in your right hand. Carefully but firmly pull apart.

Inside the main part of the body (mantle) is a long, thin, almost transparent backbone, or quill. Hold the mantle with one hand, and with your other pull out the backbone; discard. Scoop out the eggs and discard along with the entrails.

The tentacle end is the prized part of the squid. To clean, pop out the birdlike "beak," positioned between the tentacles, and carefully pull out the ink pocket near the neck. With the point of a sharp knife, slice around the eyes and then cut them out. Be careful not to puncture them, or you'll be squirted with black ink. Discard these pieces. Rinse well.

DASHI

Approximately 2 cups

Dashi—the essence of Japanese cooking— is the basic stock used for most Japanese recipes.

1 small piece kombu (about 4 to 5 square inches)
2 cups water
1 cup katsuo bushi

Place kombu in a pot with the water over low heat. When the liquid comes to a boil, remove kombu. Increase heat and add the katsuo bushi. When the liquid returns to a boil, remove from heat. After the flakes sink, pour liquid through a strainer. The dashi is ready.

For greater quantities of dashi, the basic formula is: For each cup water, use one 2- to 3-square-inch piece kombu and ½ cup katsuo bushi.

Instant dashi, similar to tea bags or bouillon cubes, is also available.

Mail Order Sources

If you are trying to locate specific ingredients, supplies, or utensils:

1. Look in supermarkets, gourmet shops, ethnic markets, or health-food stores. Check the local telephone directory for stores in your area you might not be familiar with. Ask the owner or manager to special order your needs.

2. Ask ethnic restaurant manager/owners where specific items are obtained.

3. Get information from newspaper food editors or radio or television food-show hosts.

4. Check department store houseware and cooking supplies departments.

5. Look through mail-order catalogues for their cookware specialties.

In addition to local sources, you might write to the following stores. Check their current mail-order policies regarding payment and shipment and ask about minimum orders and lowest mail or delivery charges. Several of these companies print catalogues.

INTERNATIONAL

Williams-Sonoma, Mail Order Department, P.O. Box 3792, San Francisco, CA 94119

Maid of Scandinavia Co., 3244 Raleigh Ave., Minneapolis, MI 55416

Heidi's Around the World Food Shop, 1149 S. Brentwood Blvd., St. Louis, MO 63117

Aphrodisia Products, 29 Carmine St., New York, NY 10014

H. Roth & Son, 1577 1st Ave., New York, NY 10028

Hammacher Schlemmer, Mail Order Department, 39-25 Skillman Ave., Long Island City, NY 11104

Maison Glass, 52 E. 58th St., New York, NY 10022

Paprikas Weiss, 1546 2nd Ave., New York, NY 10028

Zabar's, 2245 Broadway, New York, NY 10024

Kitchen Bazaar, 4455 Connecticut Ave. N.W., Washington, D.C. 20008

EUROPEAN/MIDDLE EASTERN/INDIAN

Hamilton Foods Company, Inc., 3607 1st Ave. S., Birmingham, AL 32501

Niccolis Grocery, 623 W. Pierson Ave., Phoenix, AZ 85013

Southwestern Grocery, 127/131 E. Toole Ave., Tucson, AZ 85711

A & G Market, 1807 Robinson Ave., San Diego, CA 92103

Ann's Dutch Import Company, 4357 Tujunga Ave., North Hollywood, CA 91604

Arkalian's International Grocery, 4820 Santa Monica Blvd., Los Angeles, CA 90027

Bay Cities Importing Company, 1517 Lincoln Blvd., Santa Monica, CA 90401

Bazaar of India, 1131 University Ave., Berkeley, CA 94702

Bezjian's Grocery, 4725 Santa Monica Blvd., Hollywood, CA 90029

Bharat Bazaar, 11510 Washington Blvd., Los Angeles, CA 90066

Bucharest, 5235 Hollywood Blvd., Los Angeles, CA 90027

C & K Importing Company, 2771 W. Pico Blvd., Los Angeles, CA 93336

Dante Wholesale, 18803 Napa St., Northridge, CA 91324

Deukmedjian's Deli, 6807 Hazeltine Ave., Van Nuys, CA 91405

Domingo's, 17548 Ventura Blvd., Encino, CA 91316

Greek Importing Company, 2801 W. Pico Blvd., Los Angeles, CA 90006

Greek Village, 800 Alhambra Blvd., Sacramento, CA 95816

Gourmet Specialties, 2550 McKinnon Ave., San Francisco, CA 94103

Haig's Delicacies, 441 Clement St., San Francisco, CA 94118

Indo-European Foods, 881 N. Western Ave., Hollywood, CA 90029

International Groceries of San Diego, 3548 Ashford St., San Diego, CA 92111

Mediterranean and Middle East Import Company, 233 Valencia St., San Francisco, CA 94103

Persopolis International, P.O. Box 1984, Reseda, CA 91335

Sam's Food Market, 4356 Sepulveda Blvd., Culver City, CA 90230

India Health Foods, 1161 State St., Bridgeport, CT 06605

Manos Meat Market, 2804 Fairfield Ave., Bridgeport, CT 06605

Calavrita Importing Company, 12 E. 4 St., Wilmington, DE 19801

Angel's Market, 455 Athens St., Tarpon Springs, FL 33589

Cacciatore Brothers, 2301 W. Buffalo Ave., Tampa, FL 33607

Greek American Grocery, 2690 Coral Way, Miami, FL 33145

Greek Islands Deli, 501 Dedecanes Blvd., Tarpon Springs, FL 33589

Near East Bakery, 878 W. 8th St., Miami, FL 33130

University Bakery & Grocery, 408 S. 4th St., Pocatello, ID 83201

Astro Grocery & Meat Market, 309 W. Halstead St., Chicago, IL 66607

Athens Grocery, 811 W. Jackson Blvd., Chicago, IL 66607

India Groceries, 5022 N. Sheridan Rd., Chicago, IL 60640

India Spice Company, 437 South Blvd., Oak Park, IL 60302

Athens Imported Food, City Market 84-84, Indianapolis, IN 46204

Velona Italian Foods, 103 City Market, Indianapolis, IN 46219

Central Grocery Company, 923 Decatur St., New Orleans, LA 70116

Ideal Bakery, 2436 Ursulines Ave., New Orleans, LA 70119

Progress Grocery Company, 915 Decatur St., New Orleans, LA 70116

Dokan, Inc., 7921 Old Georgetown Rd., Bethesda, MD 20814

Caravan Imported Foods, 615 S. Frederick Ave., Gaithersburg, MD 20814

Imported Foods, Inc., 409 W. Lexington St., Baltimore, MD 21201

India Sub-Continental Stores, 908 Philadelphia Ave., Silver Springs, MD 20910

Parthenon Foods, 5414 S. Old Town St., Baltimore, MD 21224

Anthony Greek Market, 10 Central Square, Cambridge, MA 02139

Cardullo's Gourmet Shop, 6 Brattle St., Cambridge, MA 02138

Samas Importing, 346 Tremont St., Boston, MA 02116

Syrian Grocery Import Company, 270 Shawmut Ave., Boston, MA 02118

Vinod Shah, 3 Prescott St., North Woburn, MA 01801

Model Food Importers and Distributors, 113-15 Middle St., Portland, ME 04111

Athens Grocery, 527 Monroe Ave., Detroit, MI 48226

Greek Town Market, 571 E. Lafayette, Detroit, MI 48204

India Foods and Boutique, 3729 Cass, Detroit, MI 48201

International House, 75 W. Island Ave., Minneapolis, MN 55401

India Food Center, 15-43 McCausland Ave., St. Louis, MO 63117

Acropolis Grocery, 1004 Main St., Asbury Park, NJ 08608

Carmen Armentis, 13 N. Warren St., Trenton, NJ 08608

Annapurna, 127 E. 28th St., New York, NY 10016

Bremen House, Inc., 200 E. 86th St., New York, NY 10028

Central Grocery, 2843 Broadway, New York, NY 10025

Dean & De Luca, 121 Prince St., New York, NY 10012

Gold Star Trading Company, 570 Smith St., Brooklyn, NY 11231

House of Spices, 76-17 Broadway, Jackson Heights, NY 11373

Karnig Tashjian, Middle East & Oriental Foods, 380 3rd Ave., New York, NY 10016

Kassos Brothers, 570 9th Ave., New York, NY 10036

Maison Glass, 52 E. 58th St., New York, NY 10022

Malko Importing, 182 Atlantic Ave., Brooklyn, NY 11201

Manganaro Foods, 488 9th Ave., New York, NY 10018

Mediterranean Deli, 85-02 Parsons Blvd., Queens, NY 11432

New International Market, 517 9th Ave., New York, NY 10018

Sahadi Importing Company, 187-89 Atlantic Ave., Brooklyn, NY 11201

Sammy's Imported & Domestic Foods, 1348-54 Hertol Ave., Buffalo, NY 14216

Schaller and Weber, 1654 2nd Ave., New York, NY 10028

Athens Pastry Import, 2545 Lorain Ave., Cleveland, OH 44113

Antone's, 2606 Sheridan, Tulsa, OK 74129

Porter's Foods Unlimited, 125 W. 11th Ave., Eugene, OR 97401

Bombay Emporium, 3343 Forbes Ave., Pittsburgh, PA 15213

India Food Mart, 808 S. 47th St., Philadelphia, PA 19143

Indian Super Bazaar, 1401 Walnut St., Philadelphia, PA 19104

Michael's Greek Grocery, 930 Locust St., Philadelphia, PA 19147

European Grocery Store, 520 Court Pl., Pittsburgh, PA 15219

Near East Market, 602 Reservoir Ave., Cranston, RI 02910

Barizza Brothers, Inc., 351 S. Front St., Memphis, TN 38101

Antone Import Company, 807 Taft St., Houston, TX 77006

Antone's Import Company, 4234 Harry Hines Blvd., Dallas, TX 75219

Centennial Food Imports, 2932 Guadeloupe St., Austin, TX 78701

Asia Center, 303 W. Broad St., Rte. 7, Falls Church, VA 22046

Angelo Merlina & Sons, 816 6th Ave. S., Seattle, WA 22046

De Laurenti Italian & International Food, 1435 1st Ave., Seattle, WA 98101

Gino's World Food Market, 126 N. Washington St., Spokane, WA 99201

Nick Carras, 422 N. 48th St., Seattle, WA 98103

Acropolis Food Market, 1206 Underwood St. N.W., Washington, D.C. 20015

Georgetown International Market, 1226 Wisconsin Ave. N.W., Washington D.C. 20007

Hellas Greek Imports, 1245 20th St. N.W., Washington D.C. 20036

Skenderis Greek Import, 1612 20th St. N.W., Washington D.C. 20009

Indian Groceries and Spices, 2527 W. National Ave., Milwaukee, WI 53208

LATIN AMERICAN

Amherst Market, 12121 Pico Blvd., Los Angeles, CA 90024

El Molino, Inc., 1078 Santa Fe Dr., Denver, CO 80204

La Preferida, Inc., 3400 W. 35th St., Chicago, IL 60632

Central Grocery Company, 923 Decatur St., New Orleans, LA 70016

Cardullo's Gourmet Shop, 6 Brattle St., Cambridge, MA 02138

Bueno Mexican Foods, P.O. Box 293, Albuquerque, NM 87103

Josie's Best Mexican Foods, 1731 2nd St., Santa Fe, NM 87501

Theo. Roybal Store, Rear 212-16 Galistero St., Santa Fe, NM 87501

Casa Moneo, 210 W. 14th St., New York, NY 10011

Pecos River Spice Company, P.O. Box 680, New York, NY 10021

Beaverton Foods, P.O. Box 104, Beaverton, OR 97005

Stamoolis Brother's Grocery Store, 2020 Penn Ave., Pittsburgh, PA 15222

Adobe House, 127 Payne St., Dallas, TX 75207

Ashley's, Inc., 6590 Montana Ave., El Paso, TX 79925

Frank Pizzini, 202 Produce Row, San Antonio, TX 78207

La Semillera Horticultural Enterprises, P.O. Box 34082, Dallas, TX 34082

Simon David Grocery Store, 711 Inwood Rd., Dallas, TX 75209

Moctec Enterprizes, 1956 Montana Ave. N.E., Washington, D.C. 20002

ORIENTAL (includes Chinese, Filipino, Indonesian, Japanese, Korean, Thai, Vietnamese)

Anzen Hardware & Supply, 220 E. 1st St., Los Angeles, CA 90012

Bangkok Market, 4804 Melrose Ave., Los Angeles, CA 90029

Chico-San, Inc., 1144 W. 1st St., Chico, CA 95926

Filipino Market, 2525 Santa Fe Ave., Long Beach, CA 90801

Filipino Oriental Mart, 1804 Temple St., Los Angeles, CA 90052

Ginza Market, 2600 W. Jefferson Blvd., Los Angeles, CA 90018

Granada Market, 1820 Sawtelle Blvd., Los Angeles, CA 90025

Haig's Delicacies, 642 Clement St., San Francisco, CA 94118

Japan Food Corporation (major supplier of Oriental foods to U.S.), 445 Kaufman Ct., South San Francisco, CA 94080

Kinoko Company, 8139 Capwell Dr., Oakland, CA 94621

K. Sakai Company, 1656 Post St., San Francisco, CA 94115

Kwong Hang Company, 918 Grant Ave., San Francisco, CA 94108

Kwong On Lung Company, 680 N. Spring St., Los Angeles, CA 90015

Lorenzana Food Corporation, 4921-25 Santa Monica Blvd., Los Angeles, CA 90028

M & M Oriental Foods, 635-B E. Arrow Hwy., Azusa, CA 91702

Manila Oriental Goods & Bake Shop, 22102 S. Main St., Carson, CA 90745

Nozawa Trading, 870 S. Western Ave., Los Angeles, CA 90005

Orient Delight Market, 865 East El Camino Real, Mountain View, CA 94040

Philippine Grocery, 4929 Mission St., San Francisco, CA 94101

Philippine Plaza, 17610 S. Pioneer Blvd., Cerritos, CA 90701

Phil-Mart, 109 King Plaza Shopping Center, San Francisco, CA 94101

Rafu Bussan Company, 326 E. 2nd St., Los Angeles, CA 90012

Shing Chong & Company, 800 Grant Ave., San Francisco, CA 94108

Simex International, 331 Clement St., San Francisco, CA 94101

Tambuli Oriental Foods, 108 W. Carson St., Carson, CA 90745

The Chinese Grocer, 209 Post St., San Francisco, CA 94108

Yee Sing Chong, 966 N. Hill St., Los Angeles, CA 90012

Granada Fish, 1919 Lawrence St., Denver, CO 80202

Merapi, Inc., 139 White St., Danbury, CT 06810

Vietnam House, 191 Farmington Ave., Hartford, CT 06105

Keesan Imports, 9252 Bird Rd., Miami, FL 33165

South and Eastern Food Supply, 6732 N.E. 4th Ave., Miami, FL 33138

The Red Road Market, 4016 Red Rd., Miami, FL 33155

Asian Trading Company, 2581 Piedmont N.E., Atlanta, GA 30324

Cone di Savoia, 555 W. Roosevelt Rd., Chicago, IL 60607

Min Sun Trading Company, 2222-28 S. La Salle St., Chicago, IL 60616

Oriental Food Market & Cooking School, 2801 W. Howard St., Chicago, IL 60646

Oriental Food Mart, Westlake Plaza, 2208 Bloomingdale Rd., Glendale Heights, IL 60137

Philippine Food Corporation, 4547 N. Ravenswood, Chicago, IL 60625

Philippine World, 1051-57 E. Belmont Ave., Chicago, IL 60657

Star Market, 3349 N. Clark St., Chicago, IL 60657

Thai Grocery Store, 931 W. Irvine Park, Chicago, IL 60613

Asia House Grocery, 2433 Saint Paul St., Baltimore, MD 21281

Oriental Giftland, 72 Harrison Ave., Boston, MA 02109

Ming's Market, 85-91 Essex St., Boston, MA 02111

Yoshinoya, 36 Prospect St., Cambridge, MA 02139

Phil-Oriental Imports, Inc., 476 Lexington Pky., St. Paul, MI 55104

Oriental Food Groceries, 18919 W. 7th Mile, Detroit, MI 48233

Phil-Asian Tropical Food Mart, 4638 Woodward, Detroit, MI 48233

King's Trading, 3736 Broadway, Kansas City, MO 64111

Maruyama, Inc., 100 N. 18th St., St. Louis, MO 63103

Fil-Am Food Mart, Inc., 685 Newark Ave., Jersey City, NJ 07306

Mira-San Oriental Food Store, 530 Newark Ave., Jersey City, NJ 07306

Sammi Oriental Grocery Store, 444 Broad Ave., Leonia, NJ 07605

Asian Attic, Inc., 8 Briarwood Terr., Albany, NY 12203

Eastern Trading Company, 2801 Broadway, New York, NY 10025

E.V. Varieties, 349 Hempstead Ave., Elmont, NY 11003

Kam Kuo Food Corporation, 7-9 Mott St., New York, NY 10013

Kam Man Food Products, Inc., 200 Canal St., New York, NY 10013

Katagiri and Company, 224 E. 59th St., New York, NY 10022

Mabuhay, 524 9th Ave., New York, NY 10018

New Frontier Trading Corporation, 2394 Broadway, New York, NY 10024

Phil-Am Food Mart, 40-03 70th St., Woodside, NY 11377

Sam Bok Grocery Store, 127 W. 43rd St., New York, NY 10036

Sampaguita Food Store, 347 E. 14th St., New York, NY 10011

Tanaka and Company, 326 Amsterdam Ave., New York, NY 10023

Trinacria Import Company, 415 3rd Ave., New York, NY 10016

Wing Fat Company, 33-35 Mott St., New York, NY 10012

Bayanihan Food, Inc., 625 Bolivar, Cleveland, OH 44101

Far East Company, 247 W. McMillan St., Cincinnati, OH 45219

Anzen Japanese Food & Imports, 736 N.E. Union Ave., Portland, OR 97232

Dae Han, 9970 S.W. Beaverton Hwy., Beaverton, OR 97005

Bando Trading Company, 2126 Murray Ave., Pittsburgh, PA 15217

Chinese & Oriental Food Product Research Inc., 117 N. 10th St., Philadelphia, PA 19107

International Supermarket, 117 N. 10th St., Philadelphia, PA 19107

Mrs. De Wildt, Rte. 3, Bangor, PA 18013

Phil-Am Food Mart, 5601 Comac, Philadelphia, PA 19104

Jung's Oriental Food, 2519 N. Fitzhugh, Dallas, TX 75204

Little Home Bakery & Grocery, 2109 Parker Rd., #202A, Dallas, TX 75203

Queen's Fresh Produce, 5714 Locke Ave., Fort Worth, TX 76116

The Oriental Market, 502 Pampas St., Austin, TX 78752

The Vietnam-Laos Grocery, 33-26 East Lancaster, Fort Worth, TX 76103

Mekon Center, 3107 Wilson Blvd., Arlington, VA 22201

Vietnam Imports, 922 W. Browad St., Falls Church, VA 22046

Manila Mart, 3610 Lee Hwy., Arlington, VA 22207

Mikado, 4709 Wisconsin Ave., N.W., Washington, D.C. 20016

New China Supply Company, 709 H St. N.W., Washington, D.C. 20001

Fiesta Filipina Store, 522 6th Ave. S., Seattle, WA 98101

The Philippine Best, 10303 Greenwood N., Seattle, WA 98103

Umajimaya, P.O. Box 3003, Seattle, WA 98114

Index